Canoe and Kayak Building the Light and Easy Way

Canoe and Kayak Building the Light and Easy Way

How to Build Tough, Super-Safe Boats in Kevlar, Carbon, or Fiberglass

Sam Rizzetta

International Marine / McGraw-Hill

Camden, Maine New York Chicago San Francisco Lisbon London Madrid
Mexico City Milan New Delhi San Juan Seoul Singapore Sydney Toronto

The McGraw·Hill Companies

Library of Congress CIP

Rizetta, Sam.
    Canoe and kayak building the light and easy way / Sam Rizetta.
        p.   cm.
    Includes bibliographical references and index.
    ISBN 0-07-159735-2
       1. Canoes and canoeing—Design and construction.   2. Kayaks—Design and construction.   3. Boatbuilding.   I. Title.

    VM353.R59   2009
    623.82'9—dc22   2008049167

1 2 3 4 5 6 7 8 9 10 11 12 13 14 15 16 17 18 19 20 21   QPD/QPD   0 9

ISBN   978-0-07-159735-7
MHID   0-07-159735-2

Interior design by Think Design LLC

McGraw-Hill books are available at special quantity discounts to use as premiums and sales promotions or for use in corporate training programs. To contact a representative, please visit the Contact Us pages at www.mhprofessional.com.

Contents

Acknowledgments

To the many folks who have shared information, insight, criticism, encouragement, and good times on the water, thank you all. I am very grateful to Robert Holtzman for editing and for suggesting that I expand my flotation and safety information into a canoe building book. Many thanks to Carrie Rizzetta for valuable advice and some of the photography; to Dr. Mark Jones for practicing self-rescue procedures with me; to Joanie Blanton for loaning kayaks for testing safety flotation; and to Nicholas Blanton for safety assistance during cold water tests and also for helpful comments and criticism.

Canoe and Kayak Building the Light and Easy Way

Chapter 1

Introduction

Lightweight, strong, durable, safe, efficient to paddle, easy to build, and good looking—these are attributes most of us desire in a modern canoe or kayak. Materials like carbon fiber,

Kevlar, and fiberglass, reinforced with epoxy resin, have made these design goals achievable, and building such a boat yourself can not only cost less than purchasing a manufactured boat but also be more rewarding and fun.

This book describes two convenient methods for building a lightweight composite canoe or kayak. In the first method, which I call the fabric form method, a skeleton form is built from plywood and wood strips and covered with a taut fabric as a base for laminating the hull. In the second method, which is a simple modification of the first, an existing canoe or kayak is used as the form over which the fabric is stretched, further reducing labor and building time.

As you move through the chapters of this book, you will find the building process described step by step, along with the background needed to build a safe and successful small boat of composite materials. Building a boat, however, is a synthesis of numerous interconnected techniques and processes, so be sure to read and understand the entire book before planning a project and starting to build. Chapters 2 and 3 describe the construction method and the tools and materials required. In Chapters 4 and 5, you will begin cutting wood and setting up your building form.

Chapter 6 addresses how to assemble the fabric-covered form on which the composite hull will be laminated. This is the heart of the construction process, and it involves very basic, straightforward woodworking. Chapter 7 describes how to save time and cost by using an old canoe as a form to support the fabric. The process of covering the form and turning layers of cloth and ep°oxy into a hull is covered in Chapters 8 and 9. The idea of a fabric-covered form can be adapted to building in smaller scales, so you will also find a description of how to make a composite scale model canoe in Chapter 10. Building a model will allow you to become familiar with the process before risking a lot of labor and expensive materials on a full-size boat, and I especially recommend it if you are new to boat-building and working with epoxy. Chapters 11 through 14 detail the steps of converting a bare hull into a finished canoe or kayak. Readers experienced in building boats and working with epoxy may be able to safely skim or skip some sections or chapters.

Chapter 15, perhaps the most important, addresses flotation and safety. Here you will learn how to incorporate a lightweight flotation system into your canoe or kayak during construction or add flotation to a finished boat, including a factory-made one. This system allows a solo paddler to get back into a capsized canoe or kayak without assistance after an upset in deep water. Both the flotation and the reentry procedures are described in detail. This innovation provides so much more safety and assurance that I no longer venture far from shore without it. All my personal canoes and most of my kayaks are outfitted with this system. The flotation is inside the hull only and can be incorporated as a structural part of the boat, thereby saving weight and increasing

strength. Please read Chapter 15 before planning the final design details of your boat. All of the safety flotation information is assembled in this one long chapter for easy reference and sharing with others.

Chapter 16 explains the basic parameters of canoe design as they relate to performance, includes complete plans for three solo canoes, and provides advice on modifying the three designs or any other. Two of the included designs can be completed as decked recreational kayaks or safer wilderness trippers. I find solo boats so much fun that I avoid paddling tandems, but you can certainly make tandem canoes with my method, and I've included tips for tandems wherever the instructions deviate from making smaller solo canoes. You can also use the fabric form method to make other boat designs not described here. Most canoe and kayak designs intended for wood strip construction can be either used directly or readily adapted, and Appendix B includes sources for such designs.

In Chapter 17, you will learn how to build a very lightweight composite paddle. Like model building, making a paddle is another small, more manageable project that can help you gain experience working with wood, foam, epoxy, fiberglass, and carbon fiber before starting a larger boat project.

A Canoe Quest

My quest for better canoes had early roots. My earliest childhood memory is boating at age three. While on summer vacation in Michigan in July 1945, my father took me fishing. My one-year-old brother had to stay back in the cabin with my mother; there were advantages to being three years old. I remember pushing off from shore at early dawn in a rented canoe. Sitting amid the many ribs inside the wooden canoe seemed like being within the skeleton of a whale. I could see little else but the canoe ribs in the morning fog. It was scary to see the shore fade out of sight in the fog, but my father showed no concern. He assured me that the fog would go away. I couldn't believe or understand how he could know this. Nor could I imagine how he, or anyone, could find the way safely back to shore when it was out of sight in the fog.

My father put a cane fishing pole in my hands. It was so heavy that I could not hold the far end out of the water. He seemed genuinely surprised at the weakness of a three-year-old, and he chided me that my pole in the water would scare the fish from biting my hook. I did get a bite, but neither of us caught a fish, so I figured that my method was not any worse than his. I fared no better with the paddle. I could barely lift it, and moving the entire canoe with it was futile. Paddling was a task reserved for Hercules or my father. But I was initiated into the world of waters and watercraft. And I was hooked!

Since then I have had many interesting and amusing experiences in boats from the smallest kayaks to monstrous ocean liners and almost everything in between. I've been propelled by pole, oar, sail, electricity, gas, oil, coal, and steam. But I prefer to paddle the small ones, thank you. Powerboats may be fast and able to carry large loads on big waters. But they also bring noise, pollution, toxic fumes, high costs, and the complexities of maintenance, trailers, and taxes. I sold my last powerboat years ago. There is a special joy that comes from propelling oneself silently over the water by human power alone. The exercise is refreshing and invigorating. The pace allows an intimate connection with water and wildlife and time for appreciating the ever-changing beauty of nature. Trips require more careful planning, and they demand learning and practicing skills that make one ever more competent, comfortable, and independent outdoors and on the water. And perhaps mental and physical fitness are by-products of having fun messing around with boats.

Canoes and kayaks have taken me places where powerboats could never go. I've been surrounded by hundreds of curious, friendly manatees in tropical waters, and I've caught dinner to the sound of loons and the glow of northern lights on ice-rimmed wilderness lakes in boreal forests. I've portaged canoes for miles to remote, jewel-like lakes and rivers that seldom see a human being. Moose, bears, otters, beavers, and porpoises have swum alongside me without caution. Many times I have watched motionless as bald eagles and ospreys snatched fish out of the water right next to my canoe and flew overhead almost within reach. And the whitewater rivers of Appalachia have been a lovely paddle playground and natural refuge where sometimes days go by without seeing another human being. These are but samples of the wonders open to us as paddlers. A kayak or canoe can be a magic carpet to adventure and a closer connection to nature.

The Lightweight Advantage

My paddlecraft experiences have progressed through a wide range of hull materials, including wood and canvas, aluminum, plastics like Royalex, and composites like fiberglass, Kevlar, and carbon fiber. With experience and advancing age has come an ever greater appreciation for efficiency and a lighter weight, which provide some important advantages. Lightweight canoes mean independence. They don't require a second person to help move them around, put them on a car top, carry them to and from the water, or portage long distances. (See Figures 1.1 and 1.2.) They need no trailer. And they tend to paddle more efficiently. Light boats accelerate easily and maneuver with less effort. In my experience, the lighter and smaller the canoe or kayak, the more it gets used and enjoyed. Although lighter boats may require more expensive, high-tech materials, their usefulness often proves cost effective. An inexpensive but heavy boat is no bargain if it's not fun and you don't get much use out of it. While boat type, design, size, and strength

FIGURE 1.1. *The lightweight advantage. Canoe traveler Jay Hurley carries Kayoo, a decked canoe, between lakes in the Adirondack Mountains of New York.*

requirements may be largely determined by the type of water you intend to paddle, boats that are lighter and smaller are undeniably high on the fun scale.

Canoe or Kayak?

Throughout this book you will find the words *canoe* and *kayak* used somewhat interchangeably. My old college dictionary defined *kayak* as an "Eskimo canoe made of a light wooden frame covered with skins except for an opening in the center," or a "lightweight canoe similar to a kayak." The implication seems to be that a kayak is, by definition, a type of canoe. So, I will often use the word *canoe* to include both canoe and kayak.

Certainly they are both similarly propelled by paddles rather than by oars, propellers, or water jets, although some are rigged for sailing. And, unlike rowing, the paddler sits facing forward. Most people think of a canoe as being open on top and paddled with a single blade "canoe" paddle from a kneeling or high seated position. And, in the twentieth century at least, canoes were usually made to carry two people in a tandem configuration fore and aft. By comparison, most modern kayaks are solo craft with the paddler using a double-blade "kayak" paddle from a low seated position. But there are also kayaks that carry two or more people. And solo canoes, which were well known in the nineteenth century, are again gaining popularity.

Kayaks are commonly decked on top except for a small opening for the paddler. In modern times the opening typically has a coaming with a lip that can securely hold a sprayskirt to help keep water out. However, some kayaks have larger openings and some canoes are partially or mostly decked, which confuses the issue. A decked boat with a low, forward-facing seat will require a double-blade paddle for efficient paddling; such a craft reasonably fits the kayak description. A partially decked boat with a high enough seat might be used with single- or double-blade paddles and thought of as a canoe or a kayak. Some solo canoes fit this description.

FIGURE 1.2. *A light boat starts with a light hull. This strong hull, laminated with Kevlar and carbon fiber, is 14½ feet long and weighs 11.8 pounds.*

Adirondack Canoe Carry

Reel

Sam Rizzetta © 2008

Chapter 2

The Fabric Form Method

Wooden canoes and skin-on-wood-frame kayaks are beautiful and traditional. For anyone who loves wood, it is easy to become smitten with wooden boats. My profession as a designer and builder of musical instruments involves exotic woodworking, and I have loved working in wood since childhood, including working on wooden boats. But modern composite materials offer great advantages in strength-to-weight ratio, durability, and the infinite variety of complex shapes that can be readily molded. These advantages can translate into boats with excellent paddling efficiency and ease of use, and little or no maintenance requirements. Wood boats of similar size and shape are generally heavier, require much more time and work to build, may damage more easily, and demand more attention. I recall how my friends with wooden boats used to spend weeks each spring repairing, sanding, varnishing, and painting.

While I have enjoyed making fine wooden objects for museums to display, I prefer my boats to be practical and functional. I like to spend a lot of time on the water. Paddling. I can do so because my composite boats are safe, easy to transport, easy to paddle, and rather simple to build, and they require almost no maintenance, even when I accidentally bash them on submerged stumps and rocks. Turning a composite hull into a finished boat does require such parts as gunwales and decks, which are most conveniently made with wood, providing ample opportunity for attractive finishing touches of clear-varnished brightwork.

Composites

Cloth woven from strong Kevlar, stiff carbon (graphite) fiber, or inexpensive fiberglass can be reinforced with resin and laminated on or in a hard-surfaced mold to produce a tough and light boat hull. Hard molds are convenient and efficient for the manufacturer who is replicating many identical copies of a boat and needs to produce a slick outer finish with minimal labor per unit. However, making the molds is time consuming, tedious, and costly, and storing the molds afterward or discarding them can be a waste of space and money for the home builder. Fortunately, such molds are not necessary for building a single boat or experimenting with a variety of designs. My fabric form method is a faster, easier, and less costly approach to building small, one-of-a-kind composite hulls in the home workshop.

The word *composite* means something fabricated with, or composed of, more than one material, so wood covered with fiberglass and resin is technically a composite. However, the term is used most commonly to describe structures made with fiberglass, or other humanmade fibers, and a plastic resin. These structures have also been called fiber-reinforced plastic, or FRP. In small boat construction, the resin is typically polyester, vinylester, or epoxy, the choice depending on the type of fabric, the process, and considerations of strength, stability, cost, ease of use, hazards, and service life. For simplicity and concession to popular convention, I will refer to FRP as "composite."

From Planes to Boats

My method of creating a composite canoe starts with a wood framework that is the positive or male skeleton of the canoe hull to be built. The skeleton form is made of plywood and wood strips screwed together on a sturdy base, or *strongback*, and may be disassembled for storage or recycling of the materials. The wood skeleton is then covered with fabric, like the wings and fuselage of many classic airplanes. Today most fabric-covered aircraft are covered with a special polyester fabric. (See Figure 2.1.) A wonderfully convenient feature of this fabric is that it can be shrunk with heat to make it taut and wrinkle free. The tight fabric makes a smooth supporting surface, which is the key to a simplified laminating process.

Epoxy does not adhere well to polyester aircraft fabric, so the fabric can be used as a removable "peel ply" layer during fabrication. Layers of strong woven fabrics made of Kevlar, carbon fiber, and fiberglass are bonded together and reinforced with epoxy and laminated on top of the polyester fabric. After the epoxy has cured, the hull is lifted from the wooden framework and the polyester peel ply layer is peeled off, leaving the laminate with a slightly textured interior surface ready for structural bonding operations or finishing. Gunwales, stiffening ribs, stem reinforcements, decks, flotation chambers, and other outfitting can all be effectively epoxy-bonded to the textured surface with no additional surface preparation. The surface also sands easily for a smooth finish, if desired. The exterior surface may be left as is for lighter weight and simplicity or can be sanded and finished more smoothly. Figure 2.2 shows a kayak made using the fabric form process.

Instead of building a wooden, skeleton-type form, an old canoe can be used as a temporary form without harming it. This can save a lot of time and labor, as well as the cost of mold materials if you use a canoe you own or borrow or if you buy a used one specifically to use as a mold and then resell later. But you are limited to available boats and designs that are not someone

FIGURE 2.1. *Although it looks like an antique, this experimental Hatz biplane was built in 2000 by Gordon Hockman of Shenandoah Junction, West Virginia. It exhibits the fabric on wood frame and metal tube frame aircraft construction that is the inspiration and basis for building fabric form canoe hulls. The turtle deck behind the cockpit most clearly shows the construction of fabric over wood stringers. This method of building aircraft goes back to the Wright brothers and the classic biplanes of World War I and the 1920s. It is a time-proven process, and some new aircraft are still built this way. The author crafted the cockpit woodwork and performed the test flights.*

FIGURE 2.2. *Kayoo, a kayak or "decked canoe" made with the fabric form process, is packed and ready for the journey home after several weeks of travel in the Boundary Waters Canoe Area Wilderness of northern Minnesota.*

else's intellectual property. Boat designs are subject to copyright laws and should not be copied without the manufacturer's or designer's permission.

Building a boat, even a small canoe, requires a lot of work, patience, planning, and considerable expense, even though you will spend much less than the cost of a comparable new, factory or professionally made composite canoe. If your chief goal is to have an inexpensive boat, you will probably be happier buying a used one or a new one made of less costly materials. However, if you desire a more interesting design that is sized and customized just for you, if you want to experiment, and if you enjoy learning and building, then making a boat will offer you many rewards—not the least of which is the pride of accomplishment that comes with paddling a craft you made.

If you do decide to invest your time and labor, consider taking advantage of the strong modern fibers now available. Aramid fiber, popularly known by the DuPont trade name Kevlar, is ideal because it can be used to create a strong, tough hull that is light in weight. Graphite or carbon fiber is stiffer and can be used to increase the stiffness and reduce the weight of the hull and reinforcements when light weight is more important than resistance to impact and damage. And fiberglass is cheap, easy to work with, and easy to sand.

Two or more types of fiber can be used together to take advantage of their combined properties. For example, I used a combination of Kevlar and carbon fiber fabrics to build an 11.8-pound shell for a solo canoe that was 14½ feet long. The finished boat has endured class 3 rapids and many long wilderness trips without damage. Numerous bumps, bangs, and scratches have inflicted no leaks or structural failures. The shell was finished as a decked canoe, and even with extra self-rescue flotation and lots of special wilderness outfitting, it weighs only 28 pounds. The hull could have been made even lighter for use only on flat water, or heavier and stronger for use on more demanding whitewater and better impact resistance.

Although Kevlar and carbon fiber are wonderful space-age materials for making the lightest small boats, they are also quite expensive compared to fiberglass, with carbon being the most costly. If low cost is more important than light weight, then choose fiberglass; the type known as E-glass is the least expensive and is perfectly adequate. You will need to make your hull laminations about three times thicker and heavier than the recommendations for Kevlar, and heavier stiffening ribs may also be required. The very low relative cost of fiberglass is somewhat offset by the fact that you will need more of it, and more epoxy, to achieve adequate strength and safety. Although some other resins are a lot less costly than epoxy, I recommend using only high-quality epoxies for the fabric form method and for home building of composite boats in general.

Fiberglass has some useful qualities even when building a hull primarily with carbon or Kevlar. Fiberglass has good abrasion resistance, and it sands readily, making it a good choice for a hull's outer layer if you want a perfectly smooth surface as a base for a glossy painted or clear varnished finish. Being much more flexible than Kevlar or carbon fiber, fiberglass conforms better to tight bends, curves, and corners, making it handy for attaching parts like bulkheads and decks and for adding protective layers to ends and other areas of high wear. It is also almost transparent when saturated with epoxy, making it the best choice for strengthening and protecting wood parts when a "natural" wood finish is desired. More specific recommendations for the use of each fabric appear in Chapter 9 (and elsewhere where relevant).

The march of technology is likely to present future builders with ever more amazing materials and methods of constructing small boats. Until that time, however, layers of fiberglass, carbon fiber, and Kevlar cloth laminated in a mold or on a fabric form will produce excellent boats with an efficient use of time and labor.

Chapter 3

Preparation

To me the most important aspect of preparation and planning is mind-set. If you have the desire and determination to build a boat and have a can-do attitude, then you are likely

to budget the time, space, and money. It doesn't have to be done all at once. You can proceed in steps as resources permit. Persistence will be rewarded. Eventually, you will enjoy the thrill of paddling your handmade canoe. Even if you have never made a boat before or worked with composites, you can make a fine and serviceable canoe with the fabric form method.

Time

The composite method presented here is definitely less time consuming than many other ways of building a boat. With a block of free time, good planning, and your materials ready, a small and simple design with minimal finishing and outfitting might be completed in a couple of weeks or a little more. Still, making even a small boat is a relatively large project and a lengthy process. Most of us will work part time and take much longer than two weeks. A larger or more complex design with greater attention to detail and more elaborate outfitting increases time and labor exponentially. But the end product can be a joy to use and may last a lifetime.

Some parts of the process proceed quickly. Once the form is ready, laminating the hull with layers of cloth and epoxy must be done all at once. This is the most important step and can be accomplished in a long weekend or a few days of full-time effort. It may take a week or a month of part-time work to build a skeleton form or just a few hours to prepare an old canoe as a form. A few working days later, you will have a composite hull instead of just a wood skeleton. Adding gunwales, thwarts, flotation, decks, reinforcing ribs, and other outfitting may take the most time but can proceed in smaller, easy steps. Finishing a simple open canoe takes little time. Adding decks and some of the outfitting that makes extended wilderness trips more convenient takes more. My usual approach is to complete a canoe to a minimal but seaworthy condition and start paddling it. After testing, I may decide it is worth lavishing additional attention to outfit it more elaborately and finish it to look better. Composites are very convenient for this approach.

Cost

Estimating the costs depends on the size of boat, the type of cloth, the number of cloth layers, any new tools needed, the woods and plywood chosen for the form, and outfitting and finishing details. And, of course, prices change. I'll give some estimates of materials quantities for various operations as we proceed. In the past I've spent under $200 for plywood, lumber, and other materials for a strongback and form. When using an old canoe and two sawhorses instead of a form and strongback, I've had to add only the cost of a roll of plastic wrap, package sealing tape, and pieces of scrap plywood.

As I write, 5-ounce Kevlar cloth in 50-inch widths costs about $20 per linear yard. Fiberglass is roughly one-third the cost of Kevlar, while carbon can be twice as much or more.

For the canoe designs in this book, which are all less than 15 feet in length, about 5 yards of 50-inch-wide cloth will be needed for each layer of hull laminate. A minimum of three layers of 5-ounce Kevlar or a combination of 5-ounce Kevlar and 5.8-ounce carbon fiber is needed for the lightest layup. A layer of less expensive, 38-inch-wide Kevlar will do for adding an extra layer or two in the bottom if you expect rough use. Inexpensive fiberglass is an alternative to the pricier Kevlar and carbon, but many more layers and much more resin will be needed. This offsets most of the price advantage of fiberglass, although fiberglass is still ideal for some operations.

The current cost for WEST System epoxy resin along with ultraviolet-resistant hardener is approximately $126 for 1.3 gallons. Without the ultraviolet-resistant feature, the cost is about $20 less. About 2 gallons will be needed for the solo canoe designs in this book. Thus, the cost for laminating a hull with three layers of Kevlar and one outer layer of fiberglass might total around $600, plus the cost of building a form. Miscellaneous supplies and tools are likely to add to that total. Finishing an open canoe will also require gunwales, thwarts, flotation, and a seat. Total cost will depend on the materials you choose.

Workspace

Basic building space requirements are simple: there must be enough floor space to fit the finished hull dimensions and at least 2 or 3 feet of extra room to walk and work on all sides. More room is always desirable. Room temperature should be adequate for woodworking and using epoxy—in the range of 55° to 77°F. Humidity control helps because dampness is not good for the dimensional stability of wood and can change the curing time of epoxy. It is possible to do the hull laminating outdoors, but under cover is best. I have laminated some hulls under a carport during mild seasons. This provided natural ventilation while working long hours with epoxy. A deck or shed might provide similar cover. I then moved such projects into my shop—closer to tools and workbenches—for assembling other parts and finishing.

A garage can make a good boatbuilding shop. Basements may provide dry workspace but can be difficult to ventilate. The smells of epoxies, finishes, and solvents can permeate the living areas. Breathing masks that filter organic solvents are required for working with some of these materials. You don't want such solvents getting into your home. If a basement is your most practical shop option, then install a good exhaust fan or do the major epoxy and finishing operations outdoors. Dry cloudy weather is best. The heat from sunlight can cause epoxy to gel too quickly and can prevent adequate working time.

Whatever tool is needed always seems to be on the other side of the boat, so it helps to have a small, movable table for mixing epoxy and holding small tools. I use small, 16-by-30-inch carts on wheels so that I don't have to constantly go back to the workbench or storage shelves (see Figure 3.1).

Make sure you have good lighting. It is not possible to measure, cut, shape, sand, and do good finishing work without adequate light.

Tools

General woodworking tools are needed, and you can get by with hand tools. Cordless electric drills and a saber saw or hand jigsaw will get lots of use. Tool requirements will depend on whether you build a form or use an old canoe as

a form; you will need fewer tools if you use an old canoe. The list of tools below is based on building a form and will give you an idea of what you may need to get started. You will want to make your own wish list for tools as you read through the various chapters. Since tool needs will vary depending on the design and process chosen, it may be best to acquire tools and supplies as the need arises. Here are some suggestions for starters:

- Respirator with a filter for organic chemicals (for use when applying epoxy, varnish, paints, and solvents)
- Dust masks for sanding wood, epoxy, and fibers, such as Kevlar, carbon, and fiberglass
- Disposable latex or butyl gloves for working with epoxy
- Safety glasses or goggles
- Ear protectors (over-the-ear muff styles are safest, but earplugs are better than nothing)
- Baseball cap to keep dust and epoxy out of the hair
- Hand tools, including a hammer, pliers, and screwdrivers (an electric screwdriver is also useful)
- Saber saw with a variety of wood-cutting and metal-cutting blades, including blades for cutting ½-inch plywood smoothly

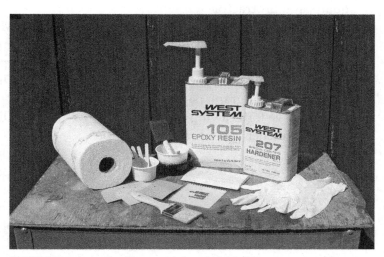

FIGURE 3.1. *A small rolling cart is handy for holding epoxy supplies.*

- Low-angle block plane
- Large, very sharp scissors for cutting fabric (you will need to be able to resharpen them when cutting Kevlar)
- Utility knife
- Sharpening stones for your plane, scissors, and knife
- Wood rasps (coarse and medium)
- Sanding block and a variety of sandpaper grits (orbital and palm sanders save time for some operations)
- Hacksaw and a mill file for cutting and smoothing aluminum brackets and thwarts
- Staple gun and staples (³/₈-inch staples are good for attaching peel ply fabric)
- C-clamps (Instrument maker's cam clamps are lightweight and especially convenient; see Figure 9.12. Eight or so will get you started, but some operations are much easier with more. You cannot have too many clamps.)
- Spring clamps (These are handy for attaching gunwales and strips for attaching decks; see Figure 11.5. If you do a practice fit with a few clamps before gluing, you will be able to decide if you need more. These are cheap, and I keep several dozen in a portable box.)
- Bungee cords (useful for holding stringers to the form temporarily)
- Measuring tools, including a tape measure, level, framing square, try square, bevel square, and protractor
- Steel straightedge rulers (in a variety of sizes; as a minimum, a 6-inch ruler and a 36-inch ruler)
- Marking gauge
- Drafting tools or graph paper and a 24-inch flexible curve for drawing stations
- Fire extinguisher and a first-aid kit (kept nearby)

Supplies

Lots of little items, such as nails, screws, package sealing tape, masking tape, yellow or white wood glue, and so on, can be purchased as you need them and as you determine what sizes fit your project. Here are some of the other major supplies you may need:

- Plywood for making a strongback and stations for the form: several sheets of ½-inch plywood
- 2 × 4 lumber for attaching stations: two or three pieces 8 feet long
- Strips of wood for making gunwales
- Thin plywood for making decks, if desired
- Aluminum tubing for thwarts
- ½-inch polystyrene foam insulation board for bulkheads and other parts
- 2.7-ounce Dacron polyester peel ply fabric: enough to cover the form, about 5 or 6 yards (It is inexpensive, and it's worth having a few yards extra.)
- Epoxy resin and hardener: 1.5 to 2 gallons required for most of the designs in this book (adding a deck will probably consume another half gallon or more)
- Reinforcing cloth, such as Kevlar or carbon fiber: three or more layers to cover the entire hull (fiberglass can also be used but may require six to eight layers)

Working with epoxy will require some additional supplies:

- Metering pumps (inexpensive minipumps are available for WEST or MAS brand epoxies).
- Disposable bristle paint brushes: many in 2- and 3-inch sizes and a few in 1-inch size)
- Disposable foam paintbrushes: several in 2- and 3-inch sizes
- Plastic epoxy spreaders or squeegees (these look like large, rectangular credit cards and are available where fiberglass is sold)
- Fine-foam paint rollers for applying seal coats of epoxy: at least two or three rollers
- Rolls of paper towels and rags for cleanup
- Acetone or lacquer thinner for cleaning epoxy from tools and the floor

Epoxy

The heart and soul of composites are the fibers that impart strength and the resins that encapsulate the fibers, providing a solid matrix that holds the desired shape. The fibers are generally flexible so that they can take on a variety of shapes. Saturate the fibers with a liquid that can be turned into a solid, and you have a solid structure quite unlike either of its components. A familiar example is the papier-mâché most of us used as schoolchildren, in which paper is mixed with paste or glue to make sculptural objects.

In modern canoe building, the matrix materials are thermosetting plastic resins. These are resins that are changed permanently from liquid to solid by a chemical reaction. The common resins in use are polyester, vinylester, and epoxy. Each of these resins is one part of a two-part system: the resin itself and a catalyst or hardener. Combining resin and hardener in the proper ratio produces a chemical reaction that gives off heat and cures the resin into a solid. The resins can be used at room temperature and at normal atmospheric pressure.

The resins cure through several stages. When the resin and hardener or catalyst are first mixed, they remain at a low viscosity so they can be applied to fibers and saturate them. After a while an exothermic reaction takes place. Heat is produced that starts the curing process. If too much heat is produced, the resin may cure too quickly or a fire may even occur. Do I have your attention? Follow the manufacturer's directions.

It is easy to prevent the exothermic reaction from proceeding too quickly by mixing resin and hardener in relatively small batches. Also, providing more surface area relative to volume will slow the reaction by dissipating heat. This can be done by pouring the mixed resin in a shallow layer in a large, flat container instead of keeping it confined in a tall, compact mixing cup.

After the initial liquid stage, the resin thickens to a point where it will no longer flow. This is the gel stage. If your mixed resin reaches this stage in the container, don't attempt to apply it to the laminate—it's past its workable stage. Just let it harden in the container, and then throw it out.

When the resin becomes dry to the touch but has not reached its full hardness, it is said to be in the "green" stage of cure. This is the time to add more layers of cloth and resin or finishing layers of resin. Because the first layer has not fully cured, it will make a strong chemical bond with the following layer, maximizing the strength of the structure. In the green state, it is relative easy to trim the edges of a laminate with a knife, whereas if you wait for full hardness, you will have to use a saw. After the green state, the resin becomes much harder and can be handled and worked on. However, it may continue to harden for several days or even weeks before reaching maximum hardness.

Polyester resins have long been used with fiberglass for boatbuilding. Polyester is cheap and easy to work with, but it does not bond well with Kevlar or carbon fiber. When combined with fiberglass, however, polyester is fine for molding larger and heavier boats, although it has a high rate of shrinkage and cannot match epoxy for impact resistance and strength. But when a combination of light weight and high strength is desirable, as in canoes, epoxy wins hands down.

Vinylester resins have some similarities to both polyester and epoxy, and vinylester is often used with Kevlar for factory-made canoes. The resin is trickier for the home builder to use and has a short shelf life. Both polyester and vinylester resins contain large amounts of styrene, which is highly flammable and severely irritates the skin, eyes, and respiratory tract. Such resins are best left to factories that have the protective equipment to use them.

Epoxy has many advantages. It has an excellent shelf life, and using it is a straightforward process. It produces strong durable laminates and is compatible with all the various fibers we may use. Epoxy is generally stronger than polyester and shrinks 40 to 50 percent less. It also works well with the peel ply layer of Dacron polyester used in the fabric form building method.

Consider these critical aspects to working with epoxy. Resin and hardener must be mixed in specific, precise ratios to cure properly. Such mixing must be very thorough, or curing and strength will be compromised. Adding excess hardener will not speed the cure rate or increase strength. Some epoxy systems offer different hardeners to shorten or extend the working time and cure rate.

Epoxy also presents some potential health hazards. The vapors, as well as the liquid, of some epoxies can cause skin irritation, rashes, and allergic reactions. Epoxy can irritate the nose, throat, and lungs and ingesting it is harmful. After using epoxy, wash your hands very thoroughly before eating or even smoking. The hardeners used with epoxy can also cause irritation and allergic reactions. If an allergic reaction is ever triggered, a person can become sensitized to epoxy so that even slight exposure causes recurrent reactions. To preserve your ability to work with epoxy, take precautions from the beginning. Wear gloves, a respirator, and glasses; cover the skin with a long-sleeved shirt and trousers; and work in an area with good ventilation. Also be cautious with the solvents, such as acetone, that are commonly used to clean up uncured epoxy. Acetone is highly flammable and is an irritant that can damage the central nervous system. The dust of cured resins and fibers can also be hazards during sawing and sanding, so take similar precautions to protect your skin and lungs during these operations.

To avoid contamination in landfills, do not discard unused epoxy in an uncured state. Mix hardener and epoxy together, and discard only after it has cured. It poses much less hazard in its solid state. Punch holes in the cans to drain them completely, and then mix the remains.

You can obtain epoxies from many manufacturers, and some of the resins now sold for home use are safer and less irritating than those of the past. I highly recommend WEST System epoxy (shown in Figure 3.1), which I have used for a long time in my musical instrument business and to build boats and aircraft parts. I have also had good success with MAS and System Three epoxies but have had less experience with them. I consider the WEST Technical Manual and Product Guide to be required reading for anyone using epoxy. Several of the suppliers in Appendix A can provide manuals for the epoxies they sell.

Because the mixing ratios of resin to hardener are so critical, it is wise to get the metering pumps for the brand of resin and hardener and the container size you wish to use. WEST and MAS both sell inexpensive plastic pumps. You will ultimately mix several gallons of epoxy in small batches, and the pumps give consistently accurate results.

Some epoxies can be used with different hardeners and a variety of additives to tailor them for various applications. Slow hardeners are best for laminating and boatbuilding. I keep small quantities of fast hardener on hand for smaller jobs that can be accomplished with a short "pot life" or working time.

Ultraviolet radiation from sunlight degrades and weakens cured epoxy. To prevent this deterioration, special UV-resistant hardeners may be used. WEST System 207 Special Coating Hardener, mixed with WEST 105 resin, provides a slow cure and ultraviolet resistance. It is still a good idea to finish the boat with paint or a UV-blocking varnish, but the use of 207 Hardener will allow you to use the boat for a while before finishing it. It also provides added protection under clear finishes and allows you to postpone touch-ups to scratches in a painted or varnished finish. Other WEST hardeners are mixed with resin at a 5:1 ratio (resin to hardener), but 207 Hardener requires a special 3:1 ratio, so make sure you buy and use the correct metering pumps.

Fillers of various types are added to epoxy to modify their working qualities and structural characteristics. These are added after the resin and hardener are mixed but before the cure begins. Several may be useful for a canoe project. Microfibers, such as WEST 403, strengthen epoxy and thicken it so that it will fill gaps. This is useful for attaching wood gunwales to the hull and for attaching decks and bulkheads. Fine wood sawdust or sanding dust makes good filler for creating fillets and matching wood colors. Colloidal silica filler increases the viscosity of liquid resin and the hardness of cured resin for improved abrasion resistance. It is a very fine powder that can harm the lungs, so put on a respirator before opening the container. Low-density WEST 410 Microlight filler creates a lightweight material that sands easily and smoothly. It is excellent for fairing large areas. It softens at high temperatures, however, so it is best to paint it with a light color to reflect sunlight and heat.

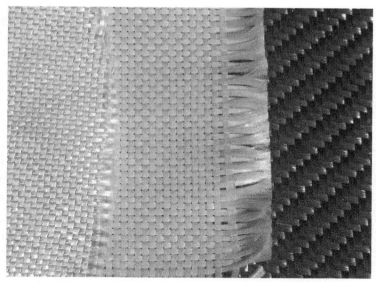

FIGURE 3.2. *Structural fabrics from left to right: fiberglass, Kevlar aramid, and carbon fiber.*

Structural Fabrics

Fibers and fabrics were introduced in Chapter 2. Currently, the most useful fabrics for canoe building are fiberglass, Kevlar, and carbon fiber. (See Figure 3.2.) Fiberglass is best known because of its longtime use in many products, including boats. E-glass, the most common form of fiberglass, is relatively strong but has poor stiffness compared to other materials. To compensate, a fiberglass laminate has to be relatively thick and heavy in applications requiring stiffness. For higher-performance applications, a somewhat stronger and stiffer fiberglass, known as S-glass, was developed. But it is costly, and its performance does not match that of Kevlar.

Kevlar 49 is an almost ideal material for canoe hulls. It is strong, tough, impact resistant, lightweight, and stiffer than fiberglass. One downside is that resin does not adhere to the fibers as well as it does to fiberglass and carbon fiber. In fact, polyester resin cannot be used at all with Kevlar. Even with epoxy, the resin-to-fiber bond reduces the strength of a Kevlar laminate, especially in compression. On the plus side, this means that laminated Kevlar does not fail in a brittle fashion all at once but instead gives and absorbs energy.

A hull is more likely to give partially as the resin fails but may stay together on impact rather than come apart catastrophically in pieces. During a portage, I once accidentally banged the side of a Kevlar canoe very hard against the small stump of an unseen tree branch. The Kevlar held and was not punctured, but the vinylester resin matrix around the Kevlar did fracture and leak. A small epoxy and fiberglass patch sealed the leak; even a bit of temporary repair tape would have gotten me home. This type of damage is common for Kevlar canoes.

Carbon fiber can be two or more times stiffer than Kevlar of the same weight. On an equal-weight basis, carbon fiber surpasses all metals, including steel, in strength and stiffness. Although Kevlar is lighter, tougher, and more impact resistant for its weight and volume, carbon's stiffness requires less weight of reinforcement to hold its shape. Therefore, for a given stiffness, it is possible to make a lighter hull from carbon fiber.

Stiffness is not without its drawbacks, however. Carbon fiber is brittle and can shatter into dust with severe impact. Since some canoes experience frequent impacts, this can be a concern. An ultralight, all-carbon hull may be adequate for open-water paddling where no obstructions are expected. But for greater safety in all-around canoe use, not to mention whitewater, one should avoid all-carbon construction. Carbon is also very expensive and occasionally in short supply.

Carbon fiber can be a plus in other ways, however. Very rigid and lightweight structures can be made by separating thin, strong layers with a lightweight core—the thicker the core, the more rigid the structure. Consider a hollow-core door as an example: if two panels of ⅛-inch-thick plywood are glued together to form a ¼-inch-thick panel, it will be quite flexible. If, instead, they are glued to a 1-inch-thick core, as in a hollow-core door, the structure becomes quite rigid. The core needs only to bond the strong outer layers together to make a stiff structure that will hold its shape.

This suggests a number of design possibilities for using carbon. Instead of making a lamination with all carbon fiber, we can use carbon for only the outer layers and still realize most of its stiffness benefits. Core layers of inexpensive fiberglass can impart greater stiffness to our structure merely by separating and holding the outer carbon layers or skins. Going a step further, we could replace the fiberglass core with a Kevlar core. This takes maximum advantage of carbon's strength and stiffness while adding Kevlar's impact protection, toughness, and resistance to tearing. Since Kevlar is lighter than fiberglass or carbon, this would also reduce weight.

This is one of the great advantages of composite structures. Different fibers can be combined to take advantage of their distinct properties for various combinations of cost, weight, stiffness, and impact resistance. It is not uncommon to incorporate a layer of Kevlar between two outer layers of carbon for making bodies and other components of race cars. When cars collide, the carbon fiber tends to shatter into dust but the Kevlar may keep the parts and pieces from flying off and creating a greater hazard.

In the previous example, Kevlar was used as a core because it is less stiff than carbon. However,

Kevlar, in turn, is much stiffer than fiberglass. Thus, Kevlar can be used as outer layers with a fiberglass core. And hull stiffness can be improved by making the core thicker by adding more layers of fiberglass, rather than using more expensive materials. The result will be heavier than a carbon-Kevlar-carbon hull, but lighter and stronger than an all-fiberglass hull.

Fiber cost could be further reduced by incorporating just one outer or inner layer of Kevlar in an otherwise all-fiberglass hull. For most general purposes, an all-Kevlar hull is a very good all-around compromise among strength, stiffness, light weight, and cost. Because Kevlar does not sand well, consider using an outer layer of fiberglass if the outer hull is to be sanded smooth.

Practice

If you have never worked with epoxy composites, it may help to get some experience before embarking on a full-size boat project. You will discover firsthand what works and what doesn't. I've seen very expensive projects ruined because someone jumped in and started building before learning to work with epoxy. The process is not at all difficult; it is just unforgiving of certain kinds of mistakes. The major problem is almost always a failure to adhere carefully to the proper mix ratios and mixing techniques. Get the mixing stick into the bottom crevasses of the mixing cup and scrape the side walls to ensure that every bit of hardener and resin is combined. Mix for a good minute or two. Read and heed the epoxy manufacturer's instructions.

Many of the epoxy systems are available in 1-quart sizes or even smaller repair kits. They can be used for test projects, such as model building with the fabric form method and paddle making. (See Chapters 10 and 17, respectively.) These projects can help you become familiar with the materials and methods, but even if you choose to skip them and have never worked with composites, you will likely be successful building a full-size canoe if you follow directions carefully. On the other hand, a model for your mantel might remind you of your goal, or some child would surely love to receive it as a gift. And a high-tech composite paddle is something you might use and enjoy long before the full-size boat is done.

Form

Building a canoe or kayak requires making a form on which to laminate the hull. The form is identical to the type used for making a wood strip canoe. The main difference is that you will need relatively few strips and you can use the strips and other materials for another project when your boat is done. The used strips are much too nice for tomato stakes, but they might be perfect for making a trellis. An optimist might save them for building the next boat!

I'll guide you step by step through constructing the skeleton form, but if you are new to boatbuilding, you may want to read some books on wood strip canoe building, which also offer designs and plans that can be used with my composite method. (See Appendix B for titles.) If possible, choose plans that have a spacing of about 12 inches between stations, which works best with the fabric form method as described. But wider spacing between stations can also be accommodated by using thicker stringers. Plans will have station drawings or station coordinates, which must be expanded to full size onto plywood. The plywood is cut out to make station forms on which wood strips are fastened to give shape to the hull form. This process is outlined in most of the books and is similar to the one I use, although the authors may differ in some details. For a preview, see Figures 6.3 and 6.4, which show stations mounted on a strongback, and Figure 6.18, which shows a completed skeleton form.

Chapter 4

The Strongback

If you wish to use an existing canoe as a form, skip ahead to Chapter 7. Assembling a skeleton form to build a canoe from plans requires some sort of support. This is the strongback. It must support everything at a convenient working height and be sturdy enough to keep everything level and in alignment as you push, pull, hammer, drill, screw, plane, sand, and do anything else necessary to conjure up a canoe. There are many ways to create a strongback. Figure 4.1 illustrates three types that are functional and easy to build. The ladder and tee strongbacks are faster to build than the box-type strongback, because they require fewer saw cuts, screws, and parts. But they require more work to level and true the station forms, because it is difficult to find lumber that is straight and warp free with straight edges.

Ladder Strongback

The ladder strongback can be made with two pieces of 2 × 6 in the length needed for the canoe.

Long lengths are usually available. If not, nail together shorter pieces with lap joints 3 to 4 feet long. The canoe form can overhang the strongback by about 6 inches at each end, so the strongback can be about a foot shorter than the boat. The strongback can be as narrow as 8 inches, but 12 to 14 inches makes leveling slightly easier. Screw a piece of lumber at each end to set the width, using #8 Phillips-head deck screws 2½ inches long. Add a piece of ⅝-inch-thick (or thicker) plywood about 18 inches long to the bottom at each end and in the center. The 2 × 4 crosspieces are added to the top to stiffen the structure. Figure 4.4 (later in this chapter) illustrates how to position the crosspieces.

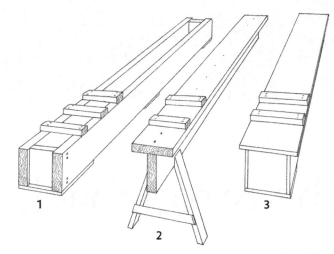

FIGURE 4.1. *Three types of strongback are shown here: (from left to right) (1) parallel beam or ladder, (2) tee, and (3) plywood box. The ladder and plywood box types can be supported on sawhorses or with legs (as shown in Figure 4.3). If sawhorses are used, it is best to screw the strongback to wooden sawhorses; using angle brackets is a convenient way to do this. The tee strongback can have sawhorse legs attached to the vertical beam, as depicted at the near end. 2 × 4 crosspieces are screwed to the top of the strongback to support plywood station forms. A few crosspieces are shown installed; one will be required for each station.*

Tee Strongback

The tee type of strongback is the fastest and simplest to make. Two pieces of 2 × 8 lumber are adequate for canoe lengths up to 15 or 16 feet. The wood must be as straight and warp free as possible. Any twist in the horizontal top of the tee will require shimming some of the station forms to make them level. If the twist is more than slight, it will be difficult to level the station forms and support them vertically against the 2 × 4 crosspieces. Assemble the tee with 2½-inch #8 deck screws. The wood beams used for the ladder and tee strongbacks can easily be unscrewed and recycled for other projects.

Plywood Box Strongback

Although the plywood box strongback takes a bit more time and work to build, it has several advantages. First, a long plywood box beam that is open on the bottom can be twisted a little, so both ends can be made level by shimming the

feet, regardless of the straightness of the floor. Also, it is easy to achieve a very flat and smooth top surface, which simplifies marking the centerline and station locations. Finally, a plywood box can be lighter than the other types and still be stiff and strong. Heavier is better in that it resists being inadvertently bumped out of place, but I work alone and have to move the strongback around and get it in and out of storage by myself. My shop is small, and there are times when I need to move the boat project out to make room for other work. I can easily lift and move the box strongback one end at a time even with the entire form attached. Of course, each time the strongback is moved, it must be shimmed and leveled again before work proceeds.

The strongback pictured in Figure 4.2 is made from 9/16-inch plywood in the form of a box section approximately 12 inches wide and 9 inches high. The bottom is open, which keeps the strongback flexible in order to adjust the twist. Plywood crosspieces at the ends and internally at 16- or 24-inch intervals brace the structure and fix the width. Drywall screws or deck screws are used to assemble the plywood pieces. There are two sections, each 8 feet long, and one slides inside the other so that it may be sized to the length needed for the hull. They must overlap in the center by at least 24 inches and be secured with plenty of screws. Because of the overlap and the 8-foot lengths of available plywood, two sections will make a strongback 14 feet long, accommodating hulls up to 15 or 16 feet. For longer hulls, make more sections. Make up the narrower section, shown on the right in Figure 4.2, first. Then make the wider section to fit.

Assemble the two sections without the top. When you are ready to screw the sections together, place them upright together on the floor. Put a nail at each end so you can tie a string taut from one end to the other along one top edge. Adjust and shim each end so that the entire assembly is as straight as possible. Then clamp the side pieces together. Put one screw in each side, and check again for straightness. It is possible to sight from the ends along the sides to ensure straightness. But if you are not already skilled at doing this, the string method is better. When everything looks near perfect, apply plenty of screws. Short drywall screws or other screws about 1¼ inches long are good for this.

Legs

For a lightweight plywood strongback, the legs can be 1 × 4 uprights, as shown in Figures 4.2 and 4.3. If your strongback is larger, heavier plywood, or the ladder or tee type, then make 2 × 4 uprights. Tie the legs together by screwing in place a plywood foot panel (as shown in Figure 4.3). The panel is ½-inch plywood 12 inches high and a minimum of 19 inches side to side. For heavier strongbacks with 2 × 4 legs, make the foot panel of ¾-inch plywood. Use at least four evenly spaced screws in each leg. Use #7

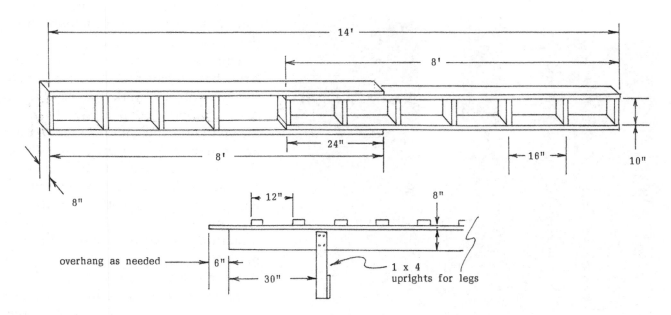

FIGURE 4.2. *Plans for a plywood strongback. At the top is a view from the underneath without the top installed. At the bottom is a side view that shows the plywood top with 2 × 4 crosspieces and an overhang at the end. Overhangs at the ends can be 6 to 8 inches.*

deck screws about 1½ inches long, or something similar.

Set the leg length to provide a comfortable working height for yourself. The top of my strongback is set at 32 inches high for building the Wasp canoe that is used as an example in most of the form assembly and laminating photographs in this book. First, place the strongback on two low sawhorses. Add blocks of wood on top of the sawhorses to prop up the strongback until the height seems good. Then screw the legs into the sides of the strongback. Height is easy to change by propping up the strongback at a different height and reinstalling screws. Do one end at a time. Sometimes I add a layer of ½-inch plywood to the bottom of the strongback just at the ends, from the ends to the legs. The ends become very stiff, allowing just the middle to twist for leveling.

Place the strongback in the location where you will build your canoe. Next, shim the legs as necessary to carefully level the entire strongback. Try to make it level along its entire length, at both ends and in the middle. Keep in mind that every time you move the strongback even a little, whether accidentally or on purpose, you will need to recheck for level.

The Top

The plywood strongback is now ready to accept a top. Fasten a piece of ½-inch plywood with screws. Since you will mark on the top surface to lay out centerline and station locations, use smooth, clear plywood. You will need two pieces 8 feet long trimmed to fit. It is handy for the top to overhang the sides by an inch or so, making a convenient ledge for temporarily clamping things in place. If you omit the overhang, much longer clamps will be needed to reach the bottom of the strongback.

Find the midpoint at each end of the strongback. Snap a chalkline between those points to mark the centerline. Another option is to place small nails at the end midpoints and tie a taut string between them. Make pencil marks along the string at intervals close enough so that you can connect them with a long metal ruler. Whether you used a chalkline or string, draw a permanent centerline with a pen or an ultrafine marker.

On a ladder strongback, there is no place to draw a centerline until the crosspieces are in place, so choose the side with the straightest beam and mark station locations on it. Draw the

FIGURE 4.3. *Strongback legs and foot.*

right-angle station lines across both beams using a framing square or T square, and attach the crosspieces to the beams using screws. Mark the centerline on top of the crosspieces from the first station to the last. Extend the centerline with a framing square to mark the end pieces of the strongback.

Marking the Station Locations

Measure and mark the station locations along the centerline, and then use a drafting square or framing square to lay out the station lines at right angles to the centerline. Use the spacing specified for the design. Figure 4.4 shows 12-inch spacing between stations, which is the distance specified for the three designs in this book.

Decide which end will be the bow and which will be the stern, and number the station locations. Figure 4.4 shows the bow to the left. Cut a 2 × 4 crosspiece for each station; the length of each crosspiece should equal the width of the strongback. Drill a couple of holes in each crosspiece to accommodate screws. If you have a power jointer, plane one 4-inch side of each of the 2 × 4 crosspieces perfectly flat. Placing that flat side against the jointer fence, run a 2-inch side over

the jointer to make an accurate right angle. The flat 4-inch side goes down on the strongback; the flat 2-inch side goes up against the station line.

For stations forward of the centermost station (for example, stations #1 through #6 for Kayoo; see the plans in Chapter 16), fasten the 2 × 4 crosspieces on the bow side of the location lines, so that the forward surface of the station forms will be right on the lines. For stations toward the stern (stations #8 through #13 for Kayoo), place the crosspieces on the stern side of the location lines, so that the aft surface of the station forms will be right on the lines. The center station (station #7 for Kayoo) can be mounted either way. The above procedure ensures that the finished hull conforms most accurately to the plans, but it is not critical.

The more complex shape of the Wasp design makes such mounting problematic. As a practical matter, I mount all of the crosspieces against the bow or forward side of the station lines, so that the forward surface of all the station forms will be on the station lines.

Figure 4.4 shows crosspieces toward the bow of each station line for stations #1 through #7 and toward the stern for station #13. Clamp each crosspiece accurately in place; then attach it securely with two Phillips-head deck screws about 2½ inches long; these can be conveniently driven with a power screwdriver or a variable-speed electric drill.

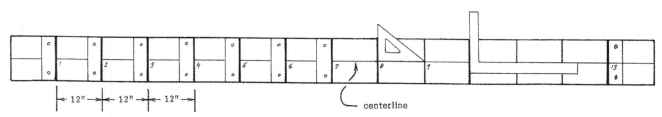

FIGURE 4.4. *Top view of strongback with the layout for centerline and 2 × 4 crosspieces for station supports.*

Chapter 5

Translating a Design into Full-Size Stations

The plans you wish to use have to be translated into full-size station templates or forms and end profile forms. Some boat designers sell full-size plans, but most provide only scale plans or coordinates—usually called "offsets" among boatbuilders—which you must plot out to make full-size drawings. You can use the designs in this book or most plans for wood strip–built canoes.

Enlarging the Drawings

I've provided three options to make it easier for you to use the designs in Chapter 16. Each design includes scale drawings of the end profiles on grids and the stations on grids. To generate full-size drawings, the grids are enlarged to 2-inch squares. The first option is to use a large photocopier to enlarge the grid to full size. A measurement of 2 inches indicated on the grid should be copied to measure 2 inches on your enlargement. It will be easier to be accurate if you measure a longer distance. For instance, make a

12-inch scale indication on the grid equal to 12 inches on your enlargement.

It may be difficult to find a suitable copier, however, and photocopiers may introduce minor distortions, especially if you are piecing together the drawings in several sections. The second option is to draw the enlargement, which is actually quite easy and sufficiently accurate. Draw a full-size grid of 2-inch squares on good heavyweight paper, taking care that the grid lines are at accurate right angles. Drafting squares are helpful, or you can buy grid paper: 17 by 22 inches is a common size that is large enough. Draw the end profiles and stations full size to look like the plans. Curved lines can be drawn with a flexible curve or French curves. Even drawing freehand can work. Minor inaccuracies are likely but are usually not very troublesome. The stringers that are applied to the forms tend to make smooth curves that eliminate minor deviations from the plans.

Using Coordinates to Make Full-Size Drawings

The third option, the most accurate way to enlarge the plans, is to use the tables of coordinates, which allow you to accurately plot many points along each curve. Each point has two measurements. For stations, one measurement is the horizontal distance from the centerline, measuring from left to right. The other is the vertical distance down from a reference line; this line represents the edge of the station form that will rest on the strongback. For end profiles, the horizontal measurement is from the first or last station. Grid paper helps make this layout a bit faster and easier, but you can use plain paper and a square or draw your own grid.

The scale drawings included with each design are an important reference for checking your work. Your full-size layouts should look similar to the scale drawings. It is easy to get confused

and make a mistake while enlarging the drawings or using the coordinates. It is also easy for the designer to make a typographical error when recording coordinates. The final check on both your accuracy and mine is to make certain that your enlargements and the scale drawings appear to be a good match. Figures 5.1 through 5.8 illustrate how to use the coordinates. The Kayoo design from Chapter 16 is used as an example; the coordinates for stations #2 and #12 are shown in Table 5.1, and the full table of coordinates is listed in Chapter 16.

TABLE 5.1 *Kayoo Coordinates for Stations #2 and #12*

	HORIZONTAL	VERTICAL
G2	7.70″	4.90″
G12	7.64	5.34
D2	7.30	7.50
D12	7.14	8.24
	6.66	10.00
	5.96	12.00
WL	4.76	14.00
	2.92	16.00
	2.00	16.68
	0.00	17.14

Stations should be grouped together to match the scale station drawings in Chapter 16. Most designs have all of the stations on one drawing; only one sheet or copy is needed. You will be able to cut and trace the largest station first, then progress in turn to the next largest station, and so on. Since your full-size station drawings will be cut out to make templates, you might choose to make safety photocopies or use the copies for cutting templates. Then, if you make a mistake with the scissors, you won't have to plot points and draw curves all over again. Businesses that provide copy services for engineers and architects can make the large copies needed. Note that the Wasp design is unusual and requires four sheets. Your paper copies will actually be half templates. They will be traced onto plywood to both the left and right of the centerline to produce full-size station forms.

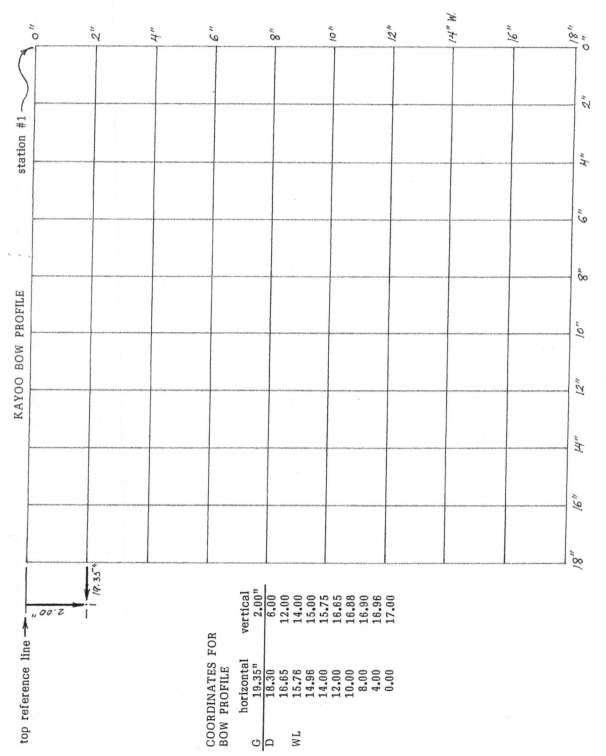

KAYOO BOW PROFILE

station #1

top reference line →

2.00"

19.35"

COORDINATES FOR
BOW PROFILE

	horizontal	vertical
	19.35"	2.00"
G	18.30	6.00
D	16.65	12.00
	15.76	14.00
WL	14.96	15.00
	14.00	15.75
	12.00	16.65
	10.00	16.88
	8.00	16.90
	4.00	16.96
	0.00	17.00

FIGURE 5.1. *Start with the coordinates for the bow profile of Kayoo, which appear to the left of the grid. The top pair of numbers locates the first point, labeled G. This is the highest point of the bow, where the gunwale meets the bow, if the boat is built as an open canoe. Start with this point even if you intend to build the decked version. Place a mark 19.35 inches to the left of the vertical line for station #1. Place another mark 2 inches down from the top reference line. Where the marks cross is point G. Although measurements are given in hundredths of an inch, it may be difficult to measure that finely or find a ruler with those graduations. Use a ruler graduated in tenths of an inch, and estimate as well as you can. For instance, .04 is almost halfway between .00 and .10. Slight variations will not hurt your boat or its performance.*

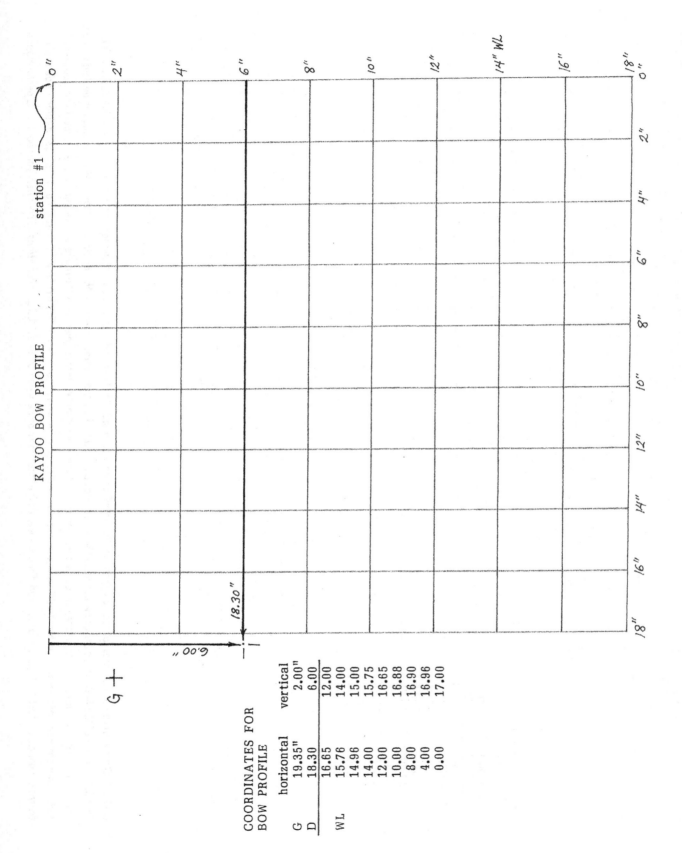

KAYOO BOW PROFILE

COORDINATES FOR
BOW PROFILE

	horizontal	vertical
G	19.35"	2.00"
D	18.30	6.00
WL	16.65	12.00
	15.76	14.00
	14.96	15.00
	14.00	15.75
	12.00	16.65
	10.00	16.88
	8.00	16.90
	4.00	16.96
	0.00	17.00

FIGURE 5.2. *The next pair of numbers locates point D. This is the highest point of the bow if Kayoo is built in a decked version. The hull is laminated a bit oversized and then trimmed to build the desired version. Place a mark 18.30 inches to the left of station #1 and 6 inches down from the top reference line. Where the marks cross is point D.*

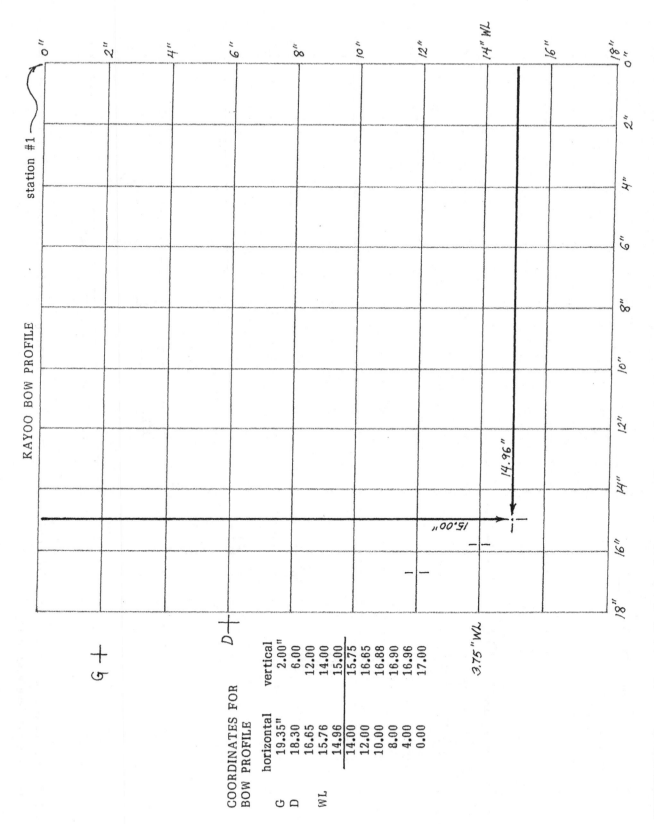

FIGURE 5.3. *Continue marking points. The fourth point is on the waterline, 14 inches down from the top. This is at the 3.75-inch waterline, a reference line chosen to represent the depth of the boat in the water with an arbitrary load. If you mark this waterline on ends and stations, it can be a handy reference while building. The fifth point, illustrated in this figure, is 14.96 inches left and 15 inches down. Continue plotting the remaining points.*

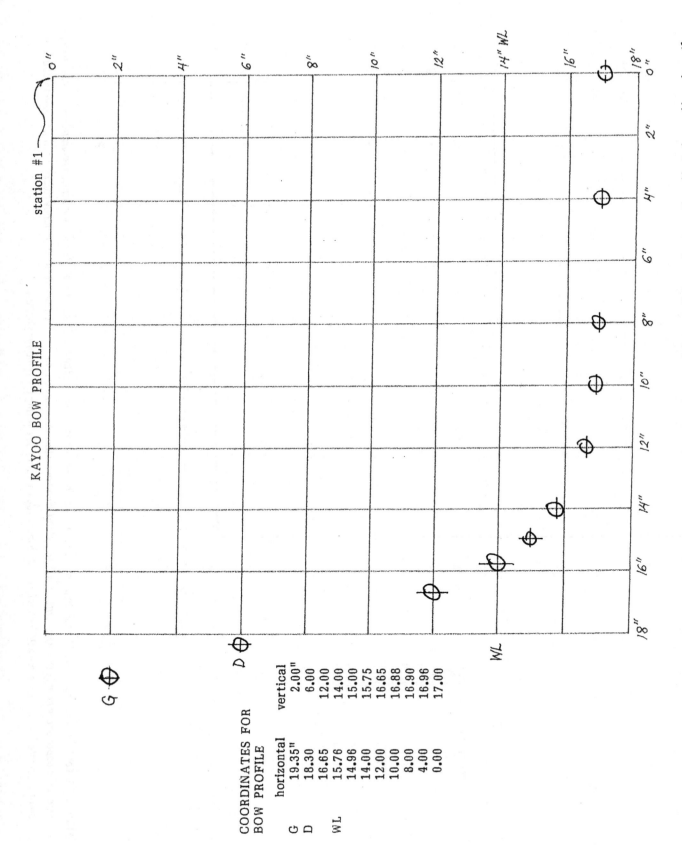

FIGURE 5.4. *All eleven points that define the bow shape have now been located. Look at them carefully to see if they make a smooth and logical curved bow shape. If any points seem questionable, measure again.*

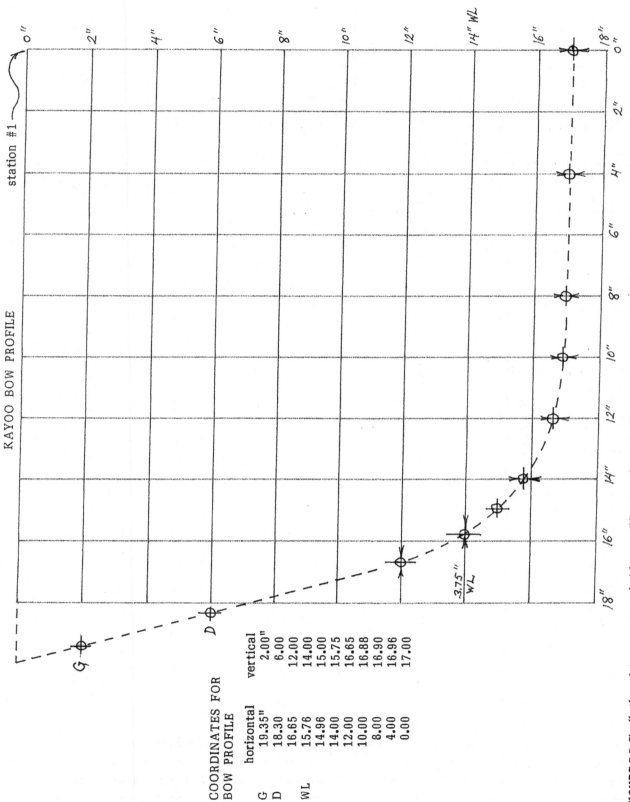

station #1

KAYOO BOW PROFILE

COORDINATES FOR BOW PROFILE

	horizontal	vertical
G	19.35"	2.00"
D	18.30	6.00
	16.65	12.00
WL	15.76	14.00
	14.96	15.00
	14.00	15.75
	12.00	16.65
	10.00	16.88
	8.00	16.90
	4.00	16.96
	0.00	17.00

FIGURE 5.5. *Finally, the points are connected with a pencil line to make a smoothly curved shape. This can be done with a combination of straight edges and a flexible curve or French curves. The curved part of the line can even be made freehand; the results might be less precise but are likely to be acceptable. Continue the line upward from point G to the top reference line. When a plywood end form is made to this pattern, the top reference line will rest on the strongback. Carefully compare your full-size layout with the plans and scale drawings. The resulting shape should match Figure 16.11, which shows the Kayoo bow profile. Next, use the coordinates for the stern profile of the design you are building to draw that pattern full size in the same manner.*

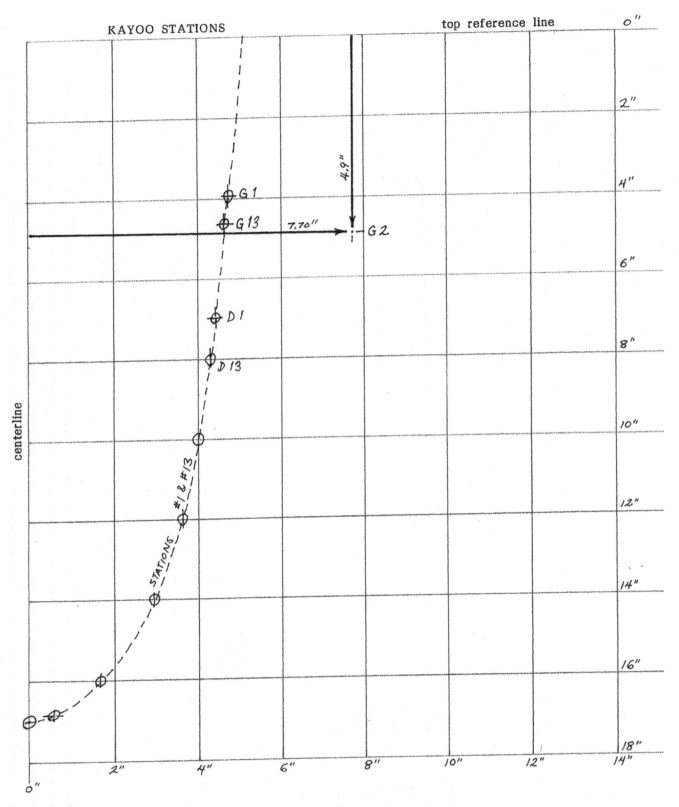

FIGURE 5.6. *Points are plotted similarly for drawing the stations. Here, Kayoo stations #1 and #13 are already drawn. Stations #1 and #13 are the same except for the gunwale heights for the open version or the deck heights for the decked version. Coordinates are in the text for the next stations, #2 and #12. Starting with the top pair of numbers, place a mark 7.70 inches to the right of the centerline. Place another mark 4.90 inches down from the top reference line. Where the marks intersect is point G2. This is the gunwale height at station #2 for the open canoe version.*

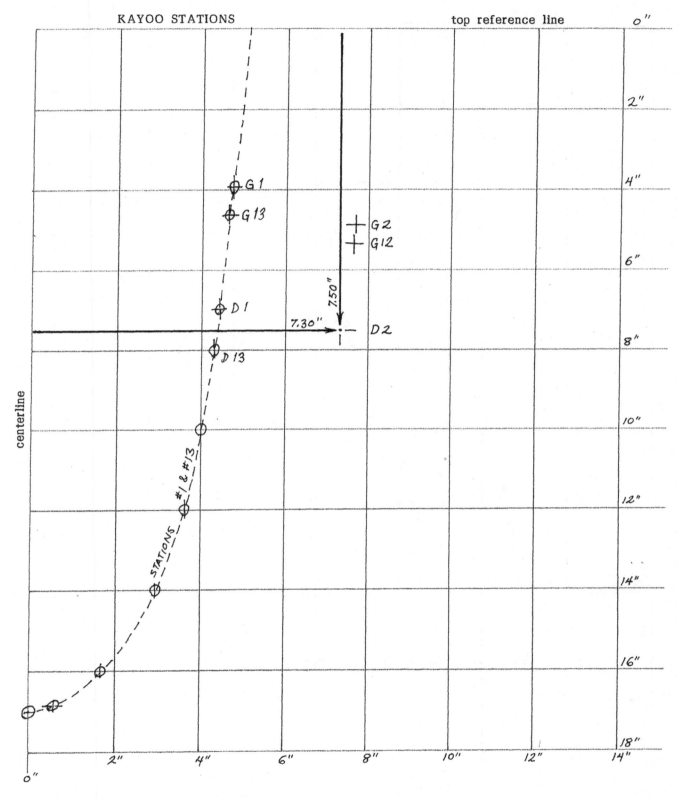

FIGURE 5.7. Points G2 and G12 are already marked. To plot point D2, place a mark 7.30 inches to the right of the centerline and a mark 7.50 inches down from the top line.

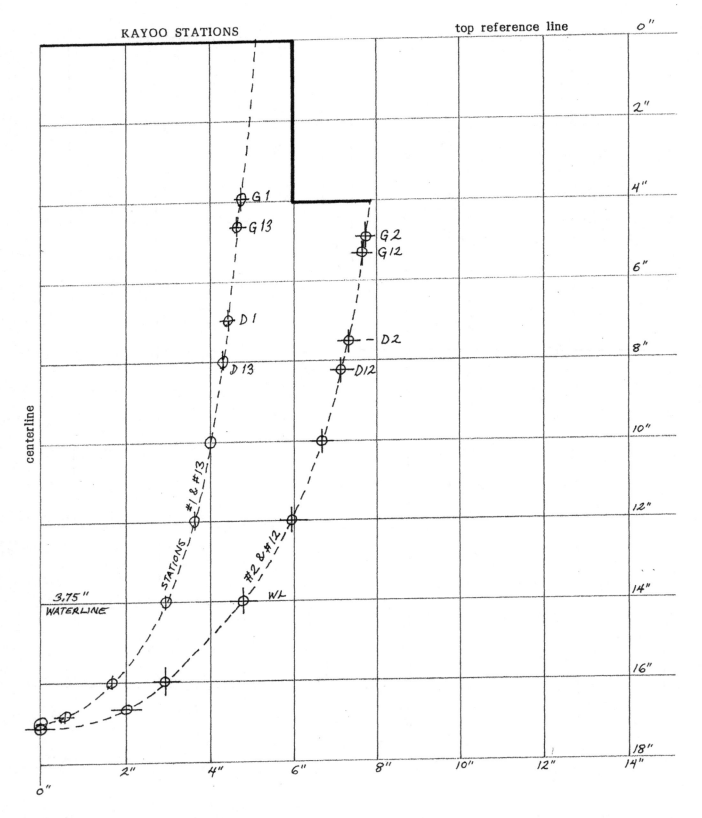

FIGURE 5.8. *After all the points have been located, draw a smooth curve through the points. Notice that the line for stations #1 and #13 continues up to the top reference line while the line for stations #2 and #12 stops 4 inches below the top. Stations #2 and #12 are wider than my 12-inch-wide strongback. Stations that are wider than the strongback have a cutout at the top. Plywood station forms will be inverted and mounted on the strongback, and the cutouts will make some operations easier.*

The Dancing Canoe

Ragtime

Sam Rizzetta © 2003

Chapter 6

Assembling the Form

Most of the photos of the building process depict the construction of Wasp, a solo canoe about 14 feet 9 inches long with a narrowed waist and flared ends, making it especially safe and

easy to paddle. (See Figure 6.1.) Wasp is used as an example because it is the most difficult of the hull designs to build and requires more detailed explanations and pictures. Any other canoe hull you choose is likely to be much simpler and easier to build. Along the way I will describe how your tasks can be simplified when building more conventional designs.

Wasp has a lot of volume to ride over waves and carry a load, yet it is light, moderately fast, maneuverable, and a joy to paddle. It has a narrow paddling station, which provides an extremely ergonomic, easy reach to the water with the paddle. The paddle stroke can be made closer to the centerline so that the canoe tracks straight with less energy wasted on correcting strokes. And the flared areas help resist capsizing. Wasp is also unique in that it is suitable for a wide range of paddler weights and sizes from small to large. Plans for Wasp appear in Chapter 16.

FIGURE 6.1. *Wasp is a partially decked solo canoe made using the fabric form process.*

Making the Station Forms

After drawing out a full-size half template on paper for each station (as described in Chapter 5), number each station and carefully cut each out with scissors. Cut along the outside hull line and also cut down the centerline. Make sure the template has marks for the waterline and the sheerline—the line that marks the top of the hull. For an open canoe, the sheerline is at the gunwale. For decked boats, it is where the hull and the deck meet. The plans for Kayoo and Wasp have alternate sheerlines for both open canoe and decked versions. Mark both if you want to preserve the option of building either way. Be sure to transfer all these marks from the paper templates to the plywood station forms.

The next task is to trace the paper template onto the plywood. An ultrafine line marker or medium-line ink pen will make the line more visible and easier to follow with a saw. Figure 10.1 shows how to cut a paper template and trace a plywood station for a model canoe. The process is the same for a full-size boat.

The outer dimensions of the stations must be reduced by an amount equal to the thickness of the wood strips you will use for stringers. I used ¼-inch-thick pine screen molding for Wasp, so I trimmed ¼ inch off the outside of the station forms. (Don't trim the bottom edge that will go against the strongback.) It would save a little plywood to trim the paper template first. But I often saw out the plywood form full size and then use a marking gauge to conveniently and accurately scribe the cut line for trimming off the thickness of the strips. This does mean cutting the plywood twice, but it allows me to double-check the work.

Trimming the plywood station forms to allow for the stringers ensures that the hull will conform more accurately to the plans. However, it is also okay to not trim the stations, and it only makes a small difference. Not trimming will result in a very slightly larger boat, which will add small amounts of weight, volume, rocker, and stability.

Use plywood that is at least ½ inch thick for the stations. It is easier to fasten the stringers to thicker plywood, but thicker is heavier and more costly. Trace one side of a paper template onto the plywood; then flip the paper template over at the centerline to trace the other side. You will now have a book-matched tracing—like a butterfly wing, left and right—on the plywood that gives the entire shape of the station form. On each plywood station form, draw lines indicating the centerline, the waterline, and the positions of the gunwales or deck sheerlines.

The plywood stations can be cut out with a band saw or a hand jigsaw or saber saw. (See Figure 6.2.) Be as accurate as you can, but very minor errors will probably not show in the end product. If you have a stationary side sander, you may cut so as to leave the tracing line visible and then sand to the line. Sanding the stations may be unnecessary. But if you have the tools, it doesn't take much time to do more accurate work. I have a 6-inch-wide belt sander mounted at right angles to a table to provide the function of a side sander. This is useful for all sorts of finishing work, including making clean scarf joints to assemble full-length wood gunwales out of shorter pieces.

Carefully level the strongback as accurately as possible by adding thin wood shims under the support legs as needed. If you are using a plywood strongback without a bottom, it will twist a bit, allowing each end to be leveled separately. Next, temporarily screw or clamp each plywood station form to

its corresponding 2 × 4 crosspiece on the strongback (as in Figure 6.3). Drill pilot holes and use screws about 1½ inches long. Notice in Figure 6.4 how the end piece is attached with pieces of 2 × 4 to the centerlines of both the first station and the top of the strongback.

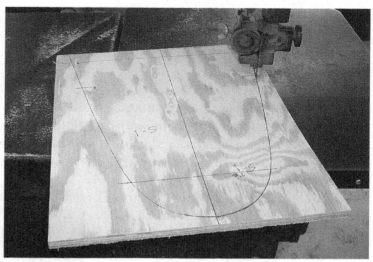

FIGURE 6.2. *A band saw makes quick work of cutting a plywood station.*

FIGURE 6.3. *Stations are assembled to the strongback.*

Shim the stations so that they are level and at the correct height and so the centerlines are aligned when a string is stretched from one end to the other. As shown in Figure 6.5, the string is elevated with pieces of scrap wood so that it does not quite touch the highest station, which should be the center station (station #7 for Wasp). The string is stretched tight between two small nails or tacks, one at each end. Place the nails exactly at the center of each end form. Loosen the clamps or screws to move the stations as needed. Drill new pilot holes if the stations have to be moved much, and then reattach them with screws. It is also possible to saw slots in the plywood stations to adjust the stations from side to side.

After all of the stations are in place, centered and level, it is time to check visually that the curves of the hull look like the plans, drawings, and pictures of the boat you are building. (See Figure 6.6.) Make sure that the curves between the stations are smooth and fair. Use a wood strip to span across several stations at several points from top to bottom of the hull, and check that the strip will make the necessary bends without some stations seeming too high or low. Sometimes plans have errors, or we don't always translate them into error-free stations. This is a good time to make corrections. Stations that seemed badly out of shape can be replaced, but that usually is not necessary. Areas on a station that stick out too much can be trimmed down. Areas that don't extend far enough to support the test strip can be shimmed out with wood scraps later on when permanent strips are attached.

Wasp is a shape with more curves and sharper curves than other boats, so it will be a little harder to judge. Look at the pictures and plans, examine the test strip carefully to ensure

FIGURE 6.4. *Pieces of 2 × 4 are screwed to the strongback, and the stations are screwed to those 2 × 4s. Note the arrangement of 2 × 4s used to attach the end forms.*

FIGURE 6.5. *A string is stretched end to end to align the stations.*

nice, fair curves, and do thorough work making adjustments where needed.

At this point the forms should be in alignment with the ends and at the correct heights to provide the desired amount of rocker (the end-to-end curve of the bottom of a hull). Attach a temporary wood keel strip down the centerline of the stations at the top of the form (as shown

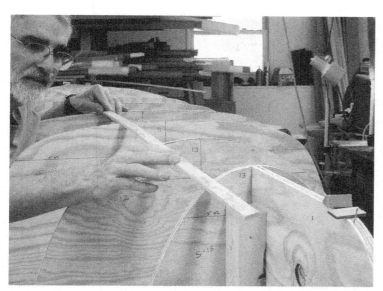

FIGURE 6.6. *Use a wood strip to check the curve between stations. The curve of the hull should be smooth, gradual, uniform, and symmetrical side to side.*

FIGURE 6.7. *A temporary keel strip is tacked in place to hold the stations vertical.*

center of a station so that the ends of both strips can be nailed down.

Attaching the Stringers

Stringers can be made from almost any clear, straight-grained, knot-free softwood; pine bends well, nails easily, and is strong enough to support the fabric covering to come later. If you have a table saw, it is easy to saw your own strips from pine boards. If you've been waiting for an excuse to buy a table saw, perhaps this is it. However, ¼-by-¾-inch pine screen molding works well and saves a lot of time since it is ready to use as is. The edges are rounded, which works well with the fabric. Cost is not prohibitive since you are not covering the entire hull as you would be if making a wood strip canoe. And you avoid the cost of a table saw, which is not really needed for the rest of the canoe building process. It is also possible to have strips cut at a lumber yard or by a supplier of canoe building materials. If you choose not to use screen molding, then you will need to round the edges of your strips with a hand plane or a router. A minimum of about thirty-one strips 8 feet long are required to make Wasp, depending on how close you choose to place the stringers. It is wise to get or make a few extra—you may break or split a few, and extras always come in handy for other tasks.

If the plans you are using call for spacing greater than 12 inches between stations, use stringers thicker than ¼-by-¾-inch molding. Otherwise, the tightened fabric that will cover the form may pull the stringers slightly out of shape between the stations. Try ³⁄₈- or ½-inch-thick strips for a station spacing of 14 to 18 inches.

in Figure 6.7). This strip can be the same as the strips used for stringers (¼-by-¾-inch pine is recommended for Wasp). Nail it in place with 1-inch wire nails or brads. Do not drive the nails in all the way; leave the heads protruding so that they will be easy to remove. You can use several strips end to end to make up the full length from bow station to stern station. Strips should meet in the

Before purchasing or cutting all the strips, try checking the curves between stations with one test strip to make sure it will make the necessary bends.

Start by attaching the stringers at the bottom of each side of the form (as shown in Figure 6.8). Two 8-foot-long strips are required to go the full length of the hull. Join them at the center station. Longer boats, such as tandem canoes, will require more strips and more joints, or longer strips (10 feet long). Proceed up each side toward the keel strip in the middle of the form. One-inch-long #6 flathead Phillips screws work well to hold the strips and can be driven with an electric screwdriver. They need not be specifically wood screws; sheet metal screws work fine. You may want to have a few #6 screws in shorter and longer sizes available. A lot of small screws have to be driven into your form, so a small power screwdriver will make the work go much faster and easier. It is a good idea to drill pilot holes in the pine stringers and perhaps into the stations, too, to prevent splitting.

After drilling the pilot holes, follow up with a countersink bit. The heads of the screws must not protrude. Make sure they are at or, better yet, slightly below the surface of the strips. It is handy to have one bit that does both hole and countersink in one operation or else have two cordless drills, one for each bit. Many holes are required, and you will save a lot of time if you are not constantly changing bits. Cordless drills are amazingly useful, and building a canoe is a fine excuse to buy extras. Make sure you have extra batteries for your drills; while you are using one battery, another can be charging.

Notice in Figure 6.9 that two strips will join end to end on the station form at the far right. Where two strips join at one station it is not possible to attach them with screws; use a couple of small, 1-inch finishing nails instead. Join strips at

FIGURE 6.8. *Attaching the stringers.*

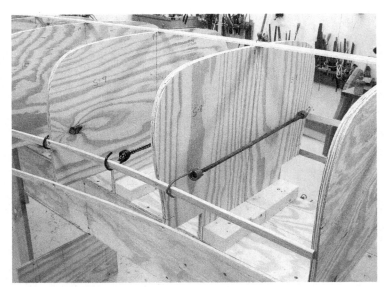

FIGURE 6.9. *Bungee cords temporarily hold strips in place for attachment.*

stations where minimal force will be required to hold the strips to the station. Drive the nailheads slightly below the surface of the strips with a punch so that the nails will not interfere with the fabric covering. Bungee cords are great for temporarily holding strips in place and to the proper curve against the stations while you drive screws or nails. (See Figures 6.9 and 6.10.)

Stringers are spaced about 4 inches apart where the station does not curve much, and closer together where it curves more sharply. Fabric pulled taut over the stringers should never touch or come closer than about ⅛ inch to the stations. See Figure 6.15, later in this chapter, for more specific fabric clearance recommendations. Space the stringers in a pleasing manner. They will likely need to be closer together near the ends of the hull than in the middle as well as where station curves are greater.

No matter how accurate your work, you may need to adjust the shape of a station—perhaps because of plan inaccuracies or minor errors that may have accumulated during the process of turning plans, station coordinates, and station locations into a form. These discrepancies will show up as the stringers are attached. In some places a stringer may seem to bend too sharply over a station. In these cases, the station may be trimmed down to achieve a fair curve with the stringer. It is usually not necessary to remove and trim the station with a saw. Just plane, rasp, or sand the station in place on the form. Try to keep both sides symmetrical.

It is also possible that a stringer may have to bow inward too much to meet a station that seems too small. Again, a fair curve of stringer from bow to stern is normally required. Of course, some plans may call for a hull shape that does bend inward, as with Wasp's tumblehome amidships and flare toward the ends. But the curve of the stringers should still be smooth and fair while touching all stations. If a station does produce a slight bow inward, the stringer can be shimmed out with a small wedge or a block of scrap wood, as shown in Figure 6.11. Use a longer #6 screw, if necessary, and place the shim alongside the screw under the stringer and

FIGURE 6.10. *Bungee cords hold one strip in place against a station form and against a spacer block (marked with an "X") while the strip is screwed in place.*

FIGURE 6.11. *A wedge of wood can be placed between a station and a stringer to support the stringer into a smooth curve. Two of the stringers here have wedges.*

Although it can be convenient to have another person's help for a few operations, it is possible to build a composite canoe alone. Tips like using bungee cords to hold strips help make this possible, and I will include such tips as we go along. You may also devise some better methods of your own.

parallel to it. You may want to keep some extralong screws on hand just in case. A wedge-shaped shim works especially well. Screw the stringer toward the station until the curve and position look just right. Then lightly tap the wedge in place with a mallet or block of wood to hold the stringer firmly.

When building wood strip canoes, the plywood end forms are planed to a V shape (as shown in Figure 6.12) so that the strips are fitted to a flat surface. A sharp block plane will perform this task. For the fabric form method, this extra work is not necessary; the strips can just be extended until they meet. However, your hull will be a little longer than the plans show if you take this approach.

Make sure that the stations will not touch the fabric covering, especially at their sharper curves. With Wasp's unusual shape, a short extra strip may be needed at station #10. (See Figures 6.13 and 6.14 for details.) For most boats, all stringers can run full length and be spaced to provide proper clearance. Check by laying a straight stick across adjacent strips wherever there are curves and measuring the clearance. (See Figure 6.15.) Where strips are relatively close together—2½

inches in Figure 6.15—a clearance of .09, or ³/₃₂, inch is adequate. Where strips are farther apart, clearance should be greater—I generally like to see ⅛ inch or more. The fabric will have some give to it, and you want to avoid having it belly inward against the stations. Move strips closer together if needed to obtain more clearance.

When you reach the keel line at the top of the form, reinstall strips there with screws. Extend and trim the keel strips so that they reach to the point at each end where the keel line starts to curve and the strips will no longer bend sufficiently.

Next, a curved pine cap is glued to each end. Filler pieces 1 inch wide or greater are added and glued between all strips. (See Figure 6.16.) Wider is better. If the end filler pieces are too narrow, the hull may be more difficult to release from the form. Any imperfections must be filled with wood filler and sanded until the end is a continuous smooth curve. The goal here is not to have a slick finish and beautiful woodwork but to avoid any unevenness and any hollows between strips that may catch on the inside of the hull and prevent your finished laminate from releasing from the form. It is okay to slather on copious quanti-

FIGURE 6.12. *Overlap and trim the strips at the ends. Notice that the end of the plywood form is planed to a V shape to accommodate the strips.*

FIGURE 6.13. *A short strip may be needed wherever there is a sharp turn of the hull. This is one end of the strip shown in Figure 6.14.*

FIGURE 6.14. *A short strip smoothes the curve and increases fabric clearance at station #10 where the hull makes a bulge and a sharp turn on Wasp. Wasp's design involves some details like this that are unnecessary on most other canoe designs.*

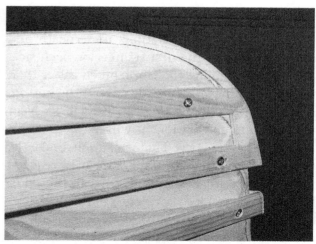

FIGURE 6.16. *Filler pieces at the stems are cut to fit and are glued lightly in place. Additional filler pieces will be added until the gaps between all the strips are filled at the ends. The ends must be smooth and continuous or the hull will not release from the form.*

FIGURE 6.15. *Measure the clearance between station curves and spans between stringers. The strips pictured are 2½ inches apart, and minimum clearance should be 0.09 or ³/₃₂ inch. Where strips are farther apart, minimum clearance should be greater; ⅛ inch is good.*

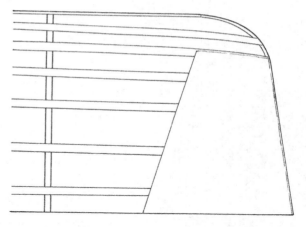

FIGURE 6.17. *Very thin trapezoidal side, or "cheek," plates added over the stringers at the ends will help prevent the finished hull from binding on the stringers. Using this method, the hull is likely to release from the form a little more easily. Some of the 1-millimeter-thick plywood that will be used later for deck covering is ideal for these plates. Glue them tightly to the stringers; spring clamps are handy for clamping. Round the edges with sandpaper, and shape the plates smoothly into the rounded bow and stern. Fill any holes or imperfections in the ends with wood filler.*

ties of wood filler and sand it to fill any hollows and surface imperfections where the strips meet the ends. Sand moderately smooth with a medium-grit sandpaper. Also see Figure 6.17 for another approach.

It is a good idea to add an extra wood strip to the bottom of the stations underneath and at right angles to the first stringer on each side. This makes stapling the fabric much easier than trying to hit the ¼-inch-wide edge of the bottom stringer with a staple through the fabric. Near the ends and end stations it will not be possible to add this extra strip. That is okay; just take the strip as far as you can or as far as it can be reached underneath with a staple gun. Near the ends, fabric can be stapled down onto the strongback.

The form itself is now done and ready to accept a fabric covering. (See Figure 6.18.) You may want to take a picture of your woodwork skeleton because you will not see it again until the hull is done. I always regretted covering the delicate and intricate framework of a fabric-covered airplane because the interior structure looks so beautiful and intriguing. The canoe form is somewhat similar.

If building a form appears to be too much time, trouble, or expense for you, Chapter 7 gives another, faster approach to making a composite canoe.

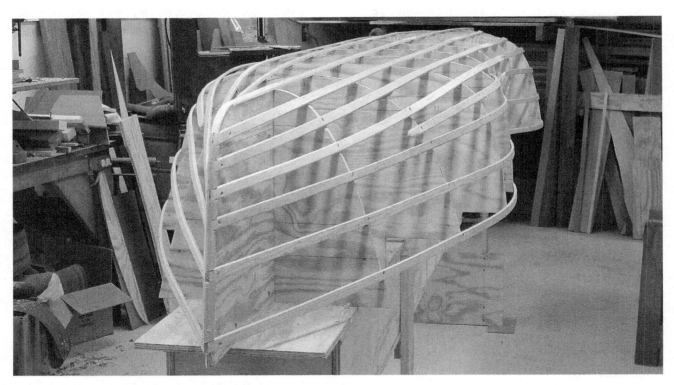

FIGURE 6.18. *A completed form viewed from the stern.*

Using an Existing Canoe for a Form

It is possible to use an existing canoe as a form if you wish to copy it or to modify it by enlarging some part of the hull a little. This can be done without hurting the original canoe. Using

this method, you can avoid making both a strongback and a wood form. You could even buy a used canoe for this purpose and sell it when you're finished, resulting in little or no cost for the form! I do not advocate copying a canoe without permission if the design is someone else's intellectual property. When in doubt, ask the designer or manufacturer for permission. But you may want to copy an old canoe model that is not otherwise available and make a composite version. Or you can use the canoe only as the basis for a form, modifying it into your own design.

Canoe Ends

Note that a composite canoe with recurved ends cannot be made on a form with the method in this book unless the ends are not closed together during laminating. Otherwise, the ends will have to be cut apart to remove the hull from the form or old canoe. There is really no good structural or performance reason for making a modern canoe with recurved ends, so I suggest avoiding those designs and the extra work they entail. Some canoe ends have a constant curve; this is okay as long as there is no vertical or recurved component. See Figure 7.1 for examples.

The ends of most canoes will generally not be vertical. Instead, they will angle outward and upward to a significant degree. Except for unusual designs, they do not make a 90-degree angle with the waterline. Ideally, the ends should angle outward from vertical about 10 degrees or greater in order to release from the form with ease. On Wasp, the bow angle is 9 degrees and the stern angle is 7 degrees; this has worked acceptably.

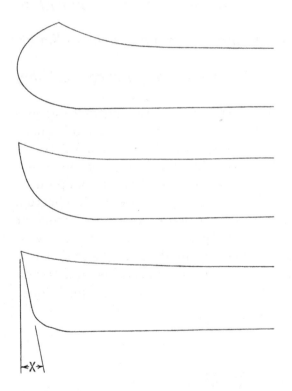

FIGURE 7.1. *The top canoe has a recurved end. The middle canoe has an end with a constant curve. The bottom canoe has a straight end. Angle X should be about 10 degrees or more. The bottom two end shapes will release from the form. The recurved end will not.*

Preparing the Hull

The first step is to get the hull surface and gunwales clean of dirt, dust, and especially wax or other surface protectors. Wash with mild soap, rinse, and let dry. Place the canoe upside down, and attach it securely to sawhorses. It may be possible to use clamps on the gunwales or thwarts. A more secure way to do this is to screw the thwarts to the sawhorses or attach the thwarts with U bolts.

Minor modifications that enlarge some part of the old hull shape can be made temporarily with Styrofoam, wood, or plywood and duct tape. I've added a few inches in length and increased flare this way. But keep in mind that the fabric may pull strongly and unevenly on flimsy modifications, so you may need creative strategies to keep foam pieces from twisting and pulling out of place when the fabric is tightened. Keep temporary foam and duct tape modifications relatively small to avoid such problems. Some modifications may telegraph visibly through the finished hull somewhat. This will not hurt the hull or paddling efficiency in any way but may require more filling and sanding if your goal is a smooth, slick exterior.

To make an exact copy of the old canoe, you must remove the gunwales; otherwise, your new hull will be the width of the gunwales instead of the original hull. Assuming the gunwales stand proud a bit from the outside of the hull, the fabric will angle out slightly from the old hull surface to the outside edge of the gunwale, and this may visually telegraph a little through the new hull. However, the laminated composite hull will be flexible until you add gunwales and thwarts, so the sides can be pulled inward or pushed outward a small amount to achieve the width at the gunwales that you desire. Final width will be fixed by the dimensions of the thwarts. The new canoe could also be finished with lower sides and less freeboard, if you choose. This has some advantages for lowering weight, making paddling easier, and reducing the influence of wind. For whitewater, waves, and heavier loads, however, more freeboard helps keep the water out.

If you wish to make a slightly larger canoe and sacrifice the old canoe, stringers and end pieces can be screwed directly to the old hull instead of using station forms, as described in Chapter 6. Follow the general directions in Chapters 6 and 8. Pay particular attention to the instructions on finishing the ends and covering ends and stringers with release tape.

A Base for Stapling the Fabric

The entire form will be covered with a layer of polyester fabric, and a rigid area of some sort must be provided for stapling the fabric under the gunwales or under the canoe being used as a form. You can staple or tack directly to the gunwales if they will hold staples or tacks and you don't mind the little holes. Staple holes in wood gunwales can be sealed over later with epoxy and varnish; holes in vinyl gunwales will cause no real harm other than cosmetic blemishes.

If you wish to leave no marks on the canoe being copied, strips of plywood or softwood approximately the width of the gunwales can be secured to the gunwales as a stapling strip. To install these strips, turn the canoe right side up. Cut pieces of plywood to fit over the ends and gunwales. The wood need not be continuous; small lengths can be placed end to end along the gunwales. Clamp the wood pieces to the gunwales from inside the canoe (as shown in Figure 7.2). This assumes that the gunwale is shaped to accept clamps.

If all else fails, inexpensive ¼- or ³⁄₈-inch soft plywood can be cut to match the bird's-eye top view outline of the canoe. Place the canoe upside down on top of a layer of plywood; two 4-by-8-foot sheets will be needed for a canoe up to 16 feet long. Trace around the gunwales onto the plywood, and cut out the resulting canoe-shaped pattern. By cutting large holes in the plywood, you should be able to make places where you can clamp the plywood to the end decks and thwarts. With the plywood in place and the canoe upside down on sawhorses, there will now be a layer of plywood under the gunwales to which you can staple the fabric.

A kayak can be used as a form for a hull, necessitating a different strategy for stapling the fabric. Cut a 2 × 6 the length of the kayak and screw it to sawhorses, wide side down. Place the kayak upside down on the 2 × 6, and clamp it to the 2 × 6 at the cockpit coaming. Use several strong clamps. The 2 × 6 will accept the staples.

For narrow craft it may be possible to avoid stapling and instead stitch the fabric together underneath the boat to make a tightly wrapped fabric cocoon. If the fabric edges do not meet under the boat, then the edges may be tied across the gap with string or other cord rather than fragile thread. While it may seem tedious to do this, string and thread are a lot less costly than wood and staples.

FIGURE 7.2. *Pieces of ¼-inch-thick softwood or plywood are clamped to a gunwale to provide a place to staple the peel ply layer of fabric covering.*

It is okay to create other strategies for fastening the fabric; the fabric is relatively wide and might be secured to other structures below the form. When the fabric is shrunk in place with heat, it will pull with a great deal of force, so it must be fastened securely. The fabric must be fastened every inch or two along the entire length of the form in order to avoid wrinkles. While quickly making a very experimental canoe, I once attached the fabric by duct taping the edges to the inside of the canoe. This held just barely long enough and just barely well enough that I was able to quickly laminate the hull, but it was risky and left a mess of tape adhesive to clean up. I would not do it again, and I recommend that you use staples to avoid risking your valuable time and materials. You will be happier with the end product.

After the stapling layer is solidly in place, return the canoe to an upside-down position and fasten it securely to the sawhorses.

FIGURE 7.3. *Package-sealing tape and plastic wrap will protect the canoe that is used for a form, enabling the new laminated hull to be easily removed. This 15-foot canoe made of Royalex is more than 20 pounds heavier than the Kevlar canoe laminated on top of it.*

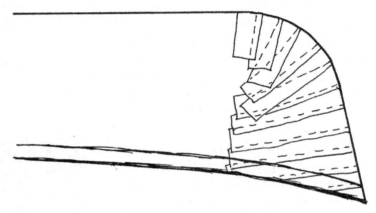

FIGURE 7.4. *The ends are taped with overlapping layers of clear package-sealing tape.*

Sealing the Old Hull

To use the old hull as is, or with modifications fastened in place, the entire hull must be covered and sealed with a layer that will not adhere to epoxy. This includes the side edges of any wood or plywood added under the gunwales for stapling the fabric. Clear package-sealing tape and plastic wrap (the same plastic wrap you might use in the kitchen) are ideal for this. (See Figure 7.3.) Start by covering the ends with 2-inch-wide tape as shown in Figure 7.4. Go horizontally around the end and along each side for a foot or two. Tape should extend a little beyond an imaginary vertical line down from where the curved end merges into a straighter keel line. Start at the bottom of the form (the part closest to the floor) and work your way up just like putting shingles on a house roof. Overlap each layer at least ½ inch. When you come to the sharper curve where the end meets the keel, narrower ¾- or 1-inch-wide Scotch tape may work better to prevent wrinkles. Wrinkles may be cut so that the cut edges can be pressed down flat. Then seal the cut with a top layer of narrow tape, and smooth it down firmly.

After the ends have been taped, the rest of the canoe form can be covered with plastic wrap. This

FIGURE 7.5. *The sawhorses and old canoe on the left took the place of a strongback with stations and stringers to produce the Kevlar hull on the right.*

is one operation that is best done with two people. I have done this step alone, but it is harder to avoid wrinkles. Start at the middle of the upside-down canoe form, with one person on each side. One person holds the roll of plastic wrap while the other pulls a length of the wrap out and over the canoe. Let the wrap lay down on the hull crossways from gunwale to gunwale—in other words, side to side, *not* end to end. Smooth it from the top down the sides to the gunwales. Cut and fasten the plastic securely under the gunwales with tape while stretching out any large wrinkles. Small wrinkles can merely be smoothed flat. Start in the middle of the boat, and work first toward one end and then the other. Overlap each strip of wrap at least 4 inches. It is even better to overlap sufficiently so that a double layer of plastic covers the hull. It is less likely that both layers will tear and let epoxy through.

If you have any holes or tears in the plastic wrap, cover them with plastic tape. Scotch tape or package-sealing tape is fine. Epoxy *must not* reach your form. Pierce any air bubbles in the wrap with a very sharp knife tip (such as a #11 X-Acto blade), or they may show through as slight bumps in your finished hull. Smooth the plastic to be as bubble free as you can, and cover the cut with a piece of Scotch tape. Any wrinkles and minor folds in the plastic can just be smoothed flat. Larger folds may telegraph slight lumps through to your finished hull, but these will not interfere with paddling performance or with sanding to achieve a smooth surface later. If you wish, bulkier folds can be cut out and the holes sealed over with package-sealing tape. It takes about two rolls of plastic wrap to cover a solo canoe.

When the plastic-wrapping operation reaches the ends of the canoe, make certain the plastic wrap overlaps the tape previously placed at the ends by several inches. The plastic wrap can be securely taped to the underlying end tape in several places. Look carefully for any remaining exposed areas of the old canoe, and cover them with tape. Check a second time. Check a third time. Check every inch. This is one part of the process that requires close attention. You want to be absolutely certain that the new laminate and the old hull will not become bonded together! So far, I have not seen this happen, and I don't even want to imagine such a mess! If you do a good job, you will be able to reuse the old canoe and it will be as good as when you started. (See Figure 7.5.)

Cover the form with fabric as described in Chapter 8. Staple the fabric to the wood or plywood underneath the gunwales, not on the vertical sides of the wood.

The Fabric Covering

*A release tape is put over the entire form, including stringers, end caps, and anything that might conceivably come in contact with the overlying fabric layer that comes next. Heavy-*duty clear plastic package-sealing tape 2 inches wide works fine. (See Figure 8.1.) The tape does not have to be put on stringers in continuous lengths, but overlap any joints in the tape by several inches. I always put some tape on the edges of any stations where the fabric may lie close. It is not a bad idea to tape all edges of the stations. Pay special attention to covering the ends. It helps to put some layers of tape vertically over the stringers where they meet at the ends and to continue out 4 or 5 inches from the ends; overlap each layer by about 1 inch. The ends of the hull are the most difficult areas to remove from the form.

The tape must lie flat without wrinkles, but it need not be continuous. Overlap small pieces of tape wherever necessary to get the tape to smoothly cover a curved area. The tape is what keeps the epoxy from bonding your hull laminate permanently to the form, so check twice

FIGURE 8.1. *The stringers and exposed portions of the form are covered with clear plastic package-sealing tape.*

FIGURE 8.2. *The form now has release tape in place.*

that there are no areas of the stringers or ends that are not well covered. A roll of ¾- or 1-inch-wide Scotch tape is handy for covering small and hard-to-reach areas. If you do have a wrinkle or air bubble, you don't need to remove and replace a long piece of package tape. Instead, cut or slit the wrinkle with a razor knife (such as a #11 X-Acto blade), and press each edge of the tape down flat. Then seal the cut area of tape with a layer of Scotch tape that is an inch or two longer than the cut. Press the tape down firmly to achieve a good seal. Figure 8.2 shows a form fully covered in release tape.

Covering the Form with Peel Ply Fabric

A layer of 2.7 ounce aircraft Dacron polyester peel ply fabric is used to cover the form. This will establish the final shape of the hull by spanning the voids between the stringers. The polyester fabric supports the layers of reinforcing cloth and epoxy that will make up the shell or skin of the hull. The polyester is later peeled away from the cured laminate, leaving a strong, lightweight composite shell.

Be certain to order shrinkable Dacron or polyester peel ply fabric from mail-order aircraft suppliers, such as Aircraft Spruce. (See Appendix A for contact information.) Aircraft-certified fabric is expensive and not required. The less costly uncertified fabric available for experimental homebuilt aircraft is fine for a canoe form. Do not buy polyester fabric from a local fabric store. It will not shrink properly and may not release from the epoxy. It is a good idea to test your fabric before installing it. Cut a small test piece (a 6-inch square is fine); measure it; and then heat it with a clothes iron just as though you were ironing a shirt. Start with a cool or moderate temperature, and keep increasing the temperature until shrinking occurs. It should shrink noticeably from your original measurement. Follow the ironing precautions that appear later in this chapter.

Unroll the fabric and cut it generously at the ends to drape over the form. (See Figure 8.3.) Smooth it by hand as much as possible. Temporarily pin the cloth with straight pins at the ends to pull the fabric snugly from one end to the other while you start working on the sides with a staple gun, as shown in Figure 8.4.

FIGURE 8.3. *A 2.7-ounce polyester fabric is draped over the form.*

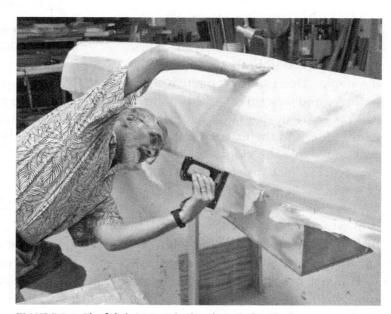

FIGURE 8.4. *The fabric is stretched and stapled to the form.*

Fabric may be stapled to the underside of bottom stringers and stations and to the strongback as needed. Staples must go *only* in places that will not be covered by the laminate. For any places difficult to staple, the fabric may be tied with string to any convenient structure or stitched to itself under the form. Near the ends it is convenient to attach the fabric to the top of the strongback. If used here, staples would cause the fabric to tear when it is shrunk, so hold it down instead with a strip of scrap wood nailed to the top of the strongback. These nailing strips are seen clearly in Figures 8.6 and 8.8 (later in this chapter). The nailheads are left sticking out so that they are easy to remove after the laminating is complete.

It is not always clear whether it is better to start stapling fabric in the middle or at the ends, but I usually start at the ends. Consider the first staples as temporary until you see how the fabric stretches onto the form. Pushpins or thumb tacks make handy temporary fasteners at this stage while you adjust the draping of the cloth. Stretch the fabric tight but not so tight that it cuts against the staples. Don't worry too much about wrinkles and wavy areas at this point. Shrinking will take care of that later. Put just a few staples in one side, and then switch to the other side to pull and staple the cloth over the form. As you proceed, readjust any staples to smooth wrinkles or waves in the fabric. If you have to move a previously stapled area of cloth onto the form, that is okay: small holes in the fabric will not detract from its performance. Larger holes, cuts, or tears can be sewn with heavy polyester thread.

It is not possible to apply the fabric without some wrinkles, so just spread them out as much as possible. (See Figure 8.5.) Many little wrinkles are better than a few large ones. The extra curves of Wasp introduce more wrinkles. Keep redistributing them and restapling until you have done the best that the form and fabric will allow. If some wrinkles seem especially worrisome, maneuver them into one large wrinkle. Then push the wrinkle into a fold toward the inside of the form and stitch across the outside of the wrinkle with heavy-duty polyester thread. Make stitches about $1/16$ inch apart. You will wind up

FIGURE 8.5. *Any wrinkles in the fabric are distributed over as wide an area as possible.*

with a fold in the cloth with stitches going across it, providing a flat layer for laminating. This will be invisible on your finished boat.

Sewing the Ends

When the fabric is stapled adequately along the length of the form, it is time to turn attention to the ends. The cut fabric is pinned tightly at the ends with straight pins and trimmed roughly to about 1-inch flaps, as shown in Figure 8.6. Sew the flaps of cloth together at their base along the line where they were pinned, using heavy-duty polyester thread only. *Do not* use cotton thread! It will stick to the epoxy resin. Sew snugly against the form. Try not to pierce the release tape underneath, although an occasional needle hole will do no harm. This first stitch line shows at the bottom of Figure 8.7.

The double flap of fabric is next trimmed to about ½ inch and then folded flat to the form

FIGURE 8.6. *The fabric is stretched over the ends, fastened snugly with straight pins, and cut as shown.*

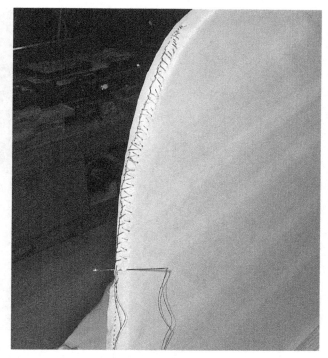

FIGURE 8.7. *Stitching the fabric over the ends.*

and sewn in place. The sewing of the folded flap is completed at the top of Figure 8.7 and will be continued to the bottom. The sewn fabric will eventually be peeled from the finished hull, discarded, and never seen. However, a moderately smooth job of sewing will make for easy release of the fabric from the laminate. Any stitch that holds the flap flat is okay. Figure 8.8 shows a completed stitching job.

Shrinking the Peel Ply Fabric

An electric clothes iron is all you need to shrink the fabric into a taut, smooth surface for laminating. (See Figure 8.9.) Be very cautious, however; the one mistake you can make is using too much heat. It is possible to burn a hole in the fabric or start a fire! The fire department does not need to be involved in your canoe project. As mentioned

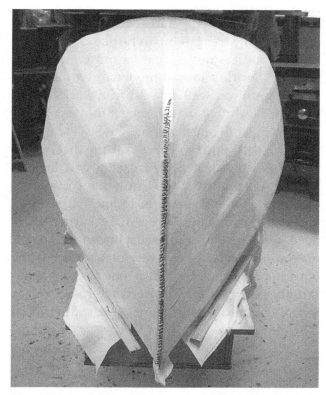

FIGURE 8.8. *Stitching at the stern is completed. The fabric is now relatively smooth with few wrinkles.*

FIGURE 8.9. *The fabric is shrunk taut with a warm clothes iron.*

in Chapter 3, it is a good idea to have a fire extinguisher on hand. It should be considered a basic shop appliance anyway.

Very accurate temperature control is required for optimum strength in aircraft covering applications, but it is not critical for our canoe form. Start first with a low to moderate temperature setting until you see how your iron works. Move the iron slowly, but *always* keep it moving. Never stop or linger in one place. Increase the temperature gradually until you find a setting that begins to shrink the fabric. Shrink each area a little at a time. After starting to shrink one section, let that area cool and move on to another section. You can return later to do more shrinking as needed. Use a temperature just hot enough to get maximum shrinkage or a very taut surface without causing the cloth to tear out at the staples. If it does start to tear, stop and add more staples before continuing. Sometimes just adding more

staples will prevent the strain from concentrating at a few staples where tearing is likely to occur. After you have reached maximum shrinkage, you will find that neither more ironing nor a hotter iron will make it shrink any tighter. Do not increase the heat further.

Any wrinkles that cannot be ironed out smooth can be sewn together into a smooth surface, as described earlier on page 58. Use only polyester thread. Stitch the cloth together on the outside, leaving the excess fold of the wrinkle on the inside. The stitching will be unnoticeable on the finished hull and much preferable to wrinkles. There is no regulation stitch for this; just sew the cloth together across the wrinkle any way you can. It only has to last long enough to make the hull. If all else fails, then replace and reshrink the fabric. This should not be required if the fabric covering instructions are followed with care.

Chapter 9

Laminating the Hull

Throughout this chapter, I describe laminating with Kevlar, but you may substitute carbon fiber or fiberglass in all of the directions except for the number of layers. Kevlar provides an excellent blend of strength, toughness, and stiffness and may be the material that most builders choose. It is a little more difficult to work with than fiberglass or carbon fiber in that it is harder to cut and does not wet out with epoxy resin quite as quickly and easily. But if you are using fiberglass or carbon, these instructions will also apply.

To build Wasp, I've chosen a layup with three layers of 5-ounce Kevlar and an outer layer of 4-ounce fiberglass, the latter in case I decide to sand the outer hull to a smooth finish and paint it. This will give me a versatile hull with light weight and moderate strength for flatwater paddling and whitewater up to class 2. For a very tough hull for serious whitewater, I recommend adding one or two more layers of Kevlar. Sometimes I put an extra, partial layer on the bottom for additional strength where the hull is most vulnerable. This partial layer is added in the core before the final layers go on.

A carbon fiber layup for flatwater utility might have inner and outer layers of 5.8-ounce carbon fiber with a core layer of 5-ounce Kevlar. This will produce a stiffer hull that requires lighter reinforcement ribs and provides a good combination of stiffness with light weight. However, a hull laminate with three layers of Kevlar only will actually be slightly lighter. So, to save weight with carbon, you will have to take advantage of carbon's stiffness by building lighter in other structural parts of the canoe, such as gunwales, bulkheads, decks, flotation chambers, and ribs.

To build a flatwater hull entirely with fiberglass, you may want a layup of fiberglass cloth layers that total approximately 45 ounces; try a minimum of seven or eight layers of 6-ounce fabric or four or five layers of 9-ounce fabric. Although fiberglass is inexpensive, more cloth and much more of the costly epoxy resin will be consumed. There may be little or no savings in building with fiberglass instead of Kevlar unless you limit the layers or switch to polyester resin, thereby reducing strength. I recommend against using polyester resin and have never tested it with the peel ply technique. Since a large investment of time and labor is required, you may prefer to use better materials and enjoy paddling a lighter, stronger craft.

One way to produce a somewhat less costly hull that is still moderately strong, stiff, and light is to use Kevlar for the outer layers and fiberglass for the inner core layers. This takes advantage of Kevlar's relative stiffness to make a stronger and stiffer hull than an all-fiberglass one. The thicker the core layers are, the stiffer the hull will be, but it will also be heavier. A minimum of two core layers of 6-ounce fiberglass should work well for flatwater use; add an outer layer of 4-ounce fiberglass fabric if you plan to sand to a perfectly smooth finish.

If you desire a smooth exterior finish, then sanding will be required. Kevlar does not sand well, so if you want a smooth finish on an otherwise all-Kevlar hull, an outer layer of fiberglass should be applied.

Handling the Laminating Fabric

After considering all of the design aspects, costs, and benefits of the various reinforcing fabrics, order enough fabric to provide the number of layers you want in your hull laminate plus a bit extra. It is disconcerting to run short in the middle of the hull layup process. And I always seem to need more fabric than I thought I would for ribs, bulkheads, and flotation chambers. However, scraps left over from hull making, and inexpensive fiberglass, are often adequate for such tasks.

Be very careful when unrolling and handling the fabric; the weave is easily disrupted. The cloth should be supplied rolled on a cardboard tube. Some suppliers will give you the option of buying it folded or rolled on a tube. For making a hull, always choose rolled. Folding makes it difficult to handle and may damage your fabric by disturbing the weave and leaving thin spots and thick spots. Rig the tube so you can unroll fabric as you need it. If you have room in your workspace, rig a stand or roll holder at one end of your canoe form. (See Figure 9.1.) A simple solution is a closet rod mounted to wall hangers about 5 feet high. I do not have any free wall space in my shop, so I use a freestanding roll holder. If possible, set up your roll holder so you can unroll fabric right onto the form from above it. Make sure the surface of the form is clean and free of any debris.

Drape the first layer of fabric carefully on the form (as shown in Figure 9.2) and cut so that the cloth reaches or comes to within an inch or so of both ends. Although you can cut Kevlar slowly with very sharp scissors, cutting will be easier and faster with special Kevlar shears, which can be purchased from some Kevlar suppliers, including Infinity Composites. (See Appendix A.)

Smooth out any wrinkles in the Kevlar, and make sure it covers the form. It is possible to overlap pieces of cloth, if needed, in case your hull size and shape are unusual or you are trying to use narrower cloth or scrap pieces. It is best to hold off trimming the fabric until after you start applying epoxy. The fabric can move around and become difficult to keep positioned if it is already cut too closely to the finished dimensions.

Working with Epoxy

The most important aspect of creating a strong hull is proper mixing and use of the epoxy. First, read the manufacturer's directions. Second, read the manufacturer's directions again. Follow them with care. A precise resin-to-hardener ratio is critical. You will probably be using 1.5 to 3 gallons of epoxy, so it is well worth buying the metering pumps that match the epoxy brand and containers. They will ensure that the ratio of resin to hardener is accurate, allowing the resin to cure properly and achieve full strength.

Choose a slow-curing hardener for your epoxy to allow maximum working time. This will be especially important if you have to work in warm temperatures, which shorten curing time. I like WEST System epoxy with 207 Special Coating Hardener, which cures slowly and provides ultraviolet resistance. The latter feature is handy if you want to use the boat for a while before painting or varnishing. Both Kevlar and epoxy are degraded by the ultraviolet radiation in sunlight, and they eventually need protection.

Mix only small amounts of epoxy as you need it, rather than making large batches, and mix it well. You can buy mixing sticks that look like

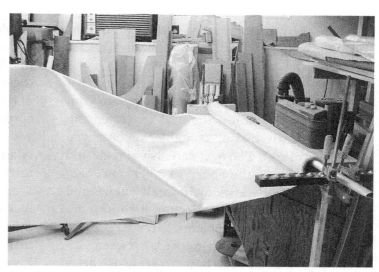

FIGURE 9.1. *Kevlar fabric is being unrolled unto the form from a makeshift holder for the fabric that was supplied rolled on a cardboard tube. Here the roll is shown placed on a scrap metal tube, which is clamped to a bench and a roller stand.*

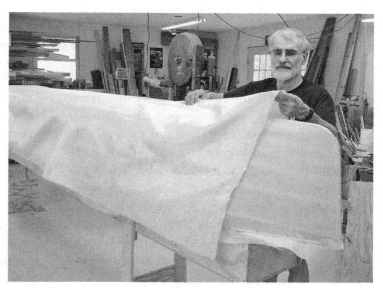

FIGURE 9.2. *The Kevlar fabric is draped carefully onto the form.*

tongue depressors, but wood scraps also work fine. One-quarter to one-third of a cup of resin and hardener combined is plenty to start. This might be one to three strokes on the pumps. Unwaxed paper cups are perhaps best for mixing epoxy. If care is taken, disposable plastic cups and tin cans can also be used for small batches.

At home we wash and save plastic butter tubs and yogurt cups, which are very handy sizes for this task.

The resin and hardener produce a reaction that creates heat. If large amounts of epoxy are confined in a small volume, the heat generated can melt your plastic mixing container or burn you through a tin can. The heat can also quickly and unexpectedly cure the epoxy to a gel state, rendering it useless. By working in small batches and when air temperatures are not too high, you are more likely to avoid problems. I try to do hull laminating when the temperature is between 55°F and 77°F—60 °F to 70°F is best. You can also delay the reaction by spreading the mixed epoxy out in a large, flat-bottom container. A paint roller tray with plastic liners is very good for this, and you will also want the tray later on for applying final epoxy layers to the hull with a fine foam roller.

Cheap, disposable paintbrushes about 3 inches wide seem to work best for applying epoxy to the hull. Smaller brushes will be useful for other bonding and finishing operations, especially on the interior. Bristle brushes can leave annoying hairs, but they are better for working epoxy into fabric than foam brushes are. Disposable foam brushes are better for smoothing the final epoxy coats, as well as for painting and varnishing in hard-to-reach places. Get lots of disposable brushes of both types; you will need them. Also, plastic applicators, scrapers, and squeegees are invaluable for spreading epoxy on the hull. Get a variety of sizes and shapes. In a pinch, an old credit card can be used as a small epoxy spreader; just be certain you don't need it to order more supplies!

You will go through disposable latex or butyl gloves at a surprising rate; get a few dozen. Use them every time you mix epoxy. Also, wear a good respirator with organic filters for working with epoxy, paints, and varnishes. Cheaper paper dust masks are okay for sanding. Keep rolls of paper towels at the ready for cleanup.

The goal with epoxy, of course, is to get it on the hull and not on you. This is easier said than done. Wearing old sacrificial clothing and shoes is necessary. A shop apron is helpful, as is an old baseball cap to keep the light out of your eyes and the glue out of your hair. Bending over to pick something up can bring hair and hull together. It is not fun to clean or cut epoxy out of the hair! No matter how careful you are, some epoxy will drip or spill onto the floor. Even if you carefully wipe up each drip, the stains will endure. The floors of my shop and carport are testaments to boats built there. If you hope to keep the floor stain free, then spread a layer of plastic just as you would for painting a ceiling. Don't forget that you will also walk in the epoxy drips and spread a trail wherever you go. I leave my old epoxy working shoes in the shop and save the house carpets.

The Laminating Schedule

Building a strong hull demands a proper schedule of timing the epoxy applications and cloth layers. Don't start until you have the time to laminate all the layers one after another as well as add two or three finish layers of epoxy to the outside of the hull. This will save sanding between layers and coats to get good adhesion. A four-layer laminate, like that used for Wasp in this example, may require about three days or a long weekend. You won't be working continuously, although it may seem like it! But you do need to be nearby and ready to add the next layer at the correct time. Depending on the epoxy, hardener, and air temperature, it may take an hour or two, or half a day, for the epoxy to cure enough to be ready for the next layer. Yes, it is okay to take a break and get a night's sleep! Plan to put a layer on late in the evening and be ready to apply another layer early the next morning.

Laminating the Ends

It can be difficult to get Kevlar, carbon fiber, or even heavy fiberglass to wrap smoothly around the ends while trying to laminate the main part of the hull, so first you will put a thin, smooth layer of light fiberglass over each end (as shown in Figure 9.3). Roll back your Kevlar or other laminating fabric from one end. Mix some epoxy, and coat the fabric form at the end. Apply a layer of 4-ounce fiberglass just to the end, over the curve of the end, and along the side for a few inches. A fiberglass strip about 6 inches wide will wrap nicely for 3 inches on each side. You should be able to wrap this light fiberglass around the end so that it lies flat to the form on both sides. Where the end makes a curve to the bottom, you may need to use small, overlapping fiberglass pieces or make cuts in from the sides of the fiberglass strip to get it to lay flat on each side. It is okay to cut or overlap the cloth. Continue the fiberglass end strip or pieces along the bottom for about 1 foot.

Structural fabrics for laminating will conform to bends more easily if the threads run at a diagonal to the bend. To get fabric to wrap more easily around the canoe ends, cut the end strips at a 45-degree angle to the threads or edges of the fabric. To make the strip conform to the curve, pull on the ends of the strip as you smooth it into the epoxy. This works best with relatively narrow strips used as outer layers. Trim as needed.

Add more epoxy on top of the fiberglass, and work it into the cloth with the brush. Use just enough epoxy to saturate or "wet out" the fabric but not so much that it runs or makes the fiberglass float up off the fabric form. Add a second layer of 4-ounce fiberglass on top of the first, and work in more epoxy to wet it out. At this stage, the ends do not have to be strong and the Kevlar or main laminating cloth does not have to wrap around or cover the ends. Additional layers of Kevlar reinforcement will go on the inside of the ends after the hull is laminated and removed from the form.

If you have decided, despite my recommendation against it, to build a design with recurved ends, leave the ends open and do not cover them with any laminating fabric at this stage. After the cured hull is removed from the form, wood stem pieces about ½ inch wide will be added at each end. You will bond them with epoxy to the two sides of the hull and then sculpt them to a rounded curve from side to side. The outside will then be reinforced with fiberglass, and the inside with Kevlar.

Extreme tumblehome in the sides can make it difficult to remove the hull from the form and may require cutting the ends apart or leaving the ends open as for a hull with recurved ends. Pulling the tumblehome outward at the sides to lift the hull off the form will pull the ends tighter. I have had no trouble with designs that have a couple of inches of tumblehome on each side. If the stems extend at a good angle forward and aft from vertical—10 degrees or so—then the hull will release from the form even with a moderate amount of tumblehome in the sides. The hull will be flexible enough that helpers pulling at the sides and ends should be able to remove most hull shapes. Some additional tumblehome can be incorporated later if desired when gunwales and thwarts are installed.

FIGURE 9.3. *To begin the laminating process, fiberglass and epoxy are applied to the ends.*

Applying Epoxy to the First Layer

It's time to begin laminating the main part of the hull, as shown in Figure 9.4. Always start your epoxy applications by putting on a respirator and disposable gloves. Mix a small batch of epoxy and hardener—two or three pumps from WEST metering pumps is enough—and start applying it to the Kevlar in the middle of the form. Epoxy can be applied with a brush or, on horizontal areas, poured on the fabric and spread with a plastic spreader or squeegee. Kevlar absorbs epoxy more slowly than fiberglass does. Work it in carefully; the fabric will darken as it becomes wetted with epoxy. It is best to work in hull sections about 2 to 4 feet long. Start at the highest point of the form and work down both sides. Keep returning to the areas where you spread epoxy earlier to ensure that the Kevlar is saturated uniformly. Add more epoxy as needed.

FIGURE 9.4. *The first layer of Kevlar is saturated with epoxy. Wear disposable latex gloves and a respirator, even though the fool in the photo (the author) has forgotten to put his on.*

Epoxy will wipe off from plastic applicators and can be cleaned off with acetone. Brushes should be discarded and replaced as soon as they start to get stiff with partially gelled epoxy.

The Kevlar cloth should cover the side or cheek areas of the hull and partially overlap the fiberglass layers that wrap around the ends. It would be difficult to make the stiff Kevlar bend sharply around the ends, so trim it just short of where the sides curve sharply together. This might be about an inch from the ends. The same applies to carbon or heavy fiberglass cloths. The ends will be reinforced later.

Generally, Kevlar will adhere to the fabric form quite well once the Kevlar is saturated. If your design has tumblehome, the Kevlar fabric may try to hang straight down rather than stick to the tumblehome area. After applying epoxy, pin the Kevlar to the bottom stringer with thumbtacks to conform to the tumblehome, if necessary. (See Figure 9.5.) You may even pin Kevlar to stringers wherever it may be needed. After the last layer of Kevlar, the finish coats of epoxy inside and out will seal any pinholes.

Laminating Additional Layers

When the epoxy is just dry to the touch, irregularities are easy to feel with your hands. Before applying each additional layer of fabric, inspect the surface of the previous layer for bumps, small wood chips, and other debris, including spiders and small insects. Each piece of debris will create a lump in your final surface, but the lumps can be easily removed with a sharp knife or razor blade at this stage. If you leave them in now, it will require much tedious work to remove lumps later, when lamination is finished and the epoxy has cured. Lumps and bubbles in the epoxy can be trimmed off with a very sharp knife or sanded flat. If any of the laminating fabric is trimmed off, those areas should be reinforced later with an equal-size patch on the inside.

Adding the second layer of Kevlar is just like doing the first. Some composite builders will advise putting the next layer on while the epoxy of the first layer is still wet. Theoretically, this is desirable so that newly added epoxy makes a chemical bond with the previous layer. If the air temperature is cool and you have a large crew of helpers working quickly to apply epoxy and help set the large cloth layers down carefully in exactly the right place, this may work. But if the epoxy gets even slightly sticky, it will become impossible to smooth out the next layer wrinkle free. It may be impossible to lift the Kevlar off and reposition it without damaging the weave, and large, unsightly lumps can result. Should this happen you will no longer be having fun and may wonder why you ever started! While your paddling dreams are going north, your materials investment may be going south.

Here is a better approach, and it is one that can be used by one person working alone. Wait until the epoxy on the previous layer is just dry to the touch and no longer tacky. Test by making sure that a piece of scrap fiberglass can be dragged across the surface without sticking or pulling. Test all areas of the hull. The epoxy surface should still dent slightly with forceful fingernail pressure, indicating that it is not fully cured. Before allowing the epoxy to cure much further, unroll the next layer, cut, and saturate as you did the first. Even when dry to the touch, the epoxy will not be fully cured to a solid state and you can achieve an excellent bond between layers. This timing is important. Do not go shopping at the mall or take the afternoon off to go fishing! Check your previous layer every half hour or so, and add the next layer when it is dry to the touch and passes the test. (See Figure 9.6.) After you've done this with a couple of layers, you will have a better idea of how much time to allow between layers, given the temperature conditions and epoxy being used. Don't forget to carefully inspect for debris, insects, lumps, and bubbles between each layer.

FIGURE 9.5. *If the design has any tumblehome, thumbtacks may be use to force the epoxy-saturated Kevlar to conform to the required shape.*

FIGURE 9.6. *After the first layer of Kevlar, additional layers are bonded in place on a carefully timed schedule.*

Experienced composite workers may advise that you apply fresh epoxy to the hull surface before adding another cloth layer. This is done by draping a new layer in place and then rolling it back from each end to the middle of the canoe. Epoxy is then applied to the previous layer for a few feet, and the new cloth is unrolled that distance, smoothed in place, and wetted out. Proceed in increments of about 2 or 3 feet to both ends. However, I find that by using more layers of lighter-weight cloth—such as 5-ounce Kevlar, 5.8-ounce carbon fiber, or 6-ounce fiberglass—the unrolling technique is not necessary. Unroll the new layer onto the entire hull, and apply epoxy just as you did for the first layer. The epoxy will soak through adequately. Plastic spreaders can help squeeze epoxy through the cloth. Hulls that I've made this way have endured years of wilderness and whitewater use without delaminating or suffering failures of any kind.

Make sure you add sufficient epoxy and spread it uniformly. Press the epoxy firmly into and through the fabric with a bristle brush, squeegee, or plastic spreader. As epoxy is absorbed, apply more until the cloth is adequately and uniformly saturated. If the fabric surface is shiny and seems to float above the previous layer, squeegee out the excess epoxy. The surface should appear evenly transparent with a smooth, uniform cloth texture.

If you don't have cloth pieces large enough to cover the entire hull, either side to side or end to end, or if you wish to make use of some scraps, pieces may be overlapped to provide the coverage needed. Overlap such joints by at least 2 or 3 inches, and make sure joints are well saturated with epoxy. Although joints may show a little, performance and strength will not be affected. Joints may be filled and sanded to be invisible under final paint, if this matters to you. Filler does add weight.

After the final Kevlar layer is in place, add another strip of lightweight fiberglass over each end. This will cover the cut edges of Kevlar, making the ends smoother and easier to fill and sand. This is a good place to use a 45-degree bias-cut strip of fabric as described earlier in this chapter.

Sealing the Outer Layer

The outer layer is given additional coats of epoxy to seal the surface and fill the fabric weave, as shown in Figure 9.7. If the weave is not filled, you can end up with a slightly porous hull that may leak. At least three coats are usually required to seal and fill adequately. If pushpins were used to hold the Kevlar or other laminating cloth to the form at a tumblehome area, as shown in Figure 9.5, they should be removed before the final epoxy coats. Fill the pinholes with dabs of thickened epoxy. A small screwdriver or square-ended mixing stick makes a good applicator for filling pinholes. You can add each of the sealer coats as soon as the previous coat is just dry to the touch. A fine foam paint roller works well for applying the last epoxy finish coats. Use the tip of a disposable foam brush to break any air bubbles and smooth them out. The brush can also be used to smooth out any runs, sags, or unevenness in the epoxy.

Despite your best efforts, you may find a few small bubbles in the cured epoxy surface. Inspect the surface for bubbles, small craters, and pinholes, which can be a potential source of very small leaks. Such minor leaks can be especially annoying if they occur below the waterline in hull locations that enclose flotation chambers, and all such imperfections should be repaired. Start by trimming off the outer part of the bubble to reveal the crater underneath. This crater area under the blister may be resin starved and may not have been filled with epoxy and sealed to the fabric underneath. Clean and roughen the interior and inside edges of the crater with the point of an awl or a small knife. Then fill the crater with fresh epoxy or epoxy slightly thickened with microfibers. Work epoxy well into

FIGURE 9.7. *Additional coats of epoxy are applied with brush or roller to seal the hull and fill the weave of the fabric. Note once more that I should be wearing a respirator.*

the crater hole with the point of a toothpick or an awl, and let the epoxy mound up slightly over the repair. If I am nearby when the epoxy starts to gel to a putty-like state, I put a piece of plastic wrap over the repair and press the epoxy firmly down into the hole with the flat side of a screwdriver or the back of a fingernail. When the epoxy has cured, it may be trimmed level with the hull surface with a knife and sanded. Repair any such bubbles and craters in each epoxy seal coat you apply.

The hull ends can be coated with extra epoxy or thickened epoxy so that they may later be sanded to a smoothly sculpted shape. If the hull will eventually be painted, which is advisable for ultraviolet protection, then microfibers or sanding filler may be added to thicken the epoxy. Very fine sawdust or sanding dust can be used as an inexpensive alternative. Mix filler and epoxy to almost the consistency of peanut butter, and apply it with a plastic applicator or squeegee. For a clear finish, add some extra layers of 4-ounce fiberglass over the ends instead of filler. Excess will later be sanded away, and the fiberglass will appear almost transparent

under a clear marine varnish. Laminating is now complete.

If you accidentally let the epoxy cure too hard before applying another layer, you will need to sand the surface to get the best adhesion. With some epoxies (especially with fast hardeners), a waxlike film or "amine blush" may appear on the cured surface. This must be removed before any further epoxy applications. It is water soluble and may be removed with clean water and an abrasive pad, such as a Scotch-Brite pad. Rinse the surface and dry it with paper towels to remove the amine blush before it dries. Then sand thoroughly with 80- or 100-grit paper.

This same surface preparation is needed before bonding the gunwales to the exterior of the hull; for any other outfitting that involves bonding to the smooth, cured exterior surface; and before varnishing or painting. Sand with 80-grit or coarser sandpaper for bonding; work up through several grits to 120 or 220 grit for paint or varnish. On the inside, the peel ply fabric will remove any amine blush and will leave a textured surface that requires no sanding before bonding interior structures.

Removing the Hull from the Form

The next step is exciting but frustrating. The hull will soon come off the form, and you will heft and admire the composite shell. Turned right side up, it will resemble a real boat. But questions remain. Will you really get it off the form? What will it look like? How light will it be? But you must be patient and wait for the epoxy to cure. It is like waiting for the store to open before a marvelous new toy goes on sale!

After the last layer of epoxy has cured dry to the touch and moderately hard, remove all staples and any hold-down strips for the polyester peel ply cloth. Get under the hull and use a fine-point marker to transfer marks for gunwale lines from the station forms onto the polyester fabric. Also mark the locations of all the stations you can reach. It is okay to trim off excess polyester fabric at this point, but leave it a few inches longer than the hull itself. Longer is better for gripping the layer to peel it, which will come later. Pull the hull and polyester fabric together away from the release tape on the form. Start at the middle of each side, and work your way toward the ends and as far up the form as you can. Pulling the hull up will release it from the center of the form. Work the ends loose, as described in Figure 9.8, and remove the hull from the form, as shown in Figure 9.9.

If there is a narrowed tumblehome area, the hull can be easily flexed to fit over and off the mold. If the tumblehome resists, it may help to have assistants to lift simultaneously at each side and each end, although with time and a little struggling I have always been able to do this solo. A moderate amount of tumblehome

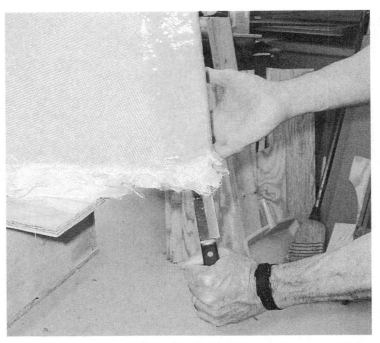

FIGURE 9.8. *Use a long knife or thin metal ruler to pry between peel ply and tape to release the laminate from the ends of the form. The ends may stick, and it could take a long time to release them. Be persistent; keep working with the long knife. It may help to tap or drive the ends of the hull upward off the form with a mallet or hammer. Place a block of wood under the end and tap, or whack, as necessary. If all else fails, it is possible to saw the ends apart to remove the hull. The ends can be rejoined with fiberglass and epoxy and reinforced on the inside later. However, persistence is usually rewarded, and I've never found it necessary to saw the ends.*

FIGURE 9.9. *Lift the hull from the form, end first. Wear leather gloves.*

can be accommodated. The more the sides have to be pulled out to fit over the form, the more the hull will bind on the ends. If this absolutely prevents removing it, you can saw the ends of the hull apart and bond them back together later. This is no problem as the real strength in the ends comes from interior Kevlar reinforcement after the hull is removed. But don't give up too soon on your attempts to pull the hull off. Try sliding long flexible knives and metal rulers between the polyester cloth and the taped form at the ends. Persistence will pay off.

Removing the Peel Ply

Gunwales, thwarts, ribs, and flotation bulkheads will eventually define the precise final shape and add stiffness, but at this stage the hull is still very flexible and it can be permanently deformed by heat and gravity. Don't leave it out in the sun! When you are not working on the hull, place it back over its form in order to maintain its shape. Although the epoxy cures to a moderately hard solid in a few hours or a day, it will continue to cure and strengthen for a week or longer. For now, it is a good idea to proceed to the steps that will allow you to remove the peel ply layer before the epoxy reaches full strength.

Turn the hull right side up onto sawhorses or, better yet, sling stands. (Building convenient sling stands is described later in this chapter.) Scribe the locations marks that you made earlier on the peel ply, using a sharp knife to cut through the fabric and precisely mark the locations of the gunwale lines and stations onto the inner surface of the hull. Then remove the peel ply polyester cloth, and prepare the hull for trimming as shown in

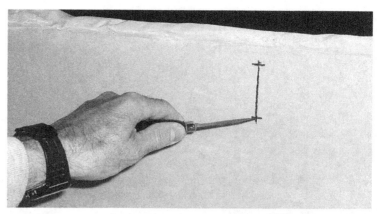

FIGURE 9.10. *Use a knife point to scribe marks through the peel ply onto the hull at the marks that were earlier transferred from the stations to the peel ply fabric. These will locate stations and gunwales or sheerlines, which will make it much easier to complete the canoe. There are alternate gunwale marks shown here for the design being built. The upper mark is the hull trim line for an open canoe with conventional raised ends. The lower mark is the trim line for completing the canoe with long and low end decks, which reduce the influence of wind and enclose large flotation chambers.*

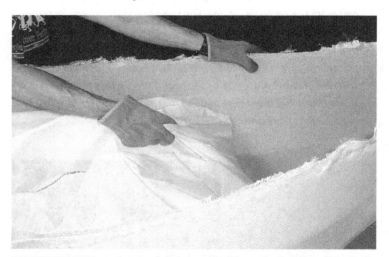

FIGURE 9.11. *The polyester fabric is peeled from the interior of the hull. This takes some effort, but the polyester will pull free. Use heavy leather gloves for protection from the sharp Kevlar edge, which is made sawlike when hardened by the epoxy. Pretend there is a shark in your canoe, or a monster muskellunge if you prefer. After the peel ply is removed, be certain to mark the station and cut-line scribes with a marker or a pencil to make them easier to locate.*

Figures 9.10 through 9.12. Pulling out the peel ply is a lot of fun. But it sounds terrible—you'll know what I mean after you've done it!

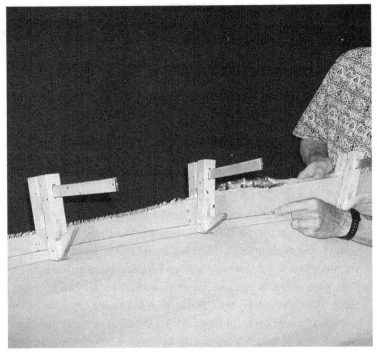

FIGURE 9.12. *A wood strip is clamped to the inside of the hull to fair and mark the gunwale cut line. The cam clamps shown are incredibly handy. They are light in weight and are available with a long throat to reach difficult places. A quick-action cam applies moderate pressure, and leather or cork pads protect finished surfaces. A good source is Stewart-MacDonald (stewmac.com), but experienced woodworkers will find them easy and fun to make. You could buy a few to see how they work and then make more.*

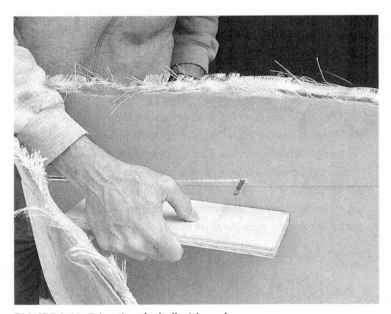

FIGURE 9.13. *Trimming the hull with a saber saw.*

Trimming the Hull

Clamp a strip of wood along the sheerline of the hull, and adjust it until it produces a perfectly sweet, fair curve. Transfer the curve to the surface of the hull with a fine-line marker, and remove the clamps and the wood strip. A saber saw is generally the most convenient tool for trimming the hull at the cut line. A block of wood is used to back up the saw and reduce vibration (as shown in Figure 9.13). Blades will dull quickly on Kevlar. A medium-tooth metal cutting blade works best and lasts longest on Kevlar. One or two blades should last long enough to trim one canoe. Protect eyes, ears, and lungs when cutting or sanding Kevlar or any of the other hull materials.

With the excess trimmed off, your hull will be close to its final dimensions and will start to really look like a boat. You may be impressed by its light weight, although there is much to add before you make a final weigh-in and go paddling. After admiring your hull, and perhaps taking a picture, return it to the form to maintain its proper shape.

Do not discard all of the excess hull laminate that you cut off. Keep a few pieces as samples. After a week or so of curing, the epoxy will have reached full strength. You can experiment with some pieces to discover in what ways it is strong and in what ways it is easily broken. If you bend a narrow piece back and forth, or force it to bend very sharply by trying to fold it in half, it will not be difficult to break in two. However, you should find it very difficult to cut or puncture it.

Also use some samples to test the ultraviolet resistance of your lamination. Place one sample outdoors exposed to weather and sunlight, one in a drawer away from light, and one or more with exposure similar to where you will store your boat. Exposure to the ultraviolet radiation in sunlight will eventually darken, degrade, and weaken the epoxy and the Kevlar. If you have used WEST epoxy with UV-resistant 207 Hardener, it will last longer. Without the UV-resistant hardener, your hull should be painted within a few months to ensure longevity. The UV-resistant epoxy will hold up longer before protection becomes necessary. Occasionally compare the color of your hull with the test samples kept away from light. When the hull starts to look darker and duller, it should be painted. If you prefer a clear finish, use a good marine varnish with UV inhibitors. But pigmented paints are much more protective and will better ensure a maximum service life.

Making Stands

Sling stands are handy for cradling the hull safely while working on the interior. They are easily made from 2 × 4s, plywood, and the web material used for repairing lawn chairs, which is available in the patio furniture sections of many stores. Size the stands to fit your boat and the most convenient working height for you. The larger and heavier the base, the sturdier and the easier it will be to work on your canoe. However, I build mine light to make them easier to move and store.

My uprights are two 40-inch-long 2 × 4s. These are set 32 inches apart for working on solo canoes and kayaks; for tandem canoes, they must be wider. Make at least one of the stands a few inches wider than the widest part of your boat. The plywood pieces can be any strong plywood. The stand in Figure 9.14 is made with ¼-inch-thick plywood to save weight. The bottom crosspieces between the 2 × 4s are 8 inches high; the end pieces, or feet, are

12 inches high and 24 inches long. Assemble the parts with finishing nails and any wood glue. At one end of the web material, fold 2 inches of web over three times to create four layers of web. Pass a wood screw with a washer through the folds and into the side of one of the 2 × 4 uprights a few inches from the top. If it is difficult to get the screw through the web material, melt a hole with a nail that has been heated in a candle flame. Hold the nail in vise grips while heating and piercing. Repeat on the other side of the stand. Screw the second web end in a place that provides the working height you want.

A bag of sand or mulch placed over the base can be used to stabilize the stand. Individual stands like this are especially handy because they can be moved to accommodate different boat lengths and various working positions and projects.

You will need at least two sling stands, one to support each end of the hull as you do the finish work. A third sling stand is handy to support the hull and help maintain the hull shape under areas being reinforced when ribs are bonded

FIGURE 9.14. *A sling stand.*

in. Of course, the web screws in the stands can be repositioned to change height. There are other ways to make rapid adjustments whenever needed. Blocks of wood or wedges can be placed under the webbing, as shown in Figure 9.15, to tighten the third stand firmly under the hull wherever you want it and at whatever height you require. Or the web can be held against the upright 2 × 4 at one side with a clamp to adjust the sling length. A pair of sturdy sawhorses will be better for some operations. They can support a canoe upside down by the gunwales for sanding and finishing the hull. Figures 9.16 and 9.17 show sling stands in action.

FIGURE 9.15. *Blocks can be placed under the web to adjust the stand height.*

FIGURE 9.16. *The roughly trimmed hull is off the form and on two sling stands ready for interior and finishing work. Wasp is pictured. The ends are trimmed low to make a partially decked canoe. This Kevlar hull shell is 14¾ feet long and weighs 16.4 pounds.*

FIGURE 9.17. *The length of the web cradle can be easily changed to suit your working height. The shape of Wasp, without gunwales and thwarts, is very slightly distorted here by the stands. To prevent permanent distortion, it must be put back in place on the form until proceeding to the next stage of adding gunwales and thwarts.*

Chapter 10

Making a Model

The previous chapters have described how the fabric form method works to build a full-size canoe. The process is also easily adapted to building in smaller sizes, and I have used it to mold musical instruments and one-of-a-kind parts for airplanes. You may skip this chapter if you are ready to forge confidently ahead and build a full-size canoe. But if you are new to boatbuilding or working with composites, you may want to build a scale-model canoe to try out the process and learn hands on what it is really like to work with epoxy, fiberglass, and peel ply. Model making can also be valuable for creating new designs and making the measurements needed to draw plans. The materials for a model are less costly; there is no need for carbon fiber or Kevlar. And the process can be simplified to shorten the working time while still making an attractive model.

Making the Templates and Station Forms

A model for the Dragonfly canoe is used as an example (see Chapter 16 for a description of the boat and working plans). It is the simplest design in this book and is ideal for making a one-quarter-scale model. All full-size dimensions are divided by 4 to produce one-quarter scale. The full-size length of Dragonfly is 11.6 feet, or 139.2 inches. So, the model length is 139.2 inches ÷ 4 = 34.8 inches.

Use a photocopier that can adjust copy size to produce templates of the stations and end profile forms. The drawings of the stations and end forms are on grids that would be 2-inch squares if full size. Copy them so that each square is ½ inch instead of 2 inches. For Dragonfly only one paper copy of the stations is needed, although it is a good idea to make a few extra copies in case you make cutting errors. Cut out and trace the largest station, station 5, first. Then cut out and trace the next largest station, and so on.

Station forms and end forms are made from plywood that is ¼ inch or 5 mm thick; plywood with a smooth hardwood surface is easiest to work with. Start by cutting the paper stations at the centerline and the top reference line. (See Figure 10.1.) Then cut out the largest station template, for station #5. Draw a centerline onto the plywood. Place the paper template against the right side of the centerline, and trace it onto the plywood. Then flip the paper template over right to left and trace the left side. (See Figure 10.2.) Be certain to mark the centerline and the sheerlines or gunwale height on both sides of each plywood station. Saw out the plywood form for station 5. A stationary belt sander can make it a bit easier

FIGURE 10.1. *Tracing station templates for the Dragonfly model.*

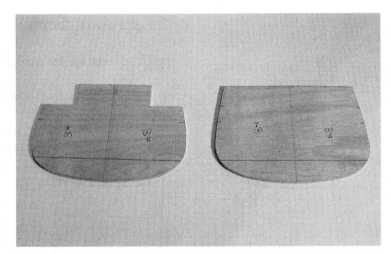

FIGURE 10.2. *Most full-size station forms will have "shoulder cutouts," as in the station on the left. The cutouts are not needed when making a model, and it is best to omit them. Continue the hull line upward to the top reference line when cutting out the paper templates and forms for model stations. The plywood station on the right is ready for assembly into the model.*

to shape the plywood forms. Cut the plywood a little proud of the tracing lines and sand to accurate finished size.

When you are satisfied with the result, cut the paper template for the next size of station. This will be stations 4 and 6, which are identical.

Assembling the Station Forms to the Strongback

A 1-by-8-inch clear pine board or piece of ¾-inch plywood will serve as a strongback. Cut the board to length (34.8 inches for Dragonfly), and draw a centerline from end to end. Mark the midpoint for station 5, and measure left and right for the other stations. Since full-size stations are 12 inches apart, one-quarter-scale stations should be 12 inches ÷ 4 = 3 inches. Use a square to draw the station location lines at right angles to the centerline on the mounting board. (See Figure 10.3.)

If you have a radial arm saw, table saw, or router, the mounting board can be slotted (as shown in Figure 10.4) so that the plywood station forms fit snugly in place. Otherwise, 1-by-1-inch strips of wood can be glued and nailed in place on the mounting board to hold the plywood stations. As with the full-size boat, station forms forward of amidships should have their forward face on the station line, and station forms aft of amidships should have their aft face on the line. The center station can go either way or dead center on the line.

Cut out the end forms. Nail the 1-by-1-inch strips to the mounting board at the ends and parallel to the centerline to hold the end forms right on the centerline. Test-fit each plywood station form. Make sure that the centerlines on the stations line up with the centerline on the board, and mark the mounting board where the sides of the stations meet the board. (See Figure 10.4.) Connect the marks with a pencil to create a canoe shape on the mounting board. Trim or shim the end forms,

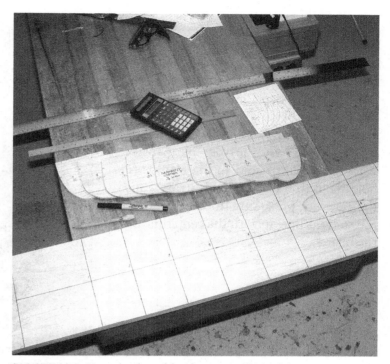

FIGURE 10.3. *Mounting board for the Dragonfly model.*

FIGURE 10.4. *The station forms and end forms are test-fitted on the mounting board.*

if needed, so that they are level with the end stations along the keel line.

Remove the forms from the mounting board, and saw the mounting board to the marked canoe shape. The side edges of the board will provide a convenient place to staple the peel ply fabric and hold it tightly to the form. Glue the stations in place with white glue, using spring clamps to hold them to the 1-by-1-inch strips while the glue sets. Make sure the centerlines of the stations line up with the centerline on the board.

Attaching Stringers

I use clear, straight-grained cedar for the stringers on models. Dimensions of about 0.1 inch thick by 0.2 inch wide are strong enough and bend well. If you don't have the planers and saws to machine small, solid wood strips, they can be easily cut from 3/32-inch or 2.5 mm plywood instead. Aircraft Spruce and Specialty Company is a good source. (See Appendix A.) Strips can be cut from such thin plywood with a sharp razor knife, a small band saw, or a benchtop jigsaw.

Attaching stringers and keeping them attached is the most difficult part of model making. There is not much surface area between the stringers and the station forms for glue to hold. Glue and tack the first strip in place at the center along the keel line to hold all the stations and end forms together and in place, as shown in Figure 10.5. White wood glue is okay. Use very fine wire nails to prevent splitting the stringers too much, and drive them into the station forms only enough to hold the stringers while the glue dries. Remove the nails after the glue sets. Dampening

FIGURE 10.5. *The mounting board is cut to shape, and the station forms and end forms are glued in place. The first stringers are attached at the keel line and near the sheerline or gunwale location. Clothespins make convenient little spring clamps.*

FIGURE 10.6. *Rubber bands and S-hooks make miniature bungee cords to hold stringers.*

the strips slightly with water will help them conform to sharper bends or to the twist that may be required at the ends. Rubber bands and S-hooks can be used as miniature bungee cords to help hold stringers to the forms and minimize the need for nails. (See Figure 10.6.) Masking tape or Scotch tape can also be used.

After the stringers have been glued, nailed, and bungeed in place, epoxy thickened with microfibers can be added to the backs of the stringers to create a fillet between each stringer and station form. Quick-setting or five-minute epoxy is fine for this application and will allow you to continue without much waiting for glue to dry.

For the model you do not need to take great pains with the woodworking at the ends of the form. However, end cheek plates of 1 mm plywood (as shown in Figures 10.7 and 10.8) will help ease hull separation from the form. Glue the end plates in place. After the glue dries, use wood filler to fill the end areas between stringers. Slather on wood filler in layers until you can sand the ends to an agreeable rounded shape.

Release Tape

Your model form is now completed. The rest of the process is similar to making a full-size canoe. Don't forget to tape the form so that the hull will release (as described in Chapter 8). Narrow plastic tape, such as Scotch tape, will do for covering stringers. Also tape the sides of the mounting board. The end cheek plates can be covered with wider package-sealing tape. Start taping from the bottom at the board and work your way up the form toward the keel, overlapping the tape like roof shingles. Figure 10.9 shows a completely taped model form.

FIGURE 10.7. *After all stringers are attached, optional 1-millimeter-thick cheek plates are glued and clamped in place with small spring clamps.*

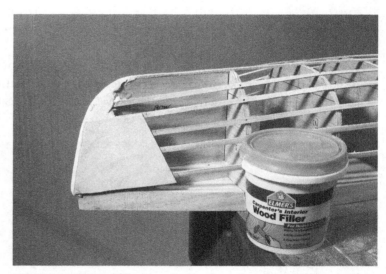

FIGURE 10.8. *Wood filler is applied to the ends and sanded to smooth curves.*

Covering the Form with Peel Ply Fabric

Peel ply for the model can be the 2.7-ounce aircraft Dacron polyester used for the full-size boat or lighter and less expensive 1.8-ounce fabric. Aircraft Spruce is a good source. (See Appendix

FIGURE 10.9. *The ends, stringers, and sides of the mounting board are covered with plastic tape so that epoxy will not stick.*

A.) Do not use polyester fabric from fabric stores or other sources. It may not shrink or release properly from the epoxy. Staple the fabric down to the side edges of the mounting board. (See Figures 10.10 and 10.11.) Sew the ends (as shown in Figures 10.12 and 10.13) and shrink the fabric just as described for full-size construction in Chapter 8. Take care not to create a hazard by using too much heat with the fabric iron.

Laminating the Hull

Laminating is similar to making a full-size canoe, but it goes much faster on the small hull. You can use a faster-setting epoxy hardener to speed the process, but a low-viscosity epoxy resin is still needed to wet out the laminating fabric. Don't try to use repair epoxy in small tubes from the hardware store! It won't have the proper viscosity. You can buy epoxy in smaller volumes before committing to a full-size canoe. WEST epoxy is available in 1.2-quart kits. This

FIGURE 10.10. *Peel ply fabric is draped over the form and cut a bit oversized.*

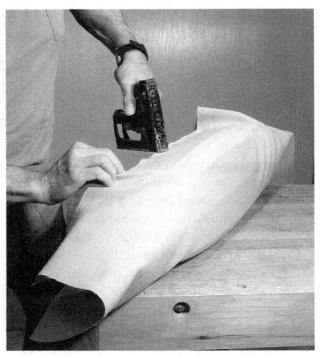

FIGURE 10.11. *The fabric is stretched over the form and stapled to the mounting board.*

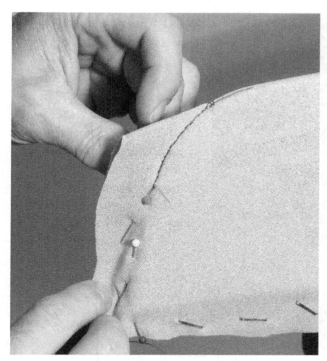

FIGURE 10.12. *At the ends, the two flaps of fabric are stretched over the ends and held together with straight pins. Then the flaps are stitched together side to side with polyester thread.*

FIGURE 10.13. *The fabric is trimmed to within about ¼ inch of the end stitches. The remaining ¼-inch flap of fabric is folded to one side and sewn to lay flat.*

is more than needed for a model, but you will surely find other uses for the remaining resin—perhaps even a full-size boat! The more costly ultraviolet resistant hardener is not necessary for the model.

Laminate with fiberglass only. (See Figure 10.14.) The structural qualities of carbon fiber and Kevlar are not required, and they are too stiff to conform to the sharper bends of the model. Use three layers of 6-ounce fiberglass or two layers of 9-ounce fiberglass. As with full-size construction, start with layers of very light weight fiberglass at the ends. The ends of the model will be much sharper than a full-size boat; therefore, even lighter-weight fiberglass should be used to wrap around the ends. "Deck cloth," or 1.45-ounce fiberglass, is ideal and is available from Aircraft Spruce. (See Appendix A.) Build up several layers. Let the first layer gel and get tacky before adding another layer. Since maximum adhesion between layers is not really necessary

for a model, there is no need to follow a strict timetable. You can let one layer cure entirely and come back at any time to add another layer.

Completing the Canoe Model

After the epoxy sets, the hull may be removed and trimmed as described for a full-size boat. It may be necessary to tap upward on the ends to encourage them to release from the form. First, clamp the mounting board to your workbench; then place a block of wood under the laminate at one end and tap upward with a mallet or hammer. Taps may turn into whacks as necessary. When one end is released, you will probably be able to lift it and tip the entire hull, which will release the other end.

FIGURE 10.14. *Fiberglass is laminated over the form just as for a full-size canoe. Marks for the gunwale trim line can be seen through the fiberglass. These were made with marker on the peel ply fabric at each station after shrinking and before laminating. The wrinkles in the fabric at the mounting board are outside the hull area beyond the gunwale trim line, so they will cause no difficulty. Pushpins hold the fiberglass tightly to stringers along the sides at the gunwales to ensure that the hull laminate conforms to the tumblehome of the form.*

Figures 10.15 through 10.22 show some finishing steps. The fiberglass may be translucent enough for you to see through to mark the station and gunwale locations. If not, use the extra paper station templates to transfer marks to the inside of the hull. After the hull is trimmed to height, the model can be finished simply. Saw wood strips for gunwales and thwarts. Install gunwale strips with epoxy and clamp them in place with spring clothespins. Other glues may not adhere to the fiberglass hull. Glue thwarts to the undersides of the interior gunwale strips. Reinforcement ribs, bulkheads, and flotation chambers are unnecessary.

A seat is optional; we can rationalize that many canoes are paddled from a kneeling position with no seat. And small pack canoes like Dragonfly can be paddled by just sitting in the bottom. I made a scale-size foam pad seat to place in the bottom of my model. The hull may be sanded and painted if you like. A small stand and a one-quarter-size paddle would be nice touches that look good on a display shelf. (Figures 10.23 and 10.24 on page 85 show a finished model.)

FIGURE 10.15. *The hull surface need not be finished any further. It is reasonable to complete the model in a simple manner and save your labors for a full-size boat. However, I've decided on a smooth painted exterior finish for my model Dragonfly. After trimming the hull to the gunwale line, a padded sanding block and 60-grit sandpaper start the smoothing process on the hull exterior. If you desire a really good-looking model, any low spots and pinholes can be built up level with layers of epoxy thickened with microfibers or Microlight filler. Sand the exterior with progressively finer sandpapers, finishing with 220-grit paper.*

FIGURE 10.16. *Wood gunwale strips are bonded to the fiberglass. Small wire nails or tacks in predrilled holes hold the gunwale strips in place on the hull for epoxy bonding. Without nails to keep the parts lined up, they will slide out of place before the epoxy sets.*

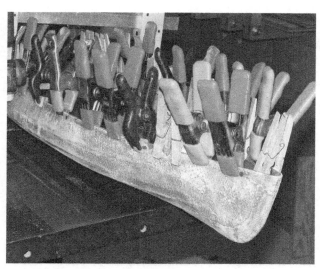

FIGURE 10.17. *Spring clamps hold gunwale strips to the hull while the epoxy sets.*

FIGURE 10.18. *Two miniature sling stands were made to display my Dragonfly model. The wood parts are scraps of walnut and pine. The slings are cut from the light nylon web material of a recycled fanny pack. Thin leather or ribbon material would work just as well.*

FIGURE 10.19. *The exterior fiberglass is sanded and ready for paint.*

FIGURE 10.20. *To avoid any sanding on the inside, the interior of this model was sprayed with a textured paint. You can find textured paints in convenient spray cans at local hardware stores. Masking tape must be used to protect the gunwales and hull exterior from overspray. The end decks were carved from scraps of rosewood veneer. One-quarter-inch mahogany dowels make scale-size thwarts.*

FIGURE 10.21. *A coat of primer on the exterior makes it easier to achieve a very smooth finish. Since I chose to spray, the interior was covered with paper and the natural wood gunwales were protected with masking tape. The primer is sanded with 320-grit paper before adding the color coats.*

FIGURE 10.22. *With a few color coats applied, the model nears completion.*

FIGURE 10.23. *After the paint dries, only a few finishing touches remain. For the finished model shown here, the wood gunwales, end decks, and thwarts were given a hand-rubbed oil finish for a non-glossy, natural wood look. Varnish or lacquer will provide a gloss finish, if you prefer.*

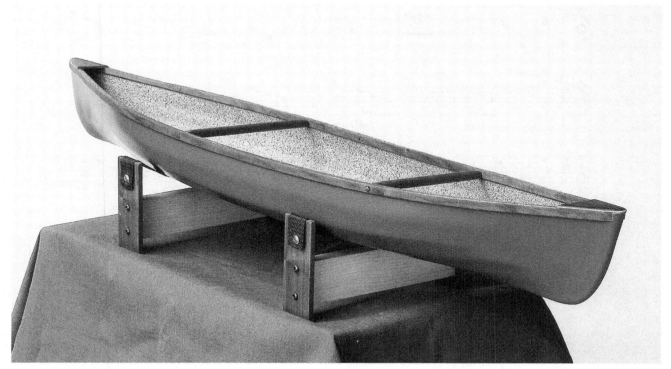

FIGURE 10.24. *The scale-model Dragonfly sits proudly on her little sling stands and is ready for display on a bookshelf or mantel. She could even become a marvelous toy for a young pre-paddler. My wife suggests that model canoes make lovely flower boxes. That is okay with me as long as I get to paddle the full-size versions!*

Sleepy Creek Waltz

Swing

Sam Rizzetta © 1997

Chapter 11

Turning the Hull into a Boat

After the full-size composite hull has been laminated, completing a canoe or kayak is straightforward. For those who have built canoes before, the process described here will be mostly familiar. Working with composites has some unique aspects, however, and care must be taken with structural bonding operations.

Completing your hull as a conventional open canoe is the simplest project. Gunwales, thwarts, ribs, flotation bulkheads, and end decks will define the precise final shape and add stiffness. Interior reinforcements will provide the strength needed to prevent damage at the vulnerable ends.

No canoe or kayak is complete or safe without adequate flotation. Composite boats absolutely must have some flotation built in. In factory-produced canoes, this is normally done by bonding a small chamber into each end. Small, inexpensive kayaks may rely on blocks of foam in the ends. Typically, however, such flotation is barely enough to keep the swamped or capsized hull from sinking; it may not be enough to also float a paddler safely or keep the boat from damage or total loss in moving water or unforeseen rough conditions.

This chapter describes how to install the minimum necessary end flotation chambers in a canoe or kayak; be aware that a variety of flotation strategies exist that are much better and safer. Some of them can be incorporated as part of a boat's structure, increasing hull stiffness and reducing the materials and weight required for other structural components. Read Chapter 15 before planning how to complete and outfit your boat.

Gunwales

If you are building an open canoe, attaching gunwales and thwarts will help determine and hold the final shape of the hull, so these are important steps. With the hull shell trimmed to the gunwale lines, the hull must next be held to the finished width. Place the hull upright, and cut several sticks of wood to prop open the hull to the correct width at several locations along the hull. (See Figure 11.1.) Use measurements at the plywood stations of the form, and transfer them to the corresponding station marks along the hull. Don't forget to include the thickness of the stringers when taking width measurements off the form. You do not need a prop stick at every station. Three or four will suffice to hold the shape of most boats, with perhaps more for a very flexible or long hull.

Before working further, the hull must be leveled as shown in Figure 11.2. It should be checked and rechecked from time to time and especially before any structural bonding operations like attaching gunwales.

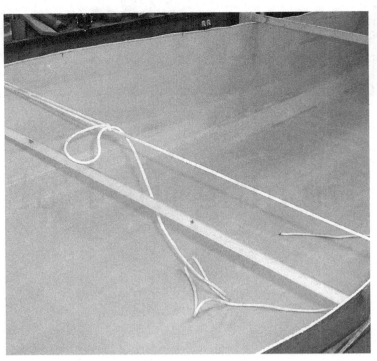

FIGURE 11.1. *A rope passed under the hull and tied across the open top at each prop stick will hold the stick in place.*

FIGURE 11.2. *Next, level the hull very carefully left to right. Check many locations from bow to stern in preparation for attaching gunwales.*

Because of the complex curves of Wasp, I laminated wood gunwales onto the hull in thin, ³/₁₆-inch-thick layers, one at a time. This time-consuming approach is not necessary with more conventional canoes. For a small, lightweight solo canoe like Dragonfly, use a ³/₈-inch-wide by 1-inch-high spruce gunwale strip on both the inside and outside of the hull. If you want extra strength, add an additional ³/₈-inch layer to the inside of Dragonfly's gunwales between stations #3 and #7.

When stronger gunwales are needed, I make them 1¼ inches high and wider than ³/₈ inch on the inside. Increase the overall gunwale width to at least 1¼ inches for a longer tandem canoe. Wasp requires gunwales 1¼ inches high and 1¼ inches wide between stations #5 and #9 to stiffen its flexible midsection. Toward the bow and stern, the gunwales have fewer layers, which total 0.8 inch wide. The decks will add strength at the ends, reducing the need for heavy gunwales there.

Ash, mahogany, oak, and other medium-hard straight-grained woods make fine gunwales. If your goal is absolute minimum weight, make the gunwales out of spruce. Douglas fir is almost equal to spruce in strength-to-weight ratio and may be easier to find in local lumberyards. The wood grain must be straight with no knots. For a decked boat, I use a lightweight wood, such as spruce, fir, or pine, ½ inch wide and attached only to the inside. This provides a gluing surface for bonding the deck, rather than any structural reinforcement. Bonding a deck to the hull and reinforcing the joint with fiberglass tape on the outside provides the necessary strength and stiffness. The same procedure can be used where decks are attached to a partially decked canoe, thereby saving materials and weight. Wasp was finished this way with sizable end decks, which enclose large flotation chambers. The internal glue strips for an end deck can be seen in Figure 11.2.

It is unlikely you will have wood long enough for a gunwale, but it is easy to make tapered scarf joints to lengthen smaller pieces. (See Figure 11.3.) As a rule of thumb to achieve good strength, the length of the scarf joint should equal fifteen times the thickness of the wood. Thus, a ½-inch-thick strip should have a joint 7½ inches long. Although jigs may be contrived to make these joints, I find it easy enough to scribe the joint with a bevel square, cut it on a band saw, and clean it up with a rasp or, even better, a stationary belt sander.

Start by preparing two or more wood strips that you want to join into one long, continuous gunwale strip. They should be planed smooth to uniform thickness and width. Cut and smooth the tapers required for the scarf joint. Screw or clamp a straight-edged board to a piece of plywood to create a jig. (See Figure 11.4.) Lay plastic wrap or wax paper over the jig. Then clamp one gunwale strip on top of the wax paper and in place against the plywood and straightedge. Apply glue, and clamp the second strip in place. A tight-fitting scarf joint with no gaps could be assembled with a one-part water-resistant glue like Titebond III. Or, use epoxy thickened with

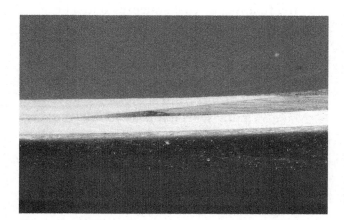

FIGURE 11.3. *This scarf joint in a gunwale strip layer is easy to see because it joins two different-colored woods. To the left are two layers of light-colored poplar that will serve as a bonding surface inside the hull under an end deck. To the right are layers of oak and walnut, which are heavier but provide more strength for an open area that is not strengthened with a deck. That open area will also have additional gunwale strips on the outside of the hull.*

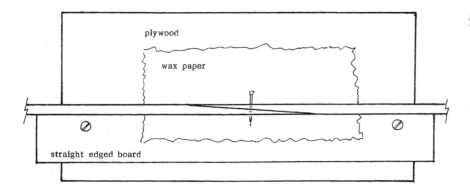

FIGURE 11.4. *A simple plywood and straight-edge jig is used to assemble two strips with a scarf joint.*

microfibers to bond the scarf joint, and it will fill any gaps. A brad or small wire nail through the joint will help hold the two strips in perfect alignment.

Drill a pilot hole first so the wood does not split, and leave the nailhead high enough to remove it after the glue sets. Add clamping pressure at the scarf joint. This is best done by placing the edge of a small wood block against the joint itself and then clamping the block. A block and clamp on each side of the nail may be needed to get a tight joint. A piece of plastic tape or plastic wrap over the block will keep it from sticking to any glue that squeezes out. The scarf joint should be clamped snugly, but do not over-tighten. Clamping too tightly may squeeze out too much epoxy, resulting in resin-starved joints that will not achieve maximum strength. In this regard, epoxy differs from some other adhesives.

Make as many scarf joints as you need to create gunwale strips of sufficient length. Make certain that any scarf joints on the inside gunwale strip are offset a few inches or more from joints on the outside strip. It is best to stagger such joints as much as possible.

The gunwales will be bonded along the top edge of the hull with epoxy. I generally bond the inner gunwale strips first and then do the outer ones after the inner ones have cured. The inside surface has a texture from the peel ply fabric and is ready for bonding. The outside surface must be sanded with coarse sandpaper to roughen the surface so that epoxy will adhere better.

Dry clamp the inner gunwales in place for a test fit, and cut them to length. Use enough clamps to make certain they will bend and fit properly. (See Figure 11.5.) Use epoxy to glue the gunwales in place just below the roughly trimmed edge of the hull. The hull can be trimmed flush later. Slightly thickening the epoxy with microfibers or sawdust will help keep the wood from sliding around while you clamp the strips in place. A few temporary finishing nails or screws are helpful to keep gunwales in register or alignment with the gunwale line marked on the hull. Drill pilot holes before driving them. Figure 10.16 (in Chapter 10) shows nails being used to keep gunwales in place on a model canoe. Clamp and allow to cure before proceeding to the outside strips.

Gunwale strips should be clamped every 2 or 3 inches along the hull. If you don't have a lot of clamps, use screws. Select stainless steel screws if you intend to leave them in place permanently.

FIGURE 11.5. *Spring clamps are inexpensive and handy for attaching wood gunwales. A couple of very small alignment nails may be visible; they keep the gunwale strips from sliding out of place while the epoxy sets.*

If the screws are to be withdrawn after the epoxy cures, wipe a little paste wax on the threads before inserting them or they will be difficult to remove. As you clamp or screw, keep checking and rechecking that the hull is level along its full length. If necessary, use clamps or weights to hold the hull in the proper shape. After the gunwales have been permanently installed, it will be impossible to correct any twist in the hull.

It is normally best to make up the full-length gunwales with scarf joints first and then attach the gunwales to the hull. However, when laminating several ³/₁₆-inch-thick layers to make up a Wasp gunwale, I scarf joint only the first layer ahead of time. Subsequent layers can be scarf jointed in place on the hull to save time. Dry clamp or screw a layer in place for fit. If no screws are used, then drill pilot holes for alignment nails, including one through the center of the scarf joint. Reassemble the layer with slightly thickened epoxy, and clamp carefully.

After the epoxy has cured, the laminated hull can be trimmed flush and level to the wood gunwales with a flush trimming router bit or power sander. If you used screws instead of clamps, you may choose to leave the screws in place because they may prevent the gunwales from coming loose should the boat suffer a severe impact or other damage. I generally remove the screws to save a little weight. Empty screw holes can be filled with small dowels or wood filler and sealed with epoxy.

If the gunwale-to-hull joint is less than attractive on top, glue a decorative thin layer of wood on top of the gunwales before planing and sanding the corners to a more rounded, hand-friendly shape. This is capped off with a layer of fiberglass to protect the top of the gunwales. For the Wasp project, I used scraps of carbon fiber. Small pieces can be overlapped slightly and sanded level later. The black carbon imparts a nice contrast to the wood.

Give the wood gunwales three thin coats of epoxy. Later on, when finishing, apply several coats of UV-resistant clear varnish to the gun-wales and all other exposed woodwork. Wood parts can be painted, if you prefer.

End Reinforcements and Rope Attachment Points

Reinforce the ends of the hull from the inside by bonding in five or more layers of 5-ounce Kevlar fabric. Scraps left over from hull laminating are handy for this. Start with a strip about 1 inch wide, and make each succeeding strip wider. The last strip should be about 4 inches wide. Where the ends curve more sharply into the keel, use several overlapping short pieces of Kevlar instead of one long piece. It will be easier to make small pieces conform to the curves, and the overlaps will add strength.

If you are building an all-fiberglass canoe, you may substitute fiberglass for the Kevlar, but double the fabric weight or number of layers. For a carbon fiber canoe, Kevlar or carbon can be used to reinforce the ends. Since the ends of the hull have only transparent fiberglass in the outer layers, whatever is added to the inside will show through somewhat. If you plan a clear finish on a carbon hull, then make the first inner layer carbon. Layers on top of that can be Kevlar.

Placing a rope attachment point directly to the hull, low and just above the waterline, will make it safer to tow or line a small boat and provides a very strong tie-down point for cartop transportation or for tying up to docks and shore. If you expect to use your canoe only on a home pond, line holes may be omitted. But they are easier to include now than add later, and it is better to have rope attachments than to wish you had them.

Wait until the end reinforcement has cured before drilling into the hull. Line holes should be several inches above the waterline, at both bow and stern. Half-inch plastic water pipe is bonded in place with epoxy through the hull. Sand or rasp a very rough surface on the pipe for better epoxy adhesion. Then drill a hole through the hull to fit the pipe. (See Figure 11.6.) A round rasp may be handy for enlarging holes in the Kevlar rather than trying to drill a hole to the exact size. A sharp knife may be needed to trim the Kevlar threads. A snug fit is okay, but a perfect fit is not necessary. Thicken the epoxy with microfibers to get a strong bond and seal the hull. (See Figure 11.7.) If the pipe fits loosely, wedge in some sticks

of wood to hold it in place. Seal any gaps with thickened epoxy.

The ends of the hull will become flotation chambers and must be strong and free of any potential leaks. When the epoxy holding the plastic pipe has cured, saw off the excess pipe and sand it flush with the hull on the outside. Later this will be finished off with a small fiberglass patch layer over the ends, covering the holes on each side. This will help to seal the joint and keep the pipe from working loose. The fiberglass cloth can be trimmed from the center of the hole with a sharp knife after the epoxy has partially cured. Bevel the inside edges of the hole and smooth them to avoid abrading the rope.

FIGURE 11.6. *A piece of plastic pipe is fitted in place to seal and reinforce the line hole.*

End Flotation Chambers

Bulkheads for end flotation chambers are made from inexpensive, ½-inch-thick polystyrene foam insulation. This lightweight, rigid foam board is available in 4-by-8-foot sheets at your local building supply store. The top of the bulkhead can be straight across to create a flat deck, which is fastest and easiest to make. This works well and looks good for small decks on open canoes. Or the deck can be raised to deflect waves bet-

FIGURE 11.7. *On the inside, add several layers of fiberglass to entirely encircle the plastic pipe and bond it to the hull. Be generous here with epoxy and thickened epoxy filler. Kevlar end reinforcement can be seen.*

FIGURE 11.8. *An end bulkhead made from ½-inch foam is dry fitted in place.*

ter and also look attractive. My Kayoo has arched bulkheads creating curved decks, while the peaked bulkhead in Wasp, shown in Figure 11.8, produces a peaked deck. The center of the bulkhead is about 2 inches higher than the gunwale.

Plan to add about 1 cubic foot of flotation volume to each end. On most canoes this can be accomplished by placing the bulkheads about 25 to 30 inches from the ends. Consider 20 inches as a minimum if your boat design is relatively small and you absolutely need the space. For Dragonfly the bulkheads are located at stations #1 and #9. On Kayoo the bulkheads are at about 28 inches from the ends. Wasp is higher in volume and has 1.6 cubic feet of flotation at each end, with bulkheads set at 30 inches. For Wasp you can use station #2 and station #12 as templates for the bulkheads. Trim the upper corners to fit the inside gunwale strips. If you are building a tandem canoe, keep in mind that there needs to be enough footroom for the bow paddler. Place the bow bulkhead accordingly.

The rigid foam cuts easily with a band saw, a handsaw, or a sharp knife. If you are using foam insulation from the local building supply store, it may have a thin layer of plastic film over each side. Be absolutely certain to peel this off before any bonding operations. After fitting it to the hull, remove the bulkhead and cover the side

that will remain exposed with a layer of scrap Kevlar or carbon or with two layers of heavy fiberglass. You can fit together several pieces of fabric scraps, if necessary, overlapping them by at least an inch.

Start by brushing epoxy directly onto the foam to cover it. Lay the fabric in place, and add enough epoxy to wet it out. Add a little extra epoxy to any overlap areas in the fabric; then place a peel ply layer of polyester fabric on top of the structural fabric and epoxy. Use a squeegee or plastic applicator to smooth the peel ply gently into the fabric and epoxy. You can squeeze out any excess resin this way, but too much pressure will result in a weaker, resin-starved fabric. If your peel ply fabric has any creases from having been folded, you will obtain a neater job if you iron it smooth first. When the epoxy has cured enough so it is no longer tacky, the peel ply fabric can be removed (as in Figure 11.9). The fabric can be trimmed with a knife if the epoxy has not yet cured hard. Otherwise, saw it to trim by cutting from the fabric side toward the foam side.

Use a very thick mixture of microfibers and epoxy to bond the bulkhead to the hull. (See Figure 11.10.) Use this same mixture to make a ½-inch concave, rounded fillet between the hull and the bulkhead on the outer, Kevlar-covered side. To make the fillet, place a bead of thickened

FIGURE 11.9. *When the epoxy has cured, peel off the polyester layer. You will have a nicely textured surface ready for structural bonding of the bulkhead. Trim off excess Kevlar.*

FIGURE 11.10. *The bulkhead is bonded in place.*

epoxy along the joint and then smooth it to a rounded, concave shape with a gloved fingertip or a stick with a rounded tip. A tongue depressor or a stick shaped like one works well. Scrape off any excess. Then reinforce this joint with 3-inch-wide fiberglass tape or hand-cut strips. Use short, overlapping pieces on the curved portions of the hull. Lap the strips equally onto the hull and the bulkhead. Carefully wet out the fiberglass with epoxy, using enough to saturate the fabric but not so much that it runs and pools at the bottom. Large bulkheads are also reinforced on the back side. (See Figure 11.11.)

Thwarts

Next is the easy but important step of adding thwarts. Before proceeding, you will want to locate the boat's center of gravity (CG). Turn the canoe upside down on a single sawhorse

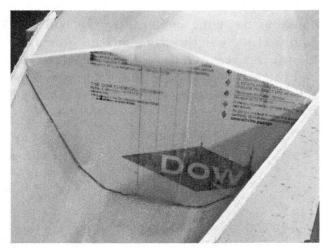

FIGURE 11.11. *The back side of the bulkhead is reinforced. If the bulkhead is rather large, as it is likely to be if it is 25 to 30 inches from the end, then it should be reinforced on the inside. Here a layer of heavy fiberglass tape 4 inches wide has been applied vertically to the middle of a bulkhead and lapped onto the hull at the bottom. Scraps of fiberglass also reinforce the joint at each side. This may be hard to see as the fiberglass is almost clear when wet with epoxy.*

and place a round dowel, rod, or pipe between the gunwales and the sawhorse. Move the hull back and forth until it balances. Make sure that the hull is exactly at right angles to the dowel by ensuring that the balance point on each side is at the same distance from a reference station mark. The CG is likely to be near the center station. When all is in adjustment and balance, mark the CG at the gunwales on both sides. Turn the boat right side up again on the cradle stands. The CG will change slightly as more outfitting is added to complete the boat, but this reference mark will help you get started. The location can be remeasured and updated from time to time.

Thwarts may be made from a variety of materials. Wood is nice, and it is easy to add portage pads to a wood center thwart on a tandem canoe. Straight-grained spruce is light and stiff; ash is tough and limber. If you are going to the effort and expense of building a very light solo canoe with high-tech materials, then you may want to make lightweight thwarts. My preference is 1-inch-diameter aluminum tubing with a minimum wall thickness of .055 inch. These thwarts will be lighter than wood and will require no maintenance. The ends are flattened in a vise, and a hole is drilled in each flattened end to accommodate a ³/₁₆-inch-diameter machine screw.

To prepare the hull for thwarts, fasten prop sticks in several places again to ensure that the hull is the correct width. This is your last chance to make some adjustments to the handling characteristics of the hull. Pulling the hull slightly narrower will generally reduce rocker, reduce stability, make turning slower, and make it easier to reach the water with the paddle. It may also improve straight-line tracking and speed. Propping the hull wider will have an opposite effect. At this stage you should not be making extreme changes—keeping them to only perhaps an inch or so either way—so these performance changes may be relatively minor. Unless you are experienced in the subtleties of handling and are familiar with the design you are building, it may be best to follow the plans. I have tweaked the handling of many finished canoes by changing the length and position of thwarts, and you may choose to experiment with this later.

With the hull propped to the correct widths, level the hull carefully at the gunwales. Mark the places on the gunwales where you will install thwarts. The center thwart of a tandem canoe should be located at the CG. The center thwart position can then be moved a little as needed so that the canoe balances slightly bow high when portaging. For a tandem canoe that will be portaged, make a wood center thwart 3 inches wide at the sides and attach it to the gunwales with two screws per side. The other thwarts can be wood or aluminum and installed according to your plans. Depending on the size and length of the canoe, there may be a thwart just behind the bow paddler's seat and a thwart in front of the stern paddler's knees. Small thwarts may be placed near the ends when end decks are small.

On a solo canoe, the rear thwart should go just to the rear of the seat without crowding the paddler. The front edge of the seat will be about 4 inches aft of the CG. Mount the thwart about 3 or 4 inches aft of the seat's estimated rear edge. Allow 11 inches for the seat's front-to-back dimension, and place the thwart 18 to 19 inches aft of the CG.

The front thwart ideally should go about halfway between the rear thwart and the front bulkhead. However, it must be far enough forward to allow ample room for the paddler's legs and feet. On small solo canoes with low sides, I sometimes mount the forward thwart at a proper distance and low enough to serve as a footrest, thus saving the weight of separate footrests.

Thwarts are usually attached to the undersides of the gunwales with vertical machine screws through the gunwales. However, to save weight on ultralight solo canoes, I make my gunwales rather narrow. A $^3/_{16}$-inch vertical machine screw might weaken the gunwale too much, so instead I make brackets from $^1/_8$-inch-thick aluminum angle. The brackets are attached to the inside of the gunwale with stainless steel wood or sheet metal screws, and the thwart is secured to them with short, $^3/_{16}$-inch-diameter stain-

less steel machine screws and locking nuts. (See Figure 11.12.) If the gunwales are a soft wood, do not rely on wood screws for attaching the brackets. Instead, use stainless steel flathead machine screws that pass all the way through the gunwales and hull. Place the heads, with finishing washers if needed, on the outside and place locking nuts on the inside.

After you have decided where and how to mount your thwarts, measure and cut the tubes. Flatten the ends in a vise, drill attachment holes, and install. In Figure 11.12, note the hole in the thwart near the end. It is convenient to have a variety of places to attach lines and ropes for lashing gear into the boat; holes in the aluminum thwarts are especially strong and handy. Smooth the edges of the aluminum holes with a countersink so that they won't cut or abrade lines.

Decks

Next, you will enclose the flotation chamber ends. For light weight, I cover the ends with thin plywood that conforms to the arch of the bulkheads. Baltic birch aircraft plywood 1 mm thick is ideal for decks. Thin mahogany plywood is also available. It is attractive but quite expensive. Trim plywood pieces to fit the bow and stern decks. Trim a little oversize. Decks

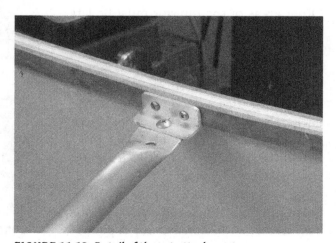

FIGURE 11.12. *Detail of thwart attachment.*

must extend 1½ or 2 inches beyond the bulkheads. Plane and sand the tops of the gunwale strips and hull as needed so that the decks fit flush. Voids in the fit, especially on the inside, can be filled with thickened epoxy.

The underside of the deck will be the inside of the flotation chamber. It must be sealed with epoxy so that it remains waterproof even if the chamber should leak or become flooded. Figure 11.13 shows epoxy coating on the interior area and the sides, which will bond to the hull. The unfinished area at the bottom will be outside the flotation chamber, beyond the bulkhead, and can be left uncoated at this stage. A large deck of 1 mm birch must be reinforced to resist flexing, and Figure 11.13 shows a crosswise layer of heavy, 4-inch-wide fiberglass tape covered with a scrap of 10-ounce carbon fiber. Two layers of scrap 5-ounce Kevlar would serve just as well. This reinforcement might be unnecessary with 1.5 mm or thicker birch plywood or smaller decks. Three-millimeter marine plywood can also be used for flat decks, but the weight will be greater.

While preparing the decks, apply two or three seal coats of epoxy to the inside of the flotation chambers only. Other areas of the interior must be left rough for epoxy bonding of ribs and other structures. The wood gunwale strips inside the end chambers should be also be sealed with epoxy, including the top edge, which will join to the decks. Coat them and the insides of the decks just before assembly. Wait until the epoxy starts to gel. Ideally, it should still be sticky. Then give the deck interiors one last coat of epoxy. Next, mix a batch of epoxy thickened with microfibers almost to the consistency of peanut butter. Apply this liberally to the gun-

FIGURE 11.13. *The inside of the deck is reinforced and sealed just before bonding to the hull.*

FIGURE 11.14. *The deck is held in place with masking tape, rope, and wood scraps while the epoxy cures.*

wale strips and bulkheads where the decks will attach.

Place each deck carefully straight down in place. Hold the deck temporarily in place with a few pieces of masking tape. Weight the deck with a few boards to make it conform to the contour of the bulkhead. Look carefully under the deck at the bulkhead to see if the plywood is tight against the bulkhead. Then proceed to fasten all the edges down firmly. (See Figure 11.14.) Masking tape will hold down 1 mm plywood. If you decide to use thicker plywood for a curved deck, then attaching small screws to the gunwale strips may be needed. Wipe off any epoxy that squeezes out.

After the epoxy sets and the boards and tape are removed, trim the edges of the decks with planes, rasps, and coarse sandpaper. A power palm sander may be handy. The edges of the decks facing the cockpit can be trimmed closer to final shape if that was not done previously. Metal shears will make a clean cut of 1 mm plywood; thicker wood needs to be sawed. Bond the bulkhead to the underside of the deck overhang with a 3- or 4-inch-wide strip of 9-ounce fiberglass. The fiberglass should lap onto the deck underside and onto the bulkhead by equal amounts. At the same time, give an epoxy coating of at least three coats to the entire deck overhang.

This is a good time to add end bumper pads (as in Figure 11.15). Then, use planes, rasps, and sandpaper to round over the outside edges of the joints between the decks and hull. The more rounded the joints are, the easier it will be to get the fiberglass tape reinforcement to conform. Kevlar and carbon are too stiff to make such sharp bends. Sand the outside of the hull down the side to about 2½ inches from the deck.

Cut 3-inch-wide strips of lightweight 4-ounce fiberglass for the first layer of the hull-deck joint. They will conform

easily to the bend if you cut them on a bias of 45 degrees to the direction of the weave. Apply epoxy to the joint area; smooth the strips in place with gloved hands and a plastic applicator, and then wet them out. After the epoxy has set enough to be very sticky but not dry, apply a layer of 4-inch-wide 9-ounce fiberglass tape or cut cloth. Press the cloth into the sticky epoxy so that it conforms tightly to the curve; then wet out with fresh epoxy. If the fiberglass tends to pull away and bubble out near the curve, you can smooth it back in place as the epoxy starts to set. I return every so often to check on it. A little extra attention at this point will result in a stronger, more attractive job.

If the fiberglass deck reinforcement did not cover the rope holes at the ends, this would be a good time to glass them over. After the epoxy cures enough to be dry to the touch, trim the glass to open the holes. Once the epoxy hardens, bevel the holes with a countersink and smooth the edges with sandpaper.

FIGURE 11.15. *It is a good idea to add some sort of a small bumper pad to protect the ends of the decks from bumps, bangs, and abrasions. A small wood pad can serve well and look good. The walnut pad shown is about 3 inches long and ⅜ inch thick. It will later be covered with two layers of 9-ounce fiberglass. If the glass ever wears through to the wood, it can be sanded down and new glass applied.*

To maintain the lightest weight, the wood decks may be finished later with three thin coats of epoxy and then varnished. They will scratch easily, however, so I like to add a layer of thin, 1.45-ounce fiberglass deck cloth, which will protect the wood from most minor bumps, bangs, and scrapes. If you expect to give the boat rough use, then you may wish to sacrifice some weight and use stronger layers. Although costly, 1.8-ounce Kevlar is tougher than the deck cloth at essentially no weight penalty. If more strength is needed, as for a whitewater boat, substitute a layer of 5-ounce Kevlar, carbon, or fiberglass. Because of the difficulty of sanding and feathering the edges of Kevlar, it is best to apply it to the decks before the fiberglass that joins deck and hull. The result will be much neater, and any sanding can be limited to the fiberglass edge.

Now would also be a good time to cover the end bumper pads with a couple of layers of 9-ounce fiberglass.

The cockpit side of the decks can be shaped in a variety of ways. A straight edge from gunwale to gunwale is easiest, lightest, and works fine. A front deck that sweeps back toward the gunwales with a raised coaming or spray rail offers a bit more protection from waves and spray and look good as well. (See Figure 11.16.) A long, curved coaming is attractive, but it will not bear much weight or rough handling unless it is built strong and heavy or is structurally supported underneath. The lighter straight spray rails shown on Wasp need little strength and no additional support. (See Figure 11.17.) I used walnut to match the gunwales and end bumpers, but any hardwood will serve. Rails are ½ inch wide. The bow rail is 1.4 inches high at the center tapering

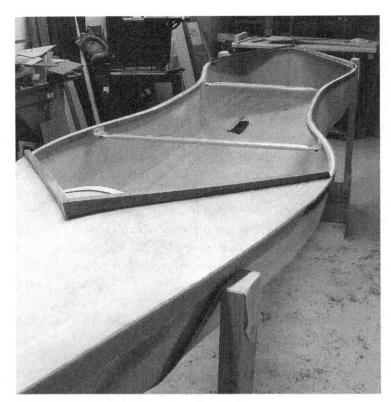

FIGURE 11.16. *A deck with spray rails added.*

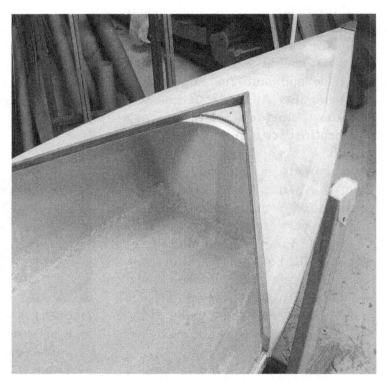

FIGURE 11.17. *Here is the deck termination above the bulkhead at the cockpit opening.*

down to 0.7 inch at the gunwales; the stern rail is slightly lower. Higher rails will give more protection from waves but will also add weight and catch wind.

Saw and trim the rails to meet in a neat miter joint. The deck shown in Figure 11.17 is raised, and the peak is curved in the middle rather than meeting at a sharp V. The bottom of each rail must be curved slightly to fit the deck curve. Cut a piece of scrap plywood as a template to fit the deck curve under one of the rails. Trim and fit by trial and error until it matches the deck curve. Then use the plywood template to transfer that curve by tracing onto the rail. Saw or plane the bottom of the rail to fit the deck. Do this for each rail. If the curves vary slightly, each rail should fit its own location.

The rails are held in place with a couple of screws from underneath the deck plywood and are bonded with thickened epoxy. Clamp as necessary. If you made thin plywood decks, they will be flexible. You may need a lot of clamps or a lot of screws to draw the plywood and rails together. A small piece of fiberglass bonded across the top of the V joint between the two rails will reinforce the joint and be invisible when finished.

A curved coaming is used with a more enclosed and arched deck, as on Kayoo (shown in Figure 11.18) and most kayaks. To make the coaming, curved sections of 3 mm plywood are clamped to bend in place after applying epoxy. (See Chapter 12 for more details on decks.) Note the handy rod holder made from PVC pipe in Figure 11.18.

Any exposed edges of the decking must be reinforced, and a drain hole must be added to each flotation chamber. (See Figure 11.19.) On Wasp I placed the spray rails in front of the drain holes. The rails also could have terminated behind the drain holes, leaving no decking behind the rails.

The plywood decking extends at least 1½ inches past the bulkhead so that the joint between the deck and the bulkhead can be reinforced underneath with fiberglass. If you made decks of thin 1 mm plywood and position the spray rails as shown in Figure 11.19, then at least two layers of 1 mm plywood strips ¾ inch wide should be bent in place and glued to the deck to thicken and strengthen the exposed edge. If your decks are 3 mm plywood, this is not necessary.

The drain hole is ½ inch in diameter and positioned near the highest point of the flotation chamber. This guarantees that the flotation chamber will drain completely when turned upside down. The inside of the hole should be coated with three or more layers of epoxy and fitted with a rubber drain plug. You will

FIGURE 11.18. *A curved and arched deck coaming on Kayoo.*

FIGURE 11.19. *A drain hole is required in the deck of each end flotation chamber.*

find a variety of plugs at marinas and boat shops. I found some convenient rubber well nut plugs at a local building supply store. They have a screw that tightens the plug in place and greatly reduces the chance of losing it.

Drain holes must be placed in hard composite or hardwood at least ³⁄₈ inch thick. In Figure 11.19, a piece of marine mahogany plywood was bonded to the deck to provide a drain hole pad. The pad must be curved to fit the deck. This is easily accomplished with the same trick—kerfs—used by guitar makers to make the curved linings that fit the sides of an acoustic guitar. Kerfs make the wood flexible.

Kerfs can be made with a handsaw, a table saw, a radial arm saw, or even a band saw. Experiment with the depth of cut and placement of kerfs until the wood will bend into the needed curve. Saw the kerfs in a larger rectangular piece of plywood, and then cut out the pads. (See Figure 11.20.) On a band saw, it helps to clamp a slotted stop behind the blade so that you don't cut all the way through. Fill the kerfs well with epoxy thickened with microfibers, and bond the pad in place with the same mixture.

On decks that have a slight arch rather than a peak, it may be possible to just sand the bottom of the pad to the more gradual curve required. A 1½-inch-diameter pad is adequate for a ½-inch-diameter hole. On most sea kayaks, you will want access hatches for decked compartments. Hatches eliminate the need for drain holes.

Ribs

The best time to bond in reinforcement ribs is just after the gunwales and bulkheads are installed. The ribs are made of a foam core with fabric bonded on top. (See Figure 11.21.) A variety of structural foams are ideal for supporting the cloth reinforcement layer. Polystyrene and urethane foams work well; they cut easily and are very light in weight. You can use the same foam insulation board material that was used for the bulkheads.

By pushing the hull up from the bottom, you can determine where reinforcement is needed and how much. The amount of hull stiffness or flexibility that is desirable in a very lightweight boat depends on how the boat will be used. A hull that has some flexibility will be more likely to give rather than break or puncture under

FIGURE 11.20. *Kerfs are sawn in the underside of the drain hole pad before bonding in place.*

FIGURE 11.21. *Bonding foam ribs into the hull.*

impact. Whitewater hulls need to be thicker and stronger but also slightly flexible. With thicker hull laminates, ribs may not be needed. A hull

that is extremely stiff theoretically may paddle with slightly greater efficiency, but it may also be brittle and puncture more easily if the hull layup is light. For most uses I prefer some flexibility, and I sense no difference in paddling efficiency.

Placing a rib across the bottom at each station location between the end bulkheads is a prudent approach. Figure 11.26, later in this chapter, clearly shows the locations for Wasp. The foam core strips for Wasp's ribs are 2¼ inches wide and ½ inch thick. For Kayoo, with side flotation chambers installed, five strips ³/₈ inch thick are needed in the middle part of the hull and should be spaced 10 inches apart.

If you are finishing your solo hull as a simple open canoe, then the three or four central ribs should continue up the hull to within an inch or two of the gunwales. For tandem canoes, all of the ribs should continue to the gunwales. I outfit some of my solo canoes with side walls that enclose side flotation and support a combination seat and portage yoke system. The side walls eliminate the need for additional stiffening of the hull at the sides. Lighter hull layups may require that all ribs extend upward to the gunwales; heavier layups may use lighter ribs, fewer ribs, or none at all. If you are experimenting with lighter or heavier laminations than described here, then test the flexibility and add ribs accordingly.

The foam ribs are beveled at a 45-degree angle on the sides and tapered at the ends. (See Figure 11.22.) A band saw with a tilt table makes quick work of this. Otherwise, they can be carved and sanded by hand. If any ribs will not conform to the bend of the hull, they may be cut and applied to the hull in short sections. Tack them in place with a quick-setting or

FIGURE 11.22. *A foam rib with beveled sides.*

FIGURE 11.23. *After wetting out carbon fiber, a layer of polyester fabric peel ply is applied.*

five-minute epoxy. Once in place, the foam can be sanded to a slightly more arched or rounded shape, which will allow the fabric layer to conform better. Polystyrene insulation board does not sand so well, and small pieces may be pulled out by the sandpaper. This is not a structural problem but may show on the outside of the rib. Urethane foam sands quite well and is so handy that I always keep some around for little fabrication tasks. It is available from Aircraft Spruce and other suppliers. (See Appendix A.)

The rib covering can be 10- to 12-ounce carbon or Kevlar fabric or 30-ounce fiberglass. Add layers to get the total cloth weight per square yard. For instance, two layers of 5-ounce Kevlar add up to the required 10 ounces. If the fabric layer over a foam rib is too flexible, the foam can be crushed slightly when you step into the boat, so it is best not to go too light on the rib reinforcement. Carbon fiber is ideal for ribs. It will provide maximum stiffness for minimum weight and will not be much exposed to impact or abrasion inside the hull. As usual, if you want to use Kevlar scraps and plan to do some interior finish-sanding, then put a layer of fiberglass over the Kevlar. I omit fiberglass to save weight.

The tops of the finished ribs will flex slightly but are spaced far enough apart so that you can easily avoid stepping on them. You can use denser structural foams or thicker fabric layers if you are willing to carry a heavier boat.

To get a nicer finished surface, add a peel ply layer after wetting out the structural fabric. Smooth the peel ply into the epoxy with a plastic applicator or squeegee (as shown in Figure 11.23). If there are white areas of air under the peel ply that cannot be squeezed out, lift the peel ply and add more epoxy. Squeeze out any excess epoxy to the fabric margins, and soak it up with a paper towel. If you omit the peel ply, the edges of the ribs may be very rough and difficult to sand.

The reinforcement fabric may conform to the foam a little better if you apply some pressure. Cover the wet peel ply with a layer of plastic wrap; on top of that, place a layer of soft foam rubber and weight it down as shown in Figure 11.24.

Composites are forgiving and make it very easy to bond in additional structures. After test paddling, you can strengthen or lengthen ribs if the hull flexes more than your liking. Just sand the bond area and add more cloth. When you are certain that all interior bonding is complete, sand the interior lightly and give it two or three seal coats of epoxy to fill the cloth weave and produce a smooth, level surface. (See Figures

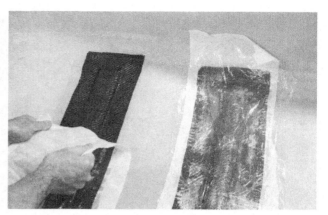

FIGURE 11.25. *When the epoxy has set and the peel ply is removed, the ribs will blend smoothly into the hull.*

FIGURE 11.24. *Soft foam 2 inches or thicker is placed on top of the ribs after the peel ply and plastic wrap. Scraps of plywood are weighted down—in this instance with paint cans—to compress the soft foam and apply pressure to the ribs as uniformly as possible. The plywood under the weights helps to distribute the load and prevents the hull from sagging down in the middle. It is best to position a third sling stand to support the hull under the rib being weighted. That will help to keep the hull from deforming from the designed shape.*

11.25 and 11.26.) If you do not seal the textured cloth surface, it may not be watertight and will also pick up mud and dirt that may be impossible to wash off.

Seats

The seat location and height may be indicated in the plans. It is quite reasonable to follow those plans for tandem canoes, but for optimum performance and safety in a solo canoe, you should determine the location that provides perfectly level trim while paddling. If the canoe is not trimmed level, stability and directional control will be compromised, making the boat more difficult or even dangerous to control in windy conditions. Whichever end floats higher in the water will tend to swing downwind like a weather vane.

Do some test paddling without a fixed seat. It's a great excuse to take your new boat out on the water! A movable small box that you can sit on placed in the bottom of the canoe is ideal. Make the box low, and bring some seat pads and pieces of plywood to experiment with different heights. For many kayaks and for a very small and narrow solo canoe like Dragonfly, the seat will be on or close to the floor and a few pads may be sufficient. If the kayak has a small cockpit opening, then the seat location is predetermined.

A good starting point is to place the front edge of the temporary seat 2 to 4 inches aft of the CG. Recheck and mark the CG as described earlier in this chapter, because it is likely to have changed a little with the additional finishing work since accomplished. But the CG alone will not tell you how the boat will trim in the water. Below the waterline, the hull may have more volume fore or aft of either the CG or the measured midpoint. Center of gravity and center of buoyancy may not be the same. Have someone observe the boat in the water while you sit in it. Move the seat fore and aft until the boat appears to have the waterline at the same distance from the bottom at both front and rear. The boat will maneuver best with that seat location. Mount the seat at that loca-

FIGURE 11.26. *The rib locations for Wasp are visible here. The bow is to the left.*

tion or an inch or two aft. Another good test is to paddle very slowly over a shallow obstruction like a stump or rock. If the boat scrapes bottom just slightly and only in the middle at your sitting position, then your trim is near perfect. Mark the seat location with a pencil or marker on the hull or gunwale.

Seat height is a matter of body size, personal preference, boat type, and paddle type. Kayaks and decked boats are generally lower and narrower, permitting lower seats; wider canoes require higher seats. A lower seat makes the center of gravity lower and results in greater stability. In an open canoe, however, the seat must be high enough that you can reach over the gunwales with your paddle or kneel with your feet under the seat. A solo canoe with tumblehome will permit the use of a lower seat than will one with wider gunwales. The tumblehome reduces secondary stability, but some stability is gained by lowering the seat and the CG. The primary net effect is an easier reach to the water with the paddle, making solo canoes with tumblehome generally more ergonomic and pleasant to paddle, especially when paddling seated.

Your paddle makes a difference, too. A double-blade paddle favors a low seat, while a single-blade paddle favors a high seat. If I don't intend to kneel, my rule of thumb for seat height is to make it as low as possible while maintaining a comfortable paddling stroke as well as back and leg comfort. If you are hitting the gunwales with the paddle too often, then the seat height may be too low or the paddle may be too short or both.

Paddling a canoe while kneeling is a time-honored technique that permits a great deal of boat control. It will also influence seat placement and height. If you want the boat set up for best paddling from the kneeling position, you will have to kneel at the center of gravity for good trim. The seat needs to be far enough to the rear to allow this. The seat mostly provides a back rest for the buttocks, and it can be angled down an inch or two at the front edge to accommodate the kneeling position. The seat must also be high enough to allow your feet, and whatever footwear you use, to fit underneath. The fit must be loose enough that your feet will not become entrapped if the boat should capsize. Keep testing the seat location and height until you are happy with it.

Cane or webbed seats are available by mail order from canoe outfitters like Piragis Northwoods Company. (See Appendix A.) The seat is cut to fit the width of your canoe and is installed under the gunwales with flathead stainless steel machine screws, finishing washers, and nuts. The screws pass vertically through the gunwales or may be attached to aluminum angle brackets, as shown earlier in Figure 11.12. Angle brackets that will support seats must be attached very securely. Mount them with flathead stainless steel screws that pass horizontally all the way through the gunwales and hull; place finishing washers on the outside and locking nuts on the inside. Spacer blocks mount between the seat and the gunwales or brackets to provide the desired seat height. (See Figure 11.27.) To save weight, I make spacer blocks from spruce with the grain running vertically, but any moderately strong wood will work okay. Wood spacer blocks should be sealed with a few coats of epoxy and painted or varnished.

On some solo canoes where the seat is to be positioned very low, it is better to mount it on the floor. This may also be necessary with decked canoes and kayaks. A closed-cell foam pad may be all that is needed. It can be glued in place or held down with Velcro tapes with self-sticking adhesive backing; these allow the seat to be repositioned easily and removed for drying or cleaning. If the required seat height is greater than 3 or 4 inches, a solid seat may be more secure. I make a solid seat with rigid foam about 14 inches wide by 11 inches front to back and at least ½ inch deep, and I cover it with three layers of 6-ounce fiberglass

FIGURE 11.27. *Traditional cane seats and web seats, like the one pictured here, are available from suppliers and are easy to mount.*

on the top, bottom, and sides. Before covering, the seat can be sculpted and the edges rounded. Use wood or foam spacers under each side to block it to the necessary height. It may be bonded to the floor with fiberglass and epoxy, but sometimes I secure it temporarily with Velcro until I am absolutely certain I like the height and the fore-and-aft location.

For yet another approach to seats, see Chapter 14, in which a combined seat and portage yoke is described.

From the Wasp Paddling Log

Today Wasp is completed to the stage that will allow some initial test paddling. But I procrastinate over breakfast, not quite ready to take the plunge.

Every year a pair of phoebes makes a nest on the floodlight under our carport. Before going out to my workshop this morning, I watch their two chicks flopping around precariously as they are fed. Suddenly one topples out of the nest as if by accident. With a lot of frantic flapping, like a crazed maple seed in a confused wind, it arrests its fall just before ground impact. It struggles up toward the second-story railing where I stand, but it can't quite fly that high or control direction so well. Landing on the ground is not an option; the cats see all. With the last of its meager and failing energy, it steers unceremoniously down onto the nearest perch, the front canoe load bar on top of my van. Little phoebe sits there a very long time, breathing hard and trying to figure out what just happened. I know the feeling. "Fee bee," it proclaims in a meek voice. I gather tie-down straps and head to the shop to coax Wasp out for her first trip to the load bar too.

The hull is now a boat, and it is ready to paddle. (See Figure 11.28.) Although there are other finishing touches and accessories that can be added, many paddlers will be happy with the canoe just as it is. Even if you plan more finish work, surely you deserve some test paddling first. Enjoy some time on the water. Take some pictures. And give yourself a pat on the back.

FIGURE 11.28. *Wasp is fully outfitted and on the water. The ends of Wasp have received a coating of epoxy, silica filler, and white pigment for extra abrasion resistance. I expect to paddle Wasp where there are submerged rocks and stumps, and the extra coating should lengthen the intervals between touch-up work and repairs on these high-wear areas. Wasp is now ready for adventures! Photo by Carrie Rizzetta.*

Chapter 12

Decked Canoes and Kayaks

Putting a deck on a hull is undeniably a lot more work than completing the hull as an open canoe. Another disadvantage is that, all else being equal, a decked boat requires more mate- rial, meaning it weighs more and costs more. The advantages may outweigh the costs, however, and composite construction can make the weight less burdensome, literally.

The Decked Advantage

For an open canoe, high freeboard is necessary to keep waves out. This presents a lot of surface area, which may make paddling difficult in windy conditions. So the canoe designer is caught in a dilemma: provide more safety from waves or provide more safety from wind. A decked boat resolves this conflict. It can be low to the water to reduce windage and to make it easier to reach the water with the paddle (two critical features for solo canoes) while the deck keeps the water out. The deck can rise up higher toward the cockpit area, providing protection from waves, but this needs to be only around the paddler or around the cockpit. For maximum protection on sea kayaks and whitewater kayaks, the cockpit opening is small and the coaming around the edge has a lip to hold a sprayskirt. With a sprayskirt in place, the interior stays relatively dry.

Some types of kayaks are low, narrow, and sleek for speed and racy looks or to improve windage and make Eskimo rolls possible. Others are wider and higher to carry more gear, leave more room for feet, increase stability, and permit a higher, more comfortable seating position. Since these beamier craft are not usually candidates for rolling maneuvers, there is no great need for small cockpit openings and sprayskirts. Such boats might be thought of as open kayaks or decked canoes. As I grow older, I spend more time in my decked canoes, like Kayoo, with higher and more comfortable seats. They are especially convenient for fishing and for camping on lakes and rivers.

It is tempting to choose a boat and deck shape based on looks. And that sexy-looking kayak might just lure you into a different type of paddling that you might enjoy. However, you may be more likely to get maximum use from a boat that suits the water activities you know you like. As you choose your style of deck, keep in mind that things usually work out best when form follows function.

Fabric Form Composite Deck

The fabric form method can be used to create a deck. After you've built a hull this way, it is easy to visualize making a deck similarly. The process follows these steps:

1. Trim the hull and place it upright on stands.
2. Design or copy deck stations to create plywood station forms. Arches of thin wood or plywood clamped to the hull can help visualize and create stations.

3. Attach station forms temporarily to the hull with screws through the hull at the sheerline.
4. Attach a temporary center stringer to hold station forms vertical. Attach stringers similarly to making a hull form.
5. Cover the stringers and areas of the hull adjacent to the deck with plastic tape so that epoxy will not stick.
6. Cover the deck form with a polyester cloth peel ply layer, and stitch it tightly under the hull.
7. Shrink the polyester cloth tight.
8. Laminate the deck, overlapping onto the hull for a few inches. Allow to cure.
9. Remove the laminated deck, remove the peel ply, and remove the station forms.
10. Trim the deck so that it will overlap the hull by an inch or more when joined.
11. Reinforce the deck from the inside with ribs, especially at the front and back of the coaming or cockpit opening.
12. Test-fit and trim the deck assembly.
13. Bond the deck to the hull with epoxy. The deck can be held in place temporarily or permanently with stainless steel sheet metal screws. If you wish to remove the screws after the epoxy hardens, coat them lightly with paste wax before driving them in.
14. Cut out the cockpit opening and add a coaming.

Plywood Deck

This is a good but time-consuming way to make a deck, and it doesn't include the structural flotation chambers that can be one advantage of making a decked boat. So I'm going to describe a different approach in more detail that uses rigid foam, reinforcing cloth, aircraft plywood, and epoxy. This chapter uses the Kayoo design for the photo illustrations, but many solo canoe hulls, including Dragonfly, will also work well with a deck. See Chapter 16 for more on both designs.

After the hull is laminated, trim it to the desired deck sheerline. Do not install reinforcing ribs yet. Use prop sticks to hold the hull to the proper widths. Bond a ½-by-½-inch wood strip on the inside of the sheerline as though you were making gunwales. Any clear straight-grained wood will do; I like to use spruce, pine, or Douglas fir. This will provide a gluing strip for attaching the deck. The strips can terminate as close as possible to the ends where the sides of the hull curve sharply into the ends.

Deck Arches

Determine the deck coverage, deck heights, and cockpit opening size you want. Figures 12.1 and 16.10 (the latter in Chapter 16) show the basic deck plan for Kayoo in top and side views. Figures 16.16 and 16.17 (also in Chapter 16) give deck arch drawings to scale on an expandable grid as well as coordinates for deriving full-size deck arch cross sections and the bulkheads for bow and stern.

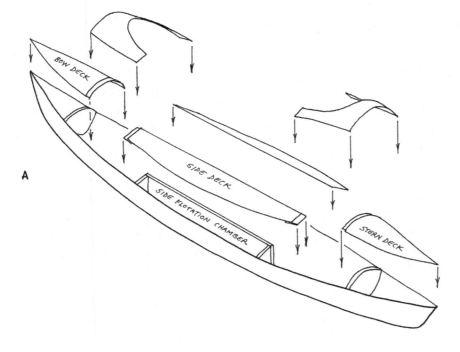

FIGURE 12.1. *Deck assembly, exploded view (A) and top view (B). Bulkheads and side chambers are constructed first. Next, bow deck, stern deck, and side deck covers are cut from plywood, fitted, and bonded in place. Joint bonding strips are added to the ends of the side and end decks. (See Figure 12.9.) The bulkheads and side chambers are covered with reinforcing cloth, bonded to the hull with fiberglass, and sealed with epoxy. Finally, the remaining decks with the fore and aft cockpit curves are fitted and bonded to the bonding strips.*

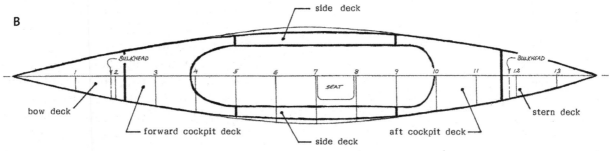

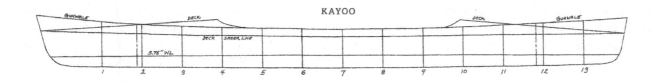

FIGURE 12.2. *Hull edge bonding strip and bow bulkhead in place.*

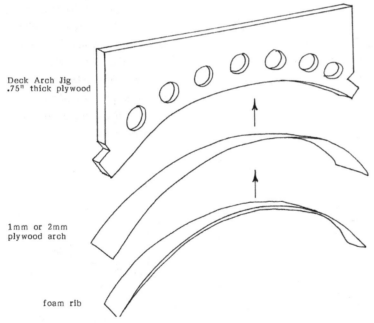

Deck Arch Jig
.75" thick plywood

1mm or 2mm
plywood arch

foam rib

FIGURE 12.3. *A deck arch jig ensures an accurate curve. The tabs at the sides and the holes in the center allow clamping of the plywood arch and reinforcing foam rib into the jig. Not much clamping pressure is required. To avoid damaging the foam, place a second strip of thin plywood between the foam and the clamps. Do not crush the foam with clamping pressure.*

Kayoo has a cockpit opening 6 feet long, and the deck does not enclose the feet. The decks are designed to be high enough to fit my favorite portage backpack under the rear deck. The front deck is just slightly higher to fend off bow waves and fit secondary dry bags. For the plywood deck skin, I chose 1 mm thick aircraft birch plywood to keep weight as low as possible. Choose 2 mm plywood if you desire more strength and puncture resistance. You may find that tin snips or metal shears are more convenient than saws for rough cutting 1 mm plywood to approximate shape.

Make the bow and stern flotation chamber bulkheads as described in Chapter 11, and fit them temporarily in place. Rest a straight board on the tip of the bow and the top of the bulkhead, extending toward the cockpit (as shown in Figure 12.5, later in the chapter). Ensure that the extended straight line will produce the required deck height at the deck arch near station #4. Make a similar check at the stern bulkhead. If all is well, bond the bulkheads in place with thickened epoxy. (See Figure 12.2.)

Deck arches support the deck at the front and rear of the cockpit opening and coaming. They also strengthen the hull from side to side, performing a function similar to thwarts in an open canoe. Arches are built similar to the hull reinforcing ribs on a foundation of a 3-inch-wide strip of plywood.

The same thin, 1 mm or 2 mm plywood used for the decks can be used for the arches. Plywood strips can be bent into a pleasing and suitable shape and clamped in place on the hull. (See Figure 12.6.) This works surprisingly well, but a simple jig (as shown in Figure 12.3) can help achieve a more accurate curve.

Cover the jig with a piece of plastic wrap and clamp it in a vise, curved side upward. The foam rib is made similarly to the hull ribs shown in Figures 11.21

and 11.22. Dimensions for the deck arch ribs are given in Figure 12.4. Place the plywood on the jig, apply a line of quick-setting epoxy down the center, and press the foam down onto it. When the epoxy has set, the arch may hold its shape adequately but, if not, do the laminating on the jig. Apply epoxy and a layer of fiberglass or carbon fiber over the foam; then cover it with a piece of polyester cloth as a peel ply. Add a layer of plastic wrap, a thick layer of soft foam rubber, and a strip of thin plywood as a clamping surface. Clamp the assemblage gently into the jig.

After it has set, remove the arch from the jig and clamp it in place on the hull. Test-fit and trim (as shown in Figures 12.5 and 12.6), but don't bond it in place yet.

Installing End Decks

When you are confident that the bulkheads and arches are to your liking, the plywood end decks can be fitted and bonded to the hull and the

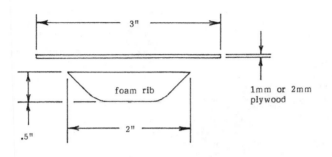

FIGURE 12.4. Deck arch and reinforcing rib, cross section. Use the same dimensions for both bow and stern arches.

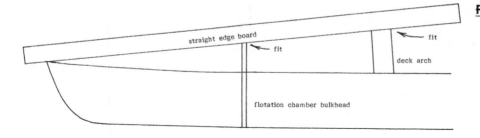

FIGURE 12.5. Use a long, straight board to test the fit of the bulkhead and deck arch at each end. The taper and fit do not need to be absolutely perfect. Thickened epoxy will fill any small gaps.

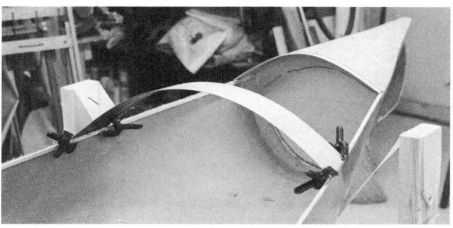

FIGURE 12.6. A plywood arch strip is clamped in place for trimming and test-fitting.

FIGURE 12.7. *Masking tape is adequate for holding Kayoo's 1 mm thick end decks in place while the epoxy sets. The spring clamps hold a bonding strip in place (see Figure 12.9).*

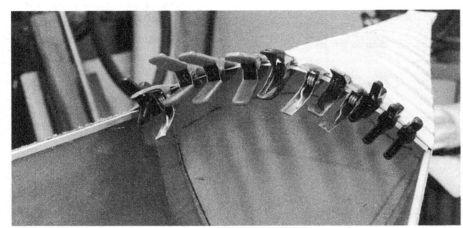

FIGURE 12.8. *Here is an end deck installation from a different angle.*

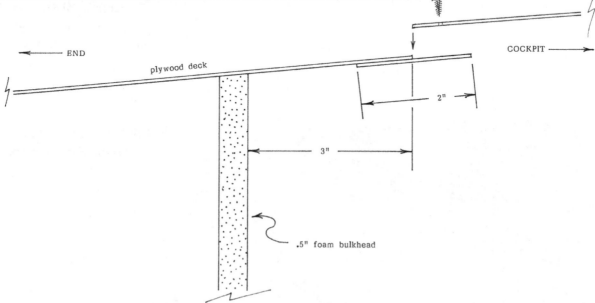

FIGURE 12.9. *This cross section of an end deck attached to a bulkhead also shows the 2-inch-wide bonding strip glued to the underside of the deck end. This strip will provide a bonding surface for the next deck section and will result in a level outer surface.*

bulkheads. Review Chapter 11 and Figure 11.13 for proper procedures and cautions for installing end decks. Kayoo's end decks are small and do not need internal reinforcement, but the interiors of the decks and hull do need to be well sealed with epoxy. Two or three seal coats are required. A well-sealed plywood surface should be smooth and glossy. The end deck needs to extend 3 inches past the bulkhead toward the cockpit, as shown in Figure 12.9.

The decks for Kayoo as shown are 1 mm thick birch plywood, although thicker material can be used. To fit the plywood deck, start by roughing out an oversize piece of plywood. Hold or tape it in place, and trace the hull shape and bulkhead location onto the underside. At the wide end, it should extend 3 inches beyond the bulkhead. Cut the deck to about ½ inch oversize all around and test fit again. Keep fitting and trimming slowly to final size. The plywood can extend past the hull by ⅛ to ¼ inch or so, to be trimmed after the deck is bonded down.

Bond the decks to the tops of the bulkheads and the gluing strips (inner gunwales) with filled epoxy. As shown in Figures 12.7 and 12.8, the sides of the deck can be held down with masking tape, while spring clamps are useful to hold the bonding strip against the underside of the deck. (See Figure 12.9.) Bonding strips should also be installed at the fore and aft ends of the plywood side chamber covers or side decks.

and #9 is used as a template for the ends of the side flotation chambers. If you intend to install a combination seat and portage yoke as described in Chapter 14, then the side walls must be perfectly parallel and vertical. The foam panels are bonded in place and bonded together with small amounts of quick-setting epoxy. Finishing nails can be used to temporarily pin the parts in alignment while the epoxy sets.

Reinforce the interiors of the boxes with 5.8-ounce carbon fiber or heavier fiberglass if rails are to be installed on the outside for hanging a seat. Otherwise, a layer of light fiberglass is adequate. Note that the top edges of the foam walls must be covered with fiberglass or carbon, as shown in Figure 12.11. Then skin the outsides of the boxes with carbon or fiberglass. Build up the side walls top to bottom to be very stiff under the locations where the seat and portage rails will attach. (See the side wall information at Figure 14.15 and accompanying text in Chapter 14.) All the side wall joints to the hull, at both ends and bottom, must be well sealed with thickened epoxy fillets and bonded with two or three layers of fiberglass lapped at least 1½ inches onto both the hull and the chamber walls. It can be annoying or difficult to track down small leaks, so it is far better to seal the joints well now and avoid the leaks later.

Close off the tops of the side boxes with 1 mm or 2 mm plywood bonded with thickened

Side Flotation Chambers

The side flotation chambers are made from the same ½-inch-thick foam used for bulkheads. (See Figure 12.10.) Figures 15.25 and 15.27 (in Chapter 15) give the general aspect and layout of the structural side chambers. Figure 16.15 (in Chapter 16) shows how a portion of the template for Kayoo stations #5

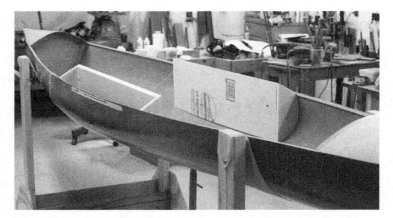

FIGURE 12.10. *Side flotation chambers are test-fitted into the hull.*

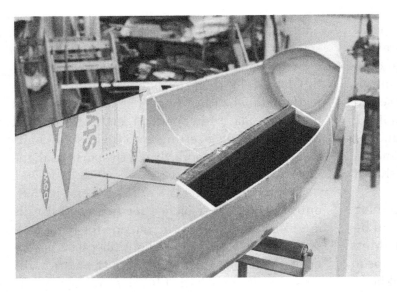

FIGURE 12.11. *These side chambers are being reinforced on the inside with carbon fiber. Fiberglass could also be used. The cloth must lap onto the hull at the bottom and roll onto the exposed edge of the foam panels at the top. This will ensure a stronger bond and a more watertight seal to the plywood deck covers that will be installed later.*

epoxy. This will create the side decks. The plywood should overhang the foam box ends by 2 inches at the front and rear. Trim carefully, as you did with the bow and stern decks. Don't forget to epoxy-seal the chamber interiors and the underside of the plywood covers. Glue plywood bonding strips under the front and rear edges similar to the strips at the bow and stern decks. This can be done after the plywood covers are bonded in place. Then bond the deck arches in place with thickened epoxy. If you did not reinforce the arches in a jig, they will be reinforced later.

Fore and Aft Cockpit Decks

The next step is to add the forward and aft cockpit decks (as shown in Figure 12.1). These are the deck sections with the front and back curves of the cockpit opening, and they connect the bow deck and the stern deck with the side decks. Cut

and trim a piece of the thin, flexible plywood to fit between the bow deck and the side deck. Make it oversize; then trim it little by little until a good fit is achieved. Helping hands or masking tape can hold a rough-cut piece in place while you trace the hull shape and mark joint locations. It should rest on the bonding strips to provide flush butt joints with the end decks and the side decks. Any unsightly gaps in the joint can be filled and sanded later, but do careful work if you want to finish the decks "bright"—that is, varnished instead of painted. Cut a curve for the front of the cockpit. See Figures 16.10 (in Chapter 16) and 12.1 (earlier in this chapter) for the cockpit curve shapes, or design your own.

Bond the plywood in place with lots of thickened epoxy, using tape, screws, and clamps as needed to hold it down. Screw it to the bow deck bonding strip and the side deck bonding strips. In order to draw up tight against the bonding strips, drill holes slightly oversize in the cockpit deck piece. Also, bond and clamp or screw the deck plywood to the deck arch. Again, masking tape can hold the deck plywood to the hull at the sides. Tape is cheap, so use a lot of it to avoid a wavy sheerline. Install the aft cockpit deck similarly. Since these sections of deck are exposed underneath, they can be sealed with epoxy later.

Waxing screws before installation can help with screw removal. Rub them against a candle or on a cloth with paste wax. Screws can be removed when the epoxy gels, and the holes can be filled later.

Trim the deck flush to the hull after the epoxy hardens; then round over the joint and cover it with fiberglass, following the deck installation procedures in Chapter 11. Also see Figures 12.12 and 12.13. If the deck arches were not formed and reinforced in a jig, as shown in Figure 12.3, then the foam and cloth reinforcement should be added now. (See Figure 12.13.) Extend the car-

FIGURE 12.12. *All deck sections are bonded in place.*

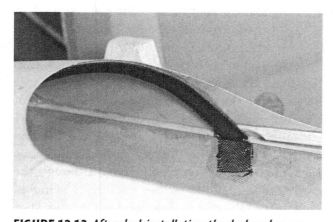

FIGURE 12.13. *After deck installation, the deck arches are reinforced underneath with foam and a layer or two of carbon cloth, if this was not done earlier in a jig. Cloth is lapped over the side gluing strip and onto the hull for a strong structural bond. To substitute fiberglass, use at least four or five layers of 6-ounce cloth.*

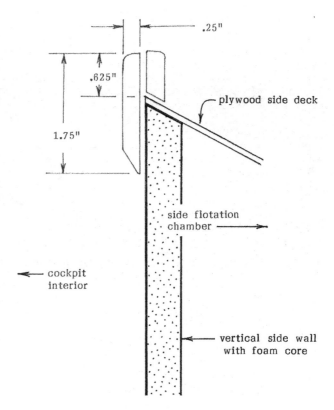

FIGURE 12.14. *This detail cross section view of a side chamber shows dimensions for the side coaming strip that finishes off and strengthens the deck. If you intend to install a combination seat and portage yoke, then the finished coaming strip should not protrude more than ¼ inch on the interior cockpit side. Instead, the strip can be widened and strengthened by installing a shorter second strip on the outboard side as depicted.*

bon or fiberglass onto the hull as shown. If the arches were reinforced earlier, add pieces of cloth and epoxy to strengthen the joints between the arches and the hull.

The Cockpit Coaming

Next, install a ¼-inch plywood coaming strip on the inside of the side walls, as shown in Figure 12.14. Marine plywood is best.

Plywood forms the curved coaming for the arched deck end openings of Kayoo, as seen in Figure 12.15. I cut curved portions of the coaming from ¼ inch or 3 mm thick oakume marine plywood and clamp them to bend in place after applying epoxy. Kayoo has just one layer, to minimize weight.

Serious whitewater and sea kayaks require smaller cockpit openings that can accommodate a sprayskirt. The coaming edge can be formed with several layers of 3 mm or ¼-inch-thick marine plywood. Layers are clamped in place

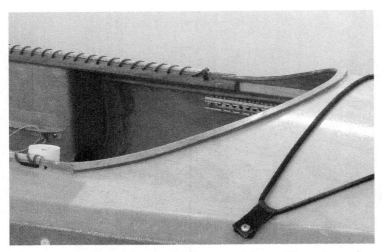

FIGURE 12.15. *A curved and arched coaming is formed from plywood.*

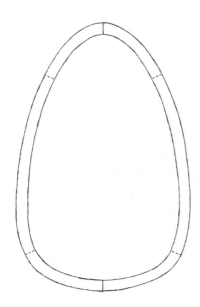

FIGURE 12.16. *Deck cockpit coaming in sections.*

with epoxy one layer at a time so that they will bend into the arch of the deck. The plywood need not be a continuous, one-piece ring but can be made up of sections with butt joints (as shown in Figure 12.16). Three or four layers are required. (See Figure 12.17.) The butt joints in each layer should be offset 3 or 4 inches from joints in other layers to avoid weak spots.

The built-in side flotation chambers will have strengthened and stiffened the hull significantly, so that fewer and shorter reinforcing ribs are required in the bottom of the hull. Pushing up from the bottom of the hull will reveal where it is flexible enough to warrant ribs. Kayoo has five ribs spaced 10 inches apart in the area between the flotation chamber side walls. Four of the five ribs can be seen in Figure 12.19, later. I chose to experiment with materials, and you can see that three of the ribs are carbon and one is Kevlar. They function equally well, although the carbon ribs are slightly stiffer. Each rib is 14 inches long. Install the ribs as described in Chapter 11.

Deck joints and screw holes can be filled with a mixture of epoxy and microfibers and then sanded level and smooth. A deck made with 2 mm or 1/16-inch plywood can be finished by applying three seal coats of epoxy. For better scratch resistance and protection on thinner, 1 mm decks, I cover them with 1.45-ounce fiberglass deck cloth

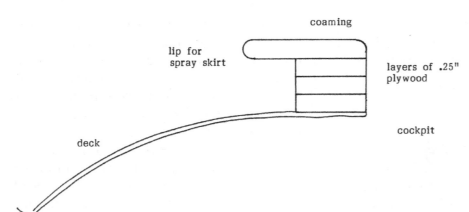

FIGURE 12.17. *Small cockpit openings that are intended for use with a sprayskirt should have a coaming with a lip. A wide top layer of plywood forms the lip. This should be rounded and sanded smooth before sealing well with epoxy and varnish. Each layer, including the lip layer, is approximately ¼ inch thick. The base layers are 1 inch wide, and the lip layer is 1¾ inches wide.*

FIGURE 12.18. *Plywood hard points are bonded in place near the floor to accommodate ropes for securing gear or bungee cords to hold a movable seat.*

FIGURE 12.19. *Rails attached to Kayoo's side chambers will support a combination seat and portage yoke as described in Chapter 14. The aluminum angle rails are held to the side chamber walls with stainless steel sheet metal screws and then bonded to the walls with a layer of fiberglass and epoxy from the top and bottom to ensure structural strength and watertight flotation chambers. The Wasp prototype lacks built-in side chambers. Instead, it has removable panels to support the rails, which are installed with machine screws. (See Figure 14.15.)*

are used on wilderness trips are turned upside down and tied to trees or boulders overnight to keep them from filling with rainwater or blowing away in storms. The thin layer of fiberglass will protect the deck wood from being scratched or gouged when the boat is overturned on hard ground, roots, rocks, and stumps. Figures 12.18 through 12.23 show additional Kayoo finishing details, including a combination movable seat and portage yoke and tie-in points for securing gear.

Using an Existing Kayak as a Form

If you have used an existing kayak as a form to laminate a composite hull, it is possible to use the existing deck as a form to laminate a composite deck to match the new hull (as shown in Figure 12.24 on page 119). Trim the new composite hull to the sheerline, and place it back on the old kayak. After adding release tape, plastic wrap, and fabric, laminate the deck the same way

before applying the seal coats. The fiberglass need not be one continuous piece. You can overlap pieces to get the coverage needed. Canoes that

FIGURE 12.20. *The combination seat and portage yoke is on the rails in the portage position and held in place with bungee cords. On the prototype Kayoo, the wood coaming at the sides is just ¼ inch wide to save weight. It is covered with neoprene tubing to softly round the edge and protect it from being marred by metal cartop load bars. The tubing was slit with a box cutter knife and tied in place with leather boot lacing to holes in the coaming. If you wish to do this, test samples of different sizes of tubing to get a good fit for your coaming. Holes are spaced 1 inch apart and sealed with epoxy. Surprisingly, the leather lacing seems to last many years between replacements. A side benefit is that the paddle makes no noise when hit or rested on the coaming, a great boon for fishing and viewing wildlife.*

FIGURE 12.22. *Cavernous volume under the rear deck accommodates portage packs or large dry bags. Tie-in points allow gear to be easily secured against possible capsizing. Although most dry bags are not intended for full submersion, they can provide extra flotation long enough for most capsize emergencies. And some flotation bags are designed to double as dry bags. The extra flotation floats a swamped boat higher in the water and reduces the bailing required after self-rescue reentry.*

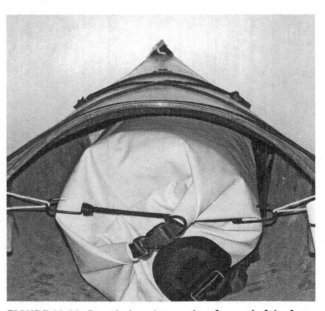

FIGURE 12.23. *Bow tie-in points are just forward of the foot rests.*

FIGURE 12.21. *In the seat position, the combination seat and yoke can be moved forward and aft to trim the balance of the boat through a wide range. Although bungee cords are pictured, spring clips were later added to hold the seat and to speed switching from portaging to paddling. The spring clips are described in Chapter 14.*

that you did the hull. Less strength is required for a deck, however, so it can be a lighter laminate than the hull. At the sides or sheerline, overlap the deck laminate onto the new hull as shown in the figure. When the cured deck is removed and trimmed, the overlap will allow the deck to be accurately and easily bonded to the hull.

If there is a large cockpit opening, it might be easiest to mold the deck in two separate pieces: a bow piece from the front of the cockpit forward and a stern piece from the rear of the cockpit aft. Bond them onto the new hull, join them with a cockpit-area center section of thin plywood (similar to the side decks shown in Figure 12.1), and add a plywood coaming.

Each deck that encloses a flotation chamber must have a drain hole and a plug. For details, see Chapter 11 at Figure 11.19 and Chapter 15 at Figure 15.28.

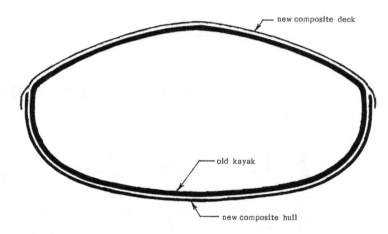

FIGURE 12.24. *This cross section depicts laminating a composite deck over an old kayak and new hull. The new deck overlaps the new hull at the sides to create an overlapping joint for epoxy bonding.*

Hoodoos On The Upper Missouri

Sam Rizzetta © 2006

Chapter 13

Finishing

If you are like me, you will want to have some fun paddling your boat before fussing over finishing touches. And it is best to let the epoxy cure a few weeks before applying any finish coat-

ing. My earlier kayaks and canoes required paint and varnish over the epoxy for ultraviolet protection. For some of my more recent boats, including Wasp and Kayoo, I used WEST 207 ultraviolet resistant epoxy hardener, and they have held up for a while before needing additional finish protection. If the boat is mostly stored indoors out of direct sunlight and just taken out for paddling trips, then it may be used for a year or even several years as is.

Eventually, however, the entire boat should be coated with a protective finish to prevent the UV radiation in sunlight from weakening the epoxy and Kevlar. Fiberglass and carbon fiber are not affected, but they will also need protection if used with epoxy. The wood parts, including decks, gunwales, and spray rails, can be sanded and finished with a clear, UV-resistant marine varnish. The hull can also be finished with clear varnish, but pigmented marine paints are more durable and protective. Colors are fun, but white is the most protective and durable. Marine varnishes and paints are available from such sources as Chesapeake Light Craft and Jamestown Distributors (see Appendix A).

Sanding and Filling

A hull made using the fabric form process will not automatically have the extremely smooth exterior of a hull made in a professional mold. This does not affect the boat's paddling performance, and it avoids the large amount of work, expense, and aggravation involved in making smooth molds. Some of my canoes get a lot of rough use and quickly show it, so giving the hull a slick finish seems like a waste of effort. A boat for mild water use and public viewing may merit more attention, however, and it is rewarding to do careful work and see the result.

If you are willing to do the sanding, your hull may be made as smooth as you desire. Sanding will usually reveal high spots and low spots in the hull surface. Sand the high spots, but do not sand through to a Kevlar or structural layer. Low spots may be filled with additional coats of epoxy, or epoxy with filler, and then sanded. Repeat the filling and sanding until all areas are level and as smooth as you want them. This step can easily be the most time-consuming part of the project, and you will certainly appreciate the labor and craftsmanship that go into the molds for fiberglass boats and other molded products.

Long areas of the hull should be sanded with sanding boards to avoid creating a wavy surface. (See Figure 13.1.) You can make simple sanding boards by gluing sandpaper to the wide side of a length of 2 × 4. Lengths of 16 to 30 inches tend to be the most useful. If you have a planer, plane flat the

side to receive the sandpaper. For more curved areas, experiment with sanding boards made of flexible plywood. The thinner the plywood, the more it will flex. Plywood that is ¼ inch or 5 mm thick makes handy sanding boards, and blocks of wood attached near each end can provide convenient handles.

Small sanding blocks invariably get the most use in my shop. I make them from scrap pieces of hardwood with a ¼-inch-thick felt pad glued to one side (see Figure 13.2). For making surfaces flat and level, you can fold a piece of coarse sandpaper over the bare wood side. For finish-sanding with finer grits, fold the sandpaper over the felt padded side.

Don't forget to protect both skin and lungs when sanding. Dust from epoxy, carbon, Kevlar,

FIGURE 13.1. *The secret to a good finish is . . . sanding! Rough shaping, leveling, and the smoothing of contours and flat areas are best done by hand with sanding boards and sanding blocks. Sanding boards help prevent wavy surfaces. The board at the top is a 16-inch length of 2 × 4, which is excellent for leveling long surfaces with coarse sand paper. Below that is a slightly flexible, 22-inch-long board made from 5 mm thick plywood. It is ideal for leveling long and curved hull surfaces with coarse and medium sandpaper. The hand grips glued near the ends are 1½-by-1½-inch pine. The 3-inch width fits self-adhesive sandpaper rolls available from Aircraft Spruce. (See Appendix A.) A 4½-by-22-inch board is also convenient; a standard-size sheet of sandpaper can be cut into two pieces and glued on end to end to cover the board. Rubber cement works okay with heavy sandpapers. The hand-sized wood blocks at the bottom are handy for many tasks. Sandpaper is just held in place on these by hand.*

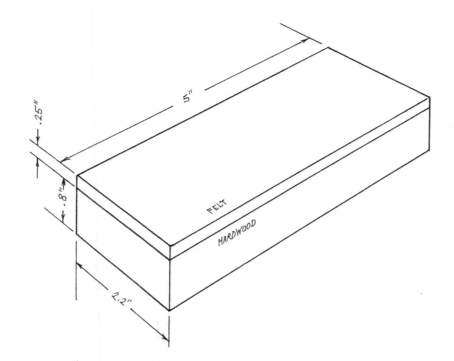

5"

.25"

.8"

2.2"

FELT

HARDWOOD

FIGURE 13.2. *Here are the dimensions for my most-used sanding blocks. Size yours to fit your hands comfortably. The wood side is planed very flat and used to level or flatten surfaces with coarser grits of sandpaper. The felt side is slightly cushioned and does a better job of final smoothing with finer grits. It is also excellent for sanding curved surfaces and edges.*

and fiberglass is irritating and hazardous to the health. Wear a very good dust mask or respirator. Cover as much skin area as possible. I sand wearing a long-sleeved shirt and long pants and a cap on my head to keep the dust out of what little hair I have. It is surprising how much dust can be transported into your living quarters in the hair! Clothing can transport a lot of dust, too. Kevlar and carbon dust are especially nasty irritants, so a long sanding session should always end with laundering and showering.

Preparing plywood decks, wood gunwales, and wood spray rails for clear varnish is relatively easy. After finish-sanding to 220 grit, bare wood may be varnished or sealed with three thin coats of epoxy. Epoxy will resist water and scratches better than varnish alone. Sand the cured epoxy surface lightly by hand or with padded hand-sanding blocks using sandpaper no coarser than necessary. This might be 120 to 150 grit. Finish sanding with 220 grit. Be careful not to sand through the epoxy into bare wood. If you do, you will need to recoat with epoxy and sand again. Sand with 220 or 320 grit between varnish coats.

The interior of the hull generally gets much less exposure to sunlight and UV since most

canoes spend most of their time in storage or upside down on top of a car or boat rack. So it is less urgent to paint or varnish the interior. Much of the interior will have a nice level surface from the building form and peel ply. A light sanding may be all that is needed before sealing with two coats of epoxy. You may have already applied epoxy seal coats to the interior while installing ribs. If you wish to paint the interior, sand it just as described for the exterior.

If you don't mind a very slightly uneven or wavy surface on the exterior of the hull, it may simply be lightly sanded and painted. This produces the very lightest weight hull. Sand by hand, or use a padded sanding block or an electric palm sander. Sand the entire surface, high spots and low spots, with 40- to 80-grit paper, depending on how much material has to be removed. Repeat with progressively finer sandpaper to remove the sanding marks made by coarser sandpaper. End with 80- or 120-grit paper if you plan to use a high-solids marine primer, or with 220-grit paper for paint. If you choose a paint system with different sanding requirements, follow the manufacturer's directions.

Leveling the Hull Surface

To produce a more level and attractive hull surface, start sanding by going over the entire hull with coarse, 40- or 50-grit sandpaper to provide a rough surface for filler. Sand the entire surface, high spots and low spots; don't try to make it level at this stage. A palm sander or random orbit sander is fine for this. (See Figure 13.3.) If necessary, sand any low spots by hand. Then fill the low spots with epoxy thickened with WEST Microlight filler. A plastic applicator works best. Next, use long sanding boards with coarse sandpaper to level the surface, being careful not to sand into the structural cloth layers. You will probably find many low spots that are still too low. Apply more filler. Continue cycles of filling and sanding until the surface is level and shaped to your satisfaction. Between waiting for filler to cure and sanding large areas, this can take many days. If you sand away most of the filler that is not needed to build up low spots, then any weight increase due to filler will be negligible.

Final Sanding

Once all the high spots and low spots are leveled out and the hull is smoothly contoured, continue sanding with progressively finer grits. Follow the sanding directions for the finish you wish to use. Generally, you will end with 80- or 120-grit paper before applying a high-solids marine primer, or with 220-grit paper to produce a smooth surface for painting. The padded side of a hand-sanding block and electric palm sanders are good for these finish-sanding operations.

Painting and Varnishing

After sanding, wash the hull surface to remove dust and any amine blush residue from the epoxy. Amine residue, which can interfere with the finish, is more common with fast-curing hardeners, and you should have been using slow hardeners for laminating the hull. Some paint and epoxy manufacturers may recommend a particular solvent for cleaning a composite hull. However, careful and thorough washing with plain water is generally adequate. Wash twice and wipe dry to remove any residue along with the water.

When varnishing or painting, wear a respirator that will filter organic solvents. A UV-resistant finish is required to protect epoxy and Kevlar. Generally, I prefer pigmented paint over Kevlar or other structural fabrics and a clear, UV-resistant varnish over the wood parts. The clear varnish I've used most often is Z-Spar 1015 Captain's Varnish, which has given me good service on wood decks and other brightwork. I like to use a natural-bristle brush to apply clear varnish. Apply a minimum of three coats. This will last several years if the boat is stored protected from sunlight and weather.

Pigmented paints can generally be applied by brush, roller, or spraying. I have seen beautiful automotive-quality spray jobs applied to kayaks and canoes. But such finishes wouldn't look good for long in my paddling environments, and I prefer a quick, simple finish that is easy to touch up and to sand and repaint as needed. One-part marine polyurethane paints, such as Interlux Brightside Polyurethane, are convenient to use and to renew. Although such paints may be intended for use above the waterline, they are fine for canoes and kayaks. They are easy to apply with a very fine foam roller and will level to a smooth surface. A short foam roller 4 or 7 inches wide works well for the large surfaces. A brush may be needed to get paint under the gunwales and into corners, if you choose to paint the interior. Brush those corner areas first, and then use the roller for large areas.

A primer, such as Interlux Pre-Kote Primer, can be applied before the color coats, if you wish. The primer is sanded to provide a more uni-

FIGURE 13.3. *It is possible to do a lot of damage with power sanders! It can be difficult to avoid wavy surfaces with power sanders, so it is often best to do the rough shaping and coarse sanding by hand with sanding boards and blocks. However, lightweight palm-size sanders are great for coarse sanding before filler is applied and for fine sanding and finish work. On the left is a random orbit sander, which is good for fast removal of material. The wedge-shaped sander on the right will sand into corners and curves inside the hull. The others are palm sanders, which are versatile, easy to use, and excellent for final sanding with fine sandpaper.*

form smooth surface, and it can help the final paint look better by hiding areas of filler and other color variations. Pre-Kote Primer requires sanding the hull only to 80 grit. The primer will fill the sanding marks and scratches. Apply one or two coats. Sand with 120-grit paper between coats, and finish up with 220-grit paper before painting. Complete your finish with two color coats, or follow the paint manufacturer's instructions.

It may take a few weeks for the paint to dry hard enough that it will not scratch or mar easily while transporting or paddling the canoe. Tie-down straps and ropes can leave marks on new paint, so painting is best done as an off-season project. Paint will scratch more easily than the colored gelcoat on many factory-made fiberglass boats, but most scratches will be on the bottom, where you won't see them. Marks and scratches are just souvenirs of your paddling adventures and, with your vessel's name (Figure 13.4), add character. And touch-ups with one-part polyurethane are quick and easy.

FIGURE 13.4. *After the hull is painted you can add a name and nose art for a final touch.*

Sanding Kevlar

Kevlar can be a problem when it comes to sanding. If you do sand into the Kevlar, you will be left with a surface of rough fuzzy fibers that do not want to sand off. Do not continue trying to sand them smooth; you will only remove more epoxy and make the situation worse. Instead, trim the fibers off with a very sharp knife or wide chisel. Place the chisel against the hull at a low angle, and cut with a slicing action. If you have more than a little trimming to do, resharpen the blade often. Then coat the fibers with a layer of fresh epoxy. When this cures, the area will feel very rough, with the coated Kevlar fibers standing up like little shark's teeth. Trim this roughness with the chisel as well as possible, and try sanding with a very fine sandpaper, such as 320 or 400 grit. Then seal with more epoxy. It may take additional coats of epoxy, but you should be able to restore a very smooth surface.

Chapter 14

Advanced Outfitting, Boat Care, and Repair

You may wish to add several outfitting items to increase your boat's comfort, efficiency, and utility. These can be added at any time you see fit. There is no need to make them part of the original construction project, and you may wish to use the boat for a while first to determine what's needed.

A backrest and a footrest are probably among the first additions you may wish to make. Very low seating positions, such as in kayaks or small canoes like Dragonfly, can be hard on the back and the legs. Footrests and backrests are welcome additions that increase comfort and reduce fatigue.

Footrests

For kayaks and solo canoes paddled from a seated position, a footrest will increase comfort and add a lot of power and control to your paddle stroke. Adjustable footrests are available from a variety of sources, including Chesapeake Light Craft. (See Appendix A.) However, for the absolute lightest-weight footrest in solo open canoes, I have the forward thwart do double duty, as shown in Figure 14.1. After some test paddling, I mount the thwart at the best location for my footrest and lower it with wood blocks to a comfortable height. This must not be so low that your feet might get trapped under the thwart if a quick exit is required.

For boats without a thwart, including decked canoes and kayaks, this approach is not an option. And boats with decks that extend over the feet will more safely avoid entrapment if the footrests are just at the sides rather than a bar all the way across. Wood blocks can be screwed to the hull to provide fixed position rests. But, if people with different leg lengths will use your boat, then adjustable footrests may be preferable. (See Figures 14.2 and 14.3.) You will just carry a little more weight on the portage trail.

FIGURE 14.1. *A spacer for the forward thwart lowers the thwart to do double duty as a footrest.*

FIGURE 14.2. *An adjustable kayak footrest is installed in Kayoo. The plastic pipe is a rod holder.*

FIGURE 14.3. *This simple and ultra-lightweight footrest works surprisingly well and is one of my favorites. A ½-inch-thick hardwood base is screwed from the back to a 1-inch-diameter hardwood dowel. The base is attached to the side of the hull with machine screws and wing nuts. The base is about 1 inch wide and 12 inches long. Holes in the base allow you to move the footrest fore and aft. The wing nuts allow it to be moved with just a pocket screwdriver.*

In Figure 14.1 note the polyethylene foam cylinders mounted against the inside of the hull. These are part of a safety flotation system that resists capsizing when swamped and aids self-rescue if you do capsize. (Please read Chapter 15 on safety flotation for more on this important topic.) Polyethylene is also available in flat gray sheets for a neater, if slightly more costly, installation.

Backrest

Many strategies exist for adding back support for paddlers who sit. For solo canoes with thwarts, the seat and rear thwart can be positioned close together so that the thwart can double as a crude backrest or hold a backrest. A simple backrest attached to the thwart (as shown in Figure 14.4) will greatly increase comfort. The backrest should be about 6 inches high and 8 to 10 inches wide. Wider backrests can interfere with pad-

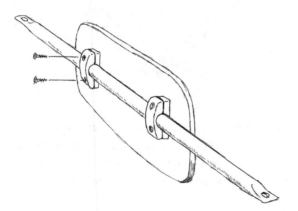

FIGURE 14.4. A simple backrest can be attached to the rear thwart of a solo canoe. The rest is a piece of 3 mm or ⅛-inch thick plywood, or a fiberglass-covered foam core panel about 6 inches high by 8 to 10 inches wide. Blocks of wood with a round cutout can clamp the backrest to an ultralight tubular aluminum thwart. If the backrest is not clamped too tightly, it can rotate to pivot out of the way when necessary. A slightly taller backrest of this style can be seen in Figure 14.14.

dling. Although some backrests are curved, I find that a relatively flat backrest is more comfortable and less restrictive. The backrest must be low or must fold down out of the way to enable inverting the canoe onto a cartop or for performing the self-rescue techniques described in Chapter 15.

Paddle Keeper

For portaging, photography, and fishing, a bungee to hold your paddle is wonderfully convenient. Such paddle keepers are becoming common on recreational kayaks and sit-on-top kayaks, but they are also a great addition for solo canoes. A bungee cord is passed through holes in the hull just under the gunwale, as shown in Figure 14.5. Holes spaced 20 to 22 inches apart seem to work well. Knot the ends of the cord on the inside of the hull. The cord can be pulled over a paddle shaft and held by a hook on the inside of the gunwale. (See Figure 14.6.) If the bungee holds the paddle at or near the center of gravity (CG), then it will automatically balance well for portaging. Installation can be similar for kayaks. However, if the kayak has built-in side flotation chambers, as on Kayoo, the bungee holder is installed externally, as shown in Figure 14.7.

I like to have convenient places to attach light ropes or bungee cords for securing packs during wilderness trips. (See Figure 14.8.) Tie-in points can be holes through the gunwales or coaming that are somewhat similar to the holes for the paddle keeper cord. Vertical or horizontal holes through a gunwale are handy if there are no convenient places inside the canoe to tie on to. Keep holes small to avoid weakening the gunwale, and seal all holes in wood with several coats of epoxy. When attaching a bungee hook, keep a small loop of line tied to the hole rather than enlarging the hole to fit the hook. You can see bungee cords hooked to loops of line in Figures 12.22 and 12.23 (in Chapter 12). Attachment points near the fore and aft deck coaming are also useful.

FIGURE 14.5. *A paddle shaft is held to the gunwale of Wasp with a bungee paddle keeper.*

FIGURE 14.6. *A hook to hold the bungee is screwed to the inside of the gunwale and pointed down so that it will not catch on clothing or cause injury. This one was cut from 1/16-by-1-inch aluminum bar stock and filed and sanded smooth. The wide end and surface are safer than smaller metal hooks. Hardware and building supply stores often stock a selection of aluminum bar stock and extrusions.*

FIGURE 14.7. *A hole through the hull is not always practical. If the best location for bungee installation is over an area of the hull or deck that encloses a flotation chamber, then the bungee should be mounted externally. Wood blocks with a hole to accommodate the bungee are bonded under the coaming with epoxy. Sand the hull bond area first. A layer of fiberglass overlapping the wood block onto the hull makes the mounting extremely strong and secure.*

FIGURE 14.8. *On Kayoo an aluminum bungee hook is screwed to one of the rails that support the combination seat and portage yoke. Make sure that you mount a hook so that it will not catch on clothing or cause injury.*

Rod Holder

If you enjoy fishing as well as paddling, you may want a rod holder. It allows trolling while pad-dling, combining exercise with recreation. What an excuse to go fishing! A piece of plastic water pipe works great. Choose pipe with an inside diameter a little larger than the handles of your favorite fishing rods.

The trick is finding a really convenient place to hold the rod. It must be out of your way for paddling, in sight for quickly detecting strikes, and easy to reach to set the hook. Most kayaks mount rod holders behind the seat, but when trolling, I lose too many strikes that way. I find the best location to be close to the feet, far enough forward to be just beyond your range of motion while paddling. If the rod is held vertically, the line will be clear of the boat while trolling and paddling straight ahead, turning, or moving the boat in any direction. Although a location between the feet or shins would be ideal, it is most convenient to mount a holder to the gunwale or coaming. Mount it just a little closer to you than where your foot rests. If you place your foot on your footrest, the rod holder should be as far forward as possible without quite touching your foot or the biggest boots you expect to wear.

In a kayak with a small cockpit opening, the best place might be through the deck in front of the coaming and between your legs. Keep in mind that the installation and the bottom of the pipe may need to be waterproof if you paddle in rough conditions and wear a sprayskirt. Also make sure that you can exit the boat quickly and smoothly in an emergency without trapping your feet on the holder. See Figures 14.9 through 14.11 for examples.

Portage Yoke

One advantage of a lightweight composite canoe is that it is easy to carry. You may want to make long-distance carrying and portaging even easier by using a portage yoke. Again, recheck and remark the CG location; the shoulder pads of any portage yoke should be near the CG or slightly forward so that the canoe balances slightly bow up when carrying. It should be comfortable for the hands to hold the gunwales in front of you while portaging, and the weight of the arms should just balance the boat with the bow high enough so you can see where you are going. Adjust the yoke

FIGURE 14.9. *In Kayoo the plastic pipe rod holder is attached at the top to the coaming with a heavy-duty plastic cable tie. At the bottom, the rod holder is screwed to a wood block, which is bonded to the hull with epoxy and fiberglass.*

FIGURE 14.10. *Here the rod holder installation in Wasp is similar to what I use in other open canoes. A length of $\frac{1}{16}$-by-1-inch aluminum strap is bent to hold the plastic pipe and is screwed to the gunwale. This is often strong enough as is for freshwater fishing. For extra security, this holder is also attached at the bottom similarly to the holder in Figure 14.9.*

FIGURE 14.11. *Rod holder strap detail.*

position fore and aft for best balance as needed. It is worth making fine adjustments because they can make a big difference in comfort on long-distance carries.

For a tandem canoe, the middle thwart can be adapted with pads to double as a portage yoke. Solo canoes present a greater problem because the seat and the portage yoke have to be close together. The portage yoke must be at the CG, which is just inches forward of the seat location required for best paddling trim. A permanent, fixed-position yoke would leave no room to step into the canoe or sit. In the past, the solution has been to clamp a temporary yoke to the gunwales when portaging. Detachable portage yokes are available from such mail order outfitters as Piragis Northwoods Company (see Appendix A), and various books offer plans for making your own. Such yokes are usually heavy, they don't always stay attached securely, and some involve hardware that can break and removable parts that eventually fall in the water and get lost.

For a detachable portage yoke, here is my favorite design. It is also the simplest and works surprisingly well with both solo canoes and kayaks. Cut a plywood panel with the outer shape and dimensions shown in Figure 14.12. Plywood ½-inch thick is strong enough for the designs in this book and other ultralight and narrow solo canoes and kayaks.

The plywood must have no voids or flaws. Seal the plywood with several coats of epoxy. Foam shoulder pads are glued to one flat side with contact cement or double-sided carpet tape. Make the shoulder pads high enough so that your head doesn't hit the bottom of the hull when carrying the boat. On the side opposite the shoulder pads, spacer bars are attached with screws to center the yoke between canoe gunwales or between the sides of a kayak coaming. The spacer bars can be positioned either inboard or outboard of the gunwales. Inboard seems to work best on most kayak coamings, and the diagram in Figure 14.12 indicates measuring for an inboard location. Figure 14.14 shows the spacer bars positioned outboard; this was done to avoid interference with a paddle keeper hook on the inboard side. Extra screw holes can be added to the yoke so that the spacer bars can be attached in different locations to fit different boats. I like the spacer bars to fit rather tightly against the gunwales, which helps to keep the yoke in place.

The yoke is held tightly in place to the canoe gunwales or kayak coaming with sticky-back, self-adhesive Velcro (fabric hook and loop fastener material) and bungee cords. Use two cords, one at each gunwale. The bungee cords can hook to D-rings, tie-in fixtures, a seat, or any structure in the bottom or sides of the boat. Chapter 15 describes how to attach tie-in fixtures and D-rings. Position the yoke near the center of gravity. Velcro is often all that is needed to hold the yoke in place for portaging the boat. If I leave the yoke in place while carrying the boat on a car top, then I also secure the yoke with bungee cords so it cannot fly off while driving. The extra security of bungee cords is also welcome on very bumpy portages.

You will find Velcro in short strips and long rolls at many fabric, craft, and building supply stores. Three-quarter-inch and 2-inch widths are common, and the Velcro is easy to cut to the widths and lengths you desire. Place the Velcro "loop" fabric on the gunwales and the "hook" fabric on the yoke. For the gunwales, cut the Velcro extra long so that the ends do not pull up when

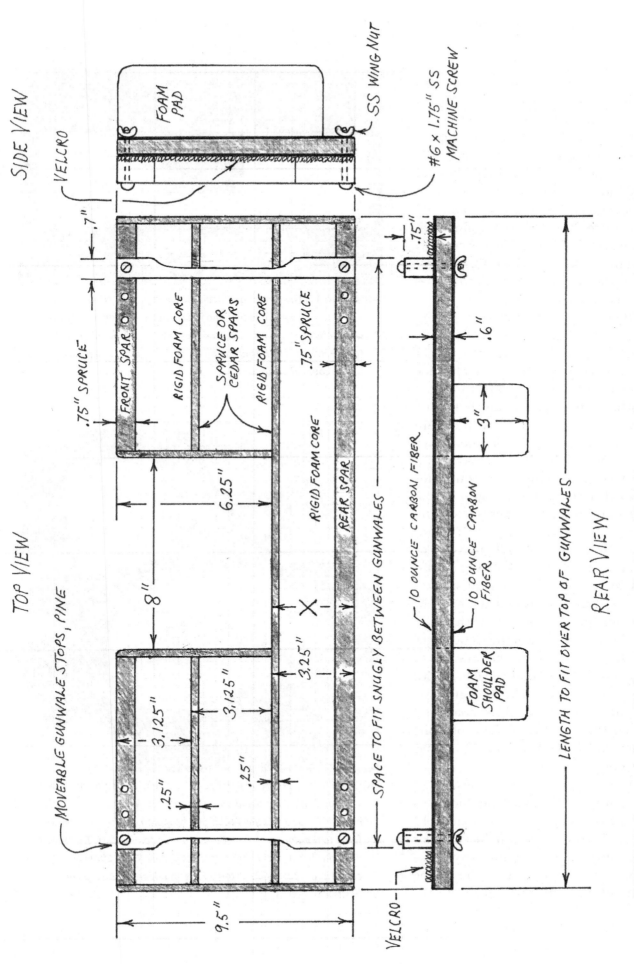

FIGURE 14.12. Portage yoke diagram. This diagram can be used for either a plywood yoke or an ultralight composite yoke. For a simple plywood yoke, cut ½-inch plywood to the outer dimensions shown and increase dimension X to 4 inches. The yoke can be made stronger for carrying heavier and wider boats by increasing X further.

removing the yoke from the gunwales. On the yoke, I make the Velcro strips long enough to wrap over the edges. Position the Velcro on the gunwales so that you can experiment with moving the yoke fore and aft a bit to obtain the best balance for carrying. Velcro, like other fabrics, tends to expand when wet, and may wrinkle. It will flatten again when dry, but cycles of wetting may eventually loosen the sticky-back adhesive. If necessary, experiment with contact adhesives for better long-term service.

Although the plywood yoke is very simple and effective, it is relatively heavy, being similar in weight to other wooden portage yokes. A ½-inch-thick foam core yoke covered with fiberglass or carbon fiber can be much lighter. Figures 14.12 and 14.13 show the foam core with wood framework necessary for a strong and durable ultralight yoke. Spruce, cedar, or pine are adequate for the wood framing, but the grain must be clear and straight. Cover the top and bottom with epoxy and 10- to 12-ounce carbon cloth for a very light yoke or several layers of 9-ounce fiberglass for a less costly yoke. The vertical sides of the wood framing around the exterior perimeter are not covered with cloth. Trim the cloth and sand the wood edges to slightly round them after the epoxy cures, and seal the wood and fabric with three coats of epoxy. The pine gunwale stops are given two or three coats of a wipe-on tung oil finish. The soft pine without an epoxy finish will not mar hardwood gunwales.

My carbon yoke weighs less than one pound, and the foam shoulder pads add only a few more ounces. This yoke combined with a small, light kayak or canoe allows me to comfortably make five-mile portages to run sections of the Upper Potomac River without a shuttle.

FIGURE 14.13. *The core of an ultralight portage yoke shows the foam and wood frame. Wood framing is assembled to foam core pieces with dabs of quick setting epoxy that temporarily hold all the pieces together. The yoke is then ready for carbon fiber or fiberglass layers on the top and bottom.*

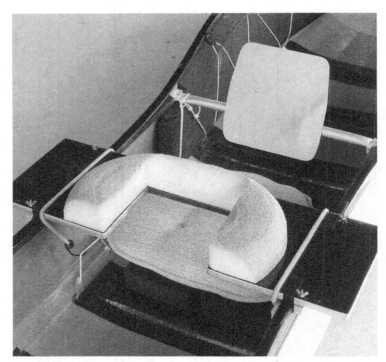

FIGURE 14.14. *The carbon portage yoke is held in position against the gunwales with Velcro and bungee cords. The Wasp canoe in this picture has a simple low seat made by gluing blocks of closed cell foam to the floor with a softer pad on top for comfort. The backrest is similar to the design in Figure 14.4. Figure 1.1 in Chapter 1 shows a canoe being carried inverted on the shoulders in the typical portage position.*

Combination Seat and Portage Yoke

Most detachable portage yokes for solo canoes are both heavy and bulky. They have to be removed for car transporting, and they require finding someplace to store and lash them safely into the boat when paddling. Although the carbon yoke is light, when paddling it still takes up room in the boat that could otherwise be used for camping, fishing, and emergency gear. My solution is to build a seat that converts to a portage yoke. Shoulder pads are under the seat, which is flipped upside down to put the shoulder pads into carrying position. I've been told that I am not the first to have done this, but since I have not seen anyone else's system, I devised my own. The combination seat and yoke weighs less than conventional seats with a separate portage yoke. It is more work to construct and fit than the detachable yoke. But if you want a greater building challenge, you will be rewarded with a slick system that is fun to use. This design has its roots in earlier solo canoe seats that I mounted on rails so that I could slide forward and backward to adjust trim, or weight balance, for various wind and load conditions. (For a basic idea of the design of a simple sliding seat, see Figures 15.25, 15.26, and 15.27 in Chapter 15.)

Figure 14.15 shows the mount for the seat/yoke in Wasp, which is similar to the installations in several of my other canoes. Extruded aluminum angle side rails support the seat. The lower rail is the seat height position; the higher rail is the portage yoke position. Pieces of aluminum bar stock ⅛ by ¾ inch are bent and hammered into clips that hold the combination seat/yoke in place. For simplicity, bungee cords could be used instead of clips to hold the seat/yoke in position.

The side walls are 21-inch-long, vertical carbon fiber panels that are screwed to the gunwales at the top and to fiberglass attachments in the hull at the bottom. The ones shown in Figure 14.16 are very light and have two layers of 9-ounce fiberglass core with outer layers of 10-ounce carbon fiber. They can be laid up on a tabletop or a piece of plywood covered with package-sealing tape. The bottom attachment between the side wall and the hull is two layers of 9-ounce fiberglass. Rather than glass the side walls directly to the hull, they are screwed on so that they may be easily removed for modification at any time. The side walls could also be made from ¼-inch-thick 5-ply marine plywood or ³/₁₆-inch-thick fiberglass, but they would be heavier.

To make the bottom attachment, the side wall is covered at the bottom with package-sealing tape so that epoxy will not adhere to it. It is screwed to the gunwale or taped in place. Make certain that both side walls are perfectly vertical and are equidistant from each other at all points. A 4-inch-wide strip of 9-ounce fiberglass

FIGURE 14.15. *Aluminum rails are installed on carbon fiber panels to support the combination seat and portage yoke.*

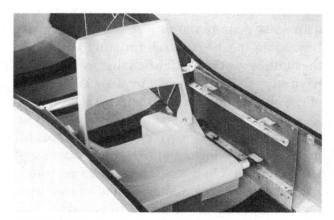

FIGURE 14.16. *The combination seat and portage yoke is in sitting position on the lower rails.*

is bonded with 2 inches lapping onto the hull and 2 inches onto the bottom of the side wall. When the epoxy has cured, the side wall can be removed, leaving a 2-inch panel of fiberglass standing up vertically from the hull. Reinforce this panel of fiberglass with a second layer. This can lap onto the hull in the direction opposite the first layer for additional strength. Side walls can then be screwed to the fiberglass at the bottom and screwed to the gunwales at the top for a secure but removable installation.

The aluminum rails are 1-inch angle stock $\frac{1}{16}$ inch thick, which is strong enough for my 140-pound weight. Heavier paddlers should use $\frac{1}{8}$-inch angle and increase the stiffness of the side walls by adding more fiberglass layers to the core. Each rail is held in place with five stainless steel machine screws with washers and nuts. Use a slow drilling speed to make the holes in the aluminum.

Plans for the seat and an optional backrest are shown in Figure 14.17. The seat is sawn and carved from 2-inch-thick urethane foam. Cut out the plywood side panels first, and glue them to the foam block with a little quick-setting epoxy. A wood gouge can be used to make hollows in the foam for the aluminum tubes to fit. It is tempting to sculpt a nice-looking seat bottom with a concave shape, but my experience argues against that. Even seats that conform nicely get uncomfortable after hours on the water. Therefore, I like to use a seat cushion. My favorites are lightweight and self-inflating. Cushions seem to work best with seats that are flat or just slightly hollowed. I found an inexpensive self-inflating cushion in the hunting section at Cabela's that works well. It has a strap that helps hold it in place. I'm not fond of the olive drab color, but the price was right!

A self-inflating cushion is especially handy on the water. If I need more cushioning, I can lift myself up a few inches, loosen the air valve, and let in more air. Or, if winds and waves get rough, I can remain sitting and let air out of the valve, thereby lowering my center of mass and increasing stability. To take advantage of this option, you should plan for any seat cushion you want to use

when fixing the height of your seat. As a rule of thumb, mount the top of the seat base about 1 to 1½ inches below where you want to sit. By using cushions or foam pads as needed, you retain the option of removing them for an instant increase in stability.

Aluminum tubes pass through the seat at the front and rear and extend out the sides to rest on the rails. They are 1 inch in diameter with a minimum wall thickness of .055 inch. The aluminum tubes must both be perfectly level for the seat to rest tightly at all four corners on the side mounting rails. Place the tubes on a level, flat workbench or tabletop. Invert the carved foam seat bottom and glue it down to the tubes with a quick-setting epoxy. The joints between wood and foam or between aluminum and foam are not structural, so just use a small amount of epoxy. A neat appearance will be much easier to achieve if epoxy does not squeeze or drip out onto the outer foam surface. The foam is so soft that it will be difficult to clean off dried epoxy and maintain the desired surface shape. The reinforcing cloth that will overlie everything will provide the needed structural strength.

The seat can be covered with fiberglass or carbon fiber. Kevlar works well structurally, but the trimming and sanding needed to finish Kevlar is a much greater chore. A layer of 10-ounce carbon, two layers of 5-ounce Kevlar, or four layers of 6-ounce fiberglass are required as a minimum. The cloth must bond onto the tubes and the plywood sides. Sand the aluminum very well with coarse sandpaper immediately before bonding. The surface oxidizes quickly, which interferes with a good bond. After the epoxy has cured, trim the cloth and round the plywood sides over a little to remove the sharp edges. Then bond a strip of very lightweight fiberglass over all corners; 1.45-ounce fiberglass deck cloth is fine. Use about a 2-inch-wide strip to lap 1 inch onto each side.

A seat backrest can add lumbar support and comfort for trips and longer paddling sessions. It helps me maintain posture and avoid back pain. My backrests are narrowed at the top so

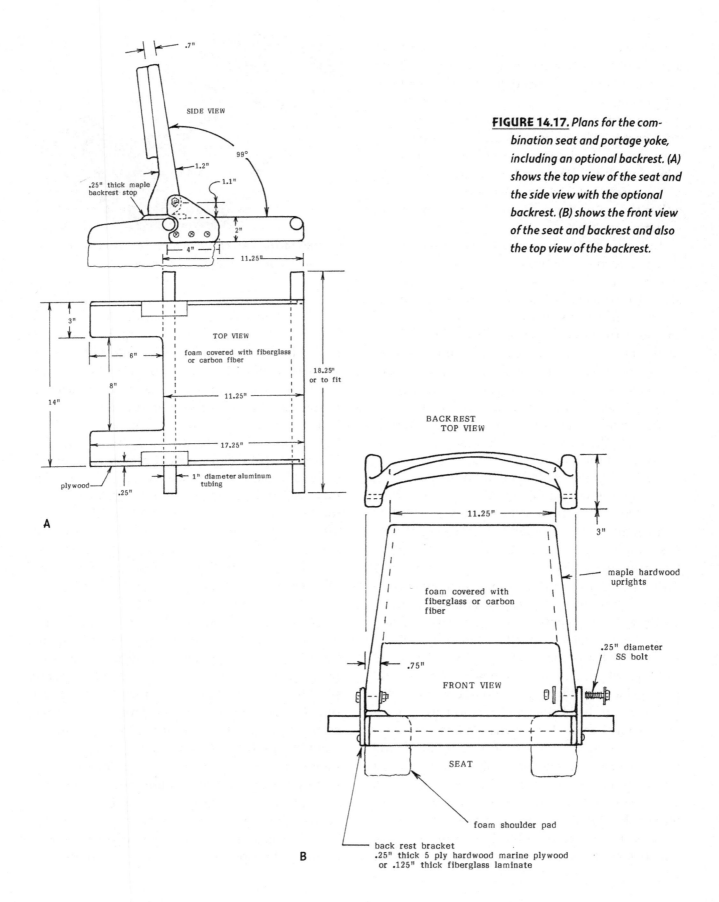

.7"

SIDE VIEW

99°

1.2"

1.1"

.25" thick maple
backrest stop

2"

4"

11.25"

3"

6"

TOP VIEW

foam covered with fiberglass
or carbon fiber

18.25"
or to fit

8"

14"

11.25"

17.25"

1" diameter aluminum
tubing

plywood

.25"

A

FIGURE 14.17. *Plans for the combination seat and portage yoke, including an optional backrest. (A) shows the top view of the seat and the side view with the optional backrest. (B) shows the front view of the seat and backrest and also the top view of the backrest.*

BACK REST
TOP VIEW

11.25"

3"

maple hardwood
uprights

foam covered with
fiberglass or carbon
fiber

.25" diameter
SS bolt

.75"

FRONT VIEW

SEAT

foam shoulder pad

back rest bracket
.25" thick 5 ply hardwood marine plywood
or .125" thick fiberglass laminate

B

that they do not interfere with rotating the torso and shoulders while paddling and fishing. Note that the seat back is hinged. It must fold flat both for portaging and for self-rescue reentry. It can also be folded and left in place for transporting on a cartop. Place a large stainless steel washer between the backrest and the backrest bracket when installing the hinge bolt. Tighten the hinge bolt enough that friction will hold the backrest in either the up or down position and keep it from swinging too freely.

In Figure 14.18, the seat/yoke is turned upside down, placed on the upper rails, and slid under the clips to secure for portaging. The 6-inch shoulder pad extensions on the seat are made as structural parts of the seat. They should be carved with the seat from one block of urethane foam. These relatively long pads allow moving the canoe forward and back on the shoulders to adjust balance, even while carrying. The opening between the pads is 8 inches to provide safe room for the head. When the canoe is turned upside down over the head for carrying, soft foam rubber rests on the shoulders.

Foam thickness will depend on the density of the foam, the weight of your boat (and anything you leave tied in it), and the amount of comfort and cushioning you require. The average thickness of my pads is around 2½ inches. I remember youthful days when a bare wood gunwale with a little neck-shaped cutout was somehow acceptable as a portage yoke. Today, comfort is more important to my happy traveling experience, and I keep trying different pad foam materials. Some are too hard, and that speaks for itself. Some are too soft, which only means they bottom out and feel too hard! Goldilocks would understand. One past solution has been to glue a soft foam layer over a hard foam layer; when combined, they can be just right. However, I have finally found the perfect foam, and it is precut into an almost ready-to-use shape. Some of the donut-shaped seat cushions that are sold in pharmacies have foam rubber inside that is just the right density for me. It is softer than hard closed-cell foams, but it doesn't soak up water as much as softer

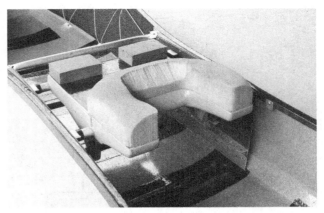

FIGURE 14.18. *The seat/yoke is turned upside down on the top rails for the portage yoke position.*

foam rubber. The cushions are a molded foam rubber with a central oval hole approximately 4 inches by 8 inches and a removable cloth cover. Make two cuts in the foam from the front to take out an 8-inch section of donut; that will leave a U-shaped pad that fits shoulders and neck.

For portaging, the yoke is clipped in place at both front and rear. However, in the seated position, only a front clip is needed. The seat/yoke can be held in place with bungee cords for a simpler installation. In that case, clips are required only for the rear tube in the portage position. None are needed for sitting, but a block or stop to limit travel to the rear is helpful if you are bracing yourself against footrests. A front clip for sitting allows you to lean a bit more on the backrest, if you are so equipped.

Besides resting on the rails, the seat can also be used flat on the floor if a very low and stable paddling position is needed. When used that way, the shoulder pads on the front and the dense pads to the rear (shown in Figure 14.18) all rest on the floor to keep the seat level. Because the seats remove to change position for portaging or paddling, they are also interchangeable. The side mounts in several of my canoes accommodate the same seat width and aluminum tube diameter.

The overhead view in Figure 14.19 gives a clearer picture of the clips that hold the aluminum tubes built into the seat/yoke. Rubber furniture leg tips cover the ends of the aluminum tubes. The clips spring a little to keep the tubes tightly in place. Wear and tear is confined to the rubber tips, which are easily replaced.

Note the small black mark on the carbon side wall near the front end of the aluminum rail, to the bottom right in Figure 14.19. This is the final CG mark after completing the canoe, including the seat/yoke. Notice that the center of the shoulder pad aligns with the CG mark. The aluminum side rails are drilled to mount the clips in different locations. If necessary, the clips can be moved in 1-inch increments fore and aft to adjust the balance of the boat better on the shoulders.

This overhead view also shows a filler piece of walnut wood toward the rear of the seat (bottom left in Figure 14.19) that acts as a spacer between the flat carbon side wall and the curved gunwale of Wasp. The side walls must be vertical, parallel, and equidistant at all points. (See Figure 14.20.) So, keep measuring and leveling constantly while making such an installation. It may save time to build a plywood or cardboard box to hold the side walls square and vertical while fitting them to the hull.

The ability to move and remove the seat is a wonderfully useful feature. It leaves enough room to recline in the bottom of a solo canoe, and I have slept that way on occasion when no usable or safe campsite was available onshore. A removable seat also makes it possible to carry large heavy cargo or an injured person in a solo canoe. The patient is placed lying down toward the bow while the paddler kneels or sits to the rear. The seat just rests on the floor. And, last but not least, on camping trips the seat with the backrest comes out of the boat and into camp to become a most welcome wilderness lounge chair. It has eased lower back strain and kept my fanny off the rocks and out of the mud on many an adventure.

Caring for Your Boat

Paint or ultraviolet-resistant varnish is the first line of defense for protecting your epoxy composite boat. The boat should also be stored away

FIGURE 14.20. *An old Kevlar solo canoe has been fitted with a combination seat/yoke mount similar to the ones in Wasp and Kayoo. The side wall is ⅛-inch-thick Kevlar 18 inches long laminated over two sides of a 2 × 10 as a form to provide the right-angle shoulder bend at the top. The attachment to the hull at the bottom is similar to the attachment in Wasp described earlier. At the top, the Kevlar side wall is screwed to aluminum angle brackets, which are in turn screwed to the gunwale. The side wall also helps hold foam side flotation (as described in Chapter 15). The rope loops at the bottom provide places to tie ropes or hook bungee cords for securing camping and safety gear.*

FIGURE 14.19. *Here is an overhead view of the seat/yoke clipped into the portage yoke position.*

from direct sunlight during the off-season or when not in use for long periods. A garage or basement is ideal. Outdoor storage locations under cover are an acceptable alternative. For many years I hoisted my handmade wooden sea kayak up under the roof of a carport, and it held up very well. Racks under a deck can also hold canoes and kayaks. If your boat must sit where sunlight can fall on it, then a tarp or cover of some sort will help preserve it. You will probably notice that the tarp also deteriorates and may need to be replaced from time to time. It is cheaper to replace the tarp than the boat.

A kayak is best supported with something like the sling stands shown in Figure 9.14 in Chapter 9. The decks are often rather delicate and not always good for supporting the weight of the boat. It may be necessary to place the kayak right side up with a cockpit cover to keep moisture, birds, and cats out. Yes, cats. A stray cat once hid her litter in one of my boats! And I have a cat now who likes to sit on the highest boat in the rack. I have to keep the top boat upside down so that she doesn't claw my cushy soft seat.

A canoe can conveniently be stored upside down with gunwales resting on sawhorses or a rack of some sort. Whatever you use to support your canoe or kayak, make sure to tie it down very securely in any semioutdoor location. One winter I thought a canoe was very safely out of wind and weather in a three-sided tractor shed. But a storm wind scooped the canoe out of the shed and tumbled it 75 feet across a clearing and into a small broken limb on a locust tree. I was not happy about having to fix the punctured Royalex hull before I could go paddling. Small boats may suffer greater risk of damage during storage or transportation than from hazards on the water.

Repairs

After you have built a composite boat, making repairs with reinforcing cloth and epoxy is relatively easy. You already know how to work with epoxy and fiberglass and how to get a good bond by sanding the bond area thoroughly. Small scratches do no harm. Large scratched areas should eventually be repainted to provide UV protection. Deep scratches or large gouges can be filled with epoxy, epoxy and filler, or fiberglass. The cured area can be sanded level and repainted to look like new.

Sometimes when a Kevlar hull is severely hit or bent, the hull may stay together but a white area or crease will show. This may be a partial or complete fracture of the resin but may not damage the Kevlar. If it remains watertight, it may be used as is. If not, sanding and a few coats of epoxy may restore watertightness. If the affected area seems more flexible than the rest of the hull, then a repair to add reinforcement is in order. This might be as simple as a patch inside the hull. A fiberglass patch is usually adequate, or you may choose whatever cloth matches the hull construction. Make it large enough to extend past the damaged area by a few inches. A very small puncture, say a pencil-sized puncture, can be covered with a patch about 2 inches in diameter. If you install patches with the same technique described for installing ribs with peel ply, then the repairs can look surprisingly good.

A composite hull with severe cracks, or even a hull that is broken in two, can still be repaired. Clean and trim the edges of the break as needed so that they can be pushed back into position. As always, sand very well with coarse sandpaper in the area to receive a patch. Then duct tape the parts together from the outside and add repair cloth layers and epoxy to the inside. Let it cure; then flip the boat upside down and remove the tape.

The exterior surface of the break must be hollowed or dished so that the repair will be flush. Sand this concave area, and taper it over several inches so that the original hull material is very thin toward the center of the repair patch. At the repair joint area, it is okay to sand right through the original hull material but not into the repair cloth that was added to the inside. Then add cloth and epoxy to the outside. Inner layers can be Kevlar if that matches the original hull, but do not build up Kevlar layers flush with the surrounding exterior surface. Use fiberglass or carbon fiber for the final exterior layers. When cured, the repaired area may be sanded level with the surrounding surface. Seal with a few coats of epoxy. Imperfections can be leveled with a filler mixture of epoxy and microfibers. Sand the surface smooth to 220 grit, and paint it to match the hull. Long sanding boards can help achieve a level surface. For more details, review Chapter 13 on finishing. It is possible to fill and sand the surface until it looks like brand new, if you take the time and care to do it.

Cartop Transporting

Most canoes and kayaks are transported to and from the water on a cartop. An important part of proper care is doing this safely; many boats are damaged during transportation rather than on the water. If your vehicle has a roof rack or a pair of load bars attached very securely, then a canoe or partially decked boat may be carried upside down tied to the load bars. Nylon web tie-down straps are especially convenient, but ¼-inch or heavier nylon rope works okay. Avoid using polypropylene rope, which does not hold knots well.

Tying only to the load bars is acceptable for short trips at slow speeds, assuming the load bars are strong and firmly attached to the roof. Otherwise, for highway travel, the canoe must also be tied to the vehicle at the front and rear. Use two ropes to tie the bow of the boat to the left and right corners of the front bumper. Similarly, use two ropes to tie the stern to the left and right corners of the rear bumper. Many vehicles have tie-down hooks underneath at the corners of the frame, which make convenient and strong tie-down points. If you have built rope holes into the ends of your boat, as suggested in Chapter 11, these will be the strongest and safest places to tie on to. For kayaks, it is best to use load bar cradles designed for carrying them.

Launching

Your technique for entering and exiting your lightweight solo canoe or kayak can also contribute to its longevity. The best practice is to never put your weight into the boat unless it is floating. Avoiding damage and abrasion usually means stepping in the water. Wear boots or plan to get your feet wet. Place the boat in the water parallel to the shore. Position it where the water is deep enough to float the boat with your weight in it—about 4 inches of water should do. Stand along the shore side of the boat and face the bow. For an open or partially decked canoe, position the paddle side to side across the gunwales a foot or so in front of the seat with the blade pointing toward the shore. (See Figure 14.21.) Grip the paddle and gunwale together with one hand. The blade can be braced against the shore for balance; this works especially well with double-blade paddles because of their length. While bracing, step into the center of the boat one foot at a time and sit.

For a kayak with a small cockpit opening, the procedure is slightly different. Instead of placing the paddle in front of the seat, place it crossways just behind the seat and coaming with one blade pointed toward the shore. Stand in front of the paddle, and face the bow with the paddle just behind your knees. Squat, grip the paddle shaft and coaming together with both hands behind you, and sit down on the paddle shaft and coaming. (See Figures 14.22 and 14.23.) Your weight can be off center a little bit so that the paddle blade braces against the shore. Slip one leg at a time into the cockpit, and slide forward onto the seat. The kayak entry works equally well for solo open canoe, and it is safer and easier on the back than the canoe entry described above. It may not feel elegant, but it works.

Many paddlers can be seen scraping the stern off the shore to launch and driving the bow onto the shore to land. Such technique may be acceptable with cheap, heavy, and expendable aluminum and plastic boats, but you may think differently after investing labor and materials in a handmade canoe. Such mistreatment can

FIGURE 14.21. *Solo canoe entry. Brace the paddle with one blade on the shore and the shaft across the gunwales or coaming. Step into the center of the hull. Photo by Carrie Rizzetta.*

FIGURE 14.22. *Kayak entry. Brace the paddle with one blade on the shore and the shaft behind you across the back of the coaming or behind the coaming. Sit on the paddle shaft with most of your weight over the boat and a little of your weight supported by the blade on shore. This allows you to enter or exit without risk of capsizing. Place one foot at a time into the center of the hull and then sit. Photo by Carrie Rizzetta.*

cause abrasion and damage, especially to ultra-lightweight hulls. Just like sanding your hull, it will eventually wear through. Putting your weight on the hull while it is resting on any hard surface can be harmful. For long tandem canoes, you may need to load gear and the bow paddler while the stern is on shore. The stern paddler can then lift the boat and push it out where it will

FIGURE 14.23. *Kayak entry, rear view. If you have a seat backrest, it should be folded down out of the way. After you are in the boat with good balance established, you can slip forward enough to raise the seat. Photo by Carrie Rizzetta.*

float before jumping in. If you enter and exit your canoe only while it is floating, it is likely to last a long time with minimal repairs.

For wilderness trips, waterproof hiking boots do double duty by usually keeping the feet dry during launching and providing adequate sup-

port for heavy loads on the portage trail. Ankle sprains are one of the most common canoe trip injuries, so good support is more important than dry feet. Boots dry relatively quickly; sprains heal slowly.

Flowing Waters

Gently and freely

Sam Rizzetta © 1993

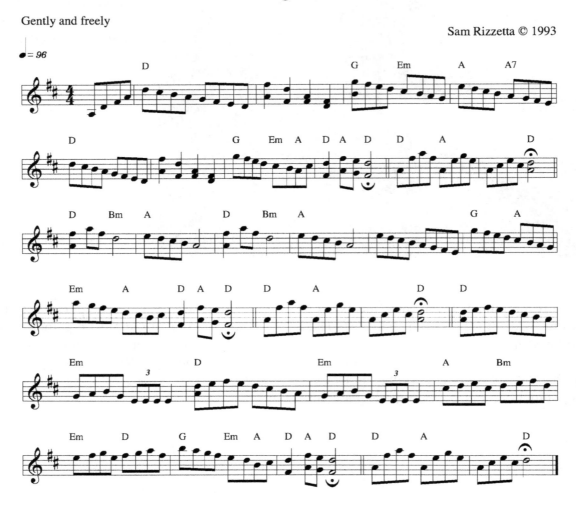

Chapter 15

Flotation and Safety

I have loved canoes and kayaks for a long time. They have been my vehicles for wondrous adventures and experiences, traveling, exploring, camping, fishing, studying nature, and

generally connecting with wild places. When I was a youngster, it was conventional wisdom that one should never go canoeing alone. It was considered unsafe. But canoes and kayaks are ideal for seeking solitude. With experience, many of us are willing to venture out solo while taking precautions and accepting the risks.

A recent study reveals a surprising number of fatalities involving canoes and kayaks, and most are the result of capsizing. Many accidents also involve fishing from canoes. The study is titled "Critical Judgment II: Understanding and Preventing Canoe and Kayak Fatalities 1996–2002" and is available from the American Canoe Association. (See Appendix B.)

My goal is not to frighten anyone away from enjoying these beautiful small boats—quite the contrary. But while emergencies are rare, dangers are real. The risks and consequences of capsizing limit where, when, and how we should use our small craft. By reducing the risks, canoes and kayaks can become more useful and more fun.

Some special-purpose boats, such as ocean outrigger canoes, are inherently stable and resist capsizing. Sit-on-top kayaks are generally wide for stability and have flotation molded in. Many of these are designed to enable reentry while snorkeling and swimming. They also tend to be slow and heavy, making them much more work to paddle and transport. They are safe and convenient if you don't have to paddle fast or far. But, for many serious paddlers, it would be ideal if we could reduce the capsize risks while keeping the versatility, efficient paddling, and light weight features of conventional canoes and sit-inside kayaks.

Over many years, I've experimented with ways to accomplish this goal. With the flotation modifications described in this chapter, a flooded canoe or kayak is less likely to capsize, and, if you should fall out, you can rescue yourself easily and quickly without assistance. The information comes from my experiments and personal experience, and I hope it will make canoes and kayaks a little safer for everyone. Please remember that you are responsible for using good judgment and assuming the risks involved in paddling.

Flotation can be installed in existing solo canoes, tandem canoes, and recreational kayaks to provide greater safety and self-rescue capability, and it can be incorporated right from the start into new boats that you build. (See Figure 15.1.) The modifications are simple and inexpensive, taking just a few hours of easy work and adding as little as 1.5 to 4 pounds of weight to the boat.

My flotation system has been successful in all of the canoes and kayaks that I have tested to date. This includes a variety of canoes as well as kayaks 27 inches wide or greater. Significantly narrower kayaks, such as sea kayaks, may not be adaptable to the flotation modifications described. They have not been tested and are not covered here.

As small, human-powered craft, canoes and kayaks are of necessity relatively narrow so that one can easily reach the water with a paddle and apply power in a useful direction. Because they are narrow, they tip more easily than most other boats; in other words, they are less stable in roll, or rotation about the fore-and-aft axis. It is possible to fall out—or to roll over . . . and then fall out! Even worse, they become much more unstable in roll if they take on water, whether from waves, leaks, mishandling, or other hazards. The more water they have inside, the less stable they become until, eventually, they will easily capsize. And it may be surprising how little water inside is needed to make staying upright difficult or impossible.

If you haven't experienced this in your kayak or canoe, test it in shallow, calm, warm water or in a swimming pool. You may be surprised. With most canoes and kayaks, you will not be able to climb back in from deep water and remain upright without assistance or special equipment. Of course, if you are on a small pond, a narrow river, or near shore, you can swim to shallow water or dry land. You might even save your boat and gear. Take the rope you tied thoughtfully to the bow earlier, grab the free end between your teeth, and swim to shore. You did have a rope tied to the bow, didn't you? It also goes without saying that one always wears a good life jacket or personal flotation device (PFD).

When you are not alone, rescue is easier. If you and your companions have rescue training, you can reenter your boat even in deep water. A variety of methods exist to accomplish this, and you can learn about them in other books and videos or, better yet, take a class. The American Canoe Association and Paddling.net (see Appendix B) are good sources of information.

But if you are alone under difficult conditions, your survival can be in doubt. When the water is cold and shore is not close, you have few options, none of them good. Trying to tow the boat with you as you swim may prevent reaching shore before hypothermia renders you helpless. On the other hand, swimming to shore without the boat may deprive you of the boat and the gear in it that may be required for survival, such as warm and dry clothing, a sleeping bag, a tent, a stove, and food. I know some folks who carry a set of

FIGURE 15.1. *On the left is a factory-made, Royalex-hull solo canoe with inflatable flotation bags in the ends and foam flotation in the sides. On the right is Kayoo, a lightweight kayak/decked canoe with flotation chambers built in.*

swim fins when they venture far from shore. That enables swimming farther and faster, but one ultimately faces the same decisions.

You may choose to paddle only in comfortable, easy conditions and with helpful companions. It is impossible to fault good judgment in that regard. Airplane pilots like to recount the following maxim: *the superior pilot uses his or her superior judgment to avoid those situations that require his or her superior skills.* The same can be said of superior paddlers. But canoes and kayaks can be modified to reduce the risks of paddling in cold weather, in remote places, and regardless of whether one has companions or goes solo.

A Cautionary Tale

It was a sunny autumn day as I paddled my slim solo canoe onto the bright, clear waters of a mountain lake in Maryland. The thin air had lost its dewy morning chill, and I looked forward to a few quiet hours on the water. As I glided out into the main lake, I noticed a couple of kayaks farther out in very deep water. Drawing within a few hundred yards, I could see one kayak had a paddler and one did not. A commotion of movement and splashing was evident. A paddler was in the water.

Approaching nearer, I saw two young boys about eleven or twelve years old. The one in the water had tried many times to climb back into his wide recreational kayak, but it rolled over each time. He had succeeded only in exhausting himself and filling the boat with water. The boat was mostly underwater, awash to the coaming, but did not quite sink. His attempts to swim while holding the cockpit rim were going nowhere. But he was unwilling to leave his kayak and swim for shore. The boy in the other kayak was frozen and didn't have a clue as to how to give assistance. He neither aided with reentry nor went for help. There was no one else in sight on the lake. The boys were clearly unprepared and frightened. I tried to put them at ease. "I bet you're glad you wore that life jacket," I offered. They were mostly worried what their parents would say when they did not return on time.

The kayak was so swamped and had so little flotation that getting much water out and the boy back in was going to be difficult, especially if I wished to avoid capsizing my own narrow canoe. The youngsters also seemed too much in shock to follow instructions. They didn't seem to be in immediate danger, so I took the simplest course. After tying my emergency rope to his boat's bow, I asked the swimmer to hold onto the stern of his boat while I towed it to shallow water. I did have a powerful double paddle onboard, which was really helpful in moving the combined mass of sunken kayak and soggy swimmer. They were lucky. Just a little later in the season, and hypothermia would have been a very real and unpleasant addition to the equation, especially if no one had noticed their plight. This story had a happy outcome. I could recount other stories that did not.

It is easy to be judgmental and say that they should not have ventured so far out without safer boats, safety instruction, emergency equipment, or supervision. But many new canoes and kayaks are sold to folks who have no idea what hazards and limitations may be involved. They may not know where to get safety information and rescue training, and they may not understand that training is prudent. Many folks assume that canoeing or kayaking is simply pulling on a paddle and that a life jacket magically removes all dangers.

It certainly would have simplified things if those boys could have done the instinctive thing and just climbed back in over the side. Heck, I wished that I could do that myself! An outrigger canoe, large inflatable boat, or sit-on-top kayak would do. But those boat options are rather special purpose and not very practical for many of the things we like to do with our canoes, such as carrying them on the car roof, portaging, handling twisty rivers, and negotiating shallow rocky and weedy areas as well as crossing bigger waters. Detachable outriggers are available but add weight, cost, and complexity. I realized that it would be ideal to be able to just make an unaided deep water reentry into the canoes and kayaks we already use and like. It was this experience, and others like it, that led me on my path to experiment with new self-rescue methods and to develop my flotation system to make canoes and kayaks safer.

Paddle Floats for Kayaks and Canoes

For narrow sea kayaks and whitewater kayaks, the Eskimo roll is the antidote to an upset in deep water. After overturning, the paddler remains seated and rolls the boat back upright with a paddle stroke. With a good sprayskirt and well-honed skills, this is quick and effective. But not all kayaks or paddlers can perform an Eskimo roll, and sometimes it is not possible or safe to stay in the boat. Even paddlers who are skilled at rolling may sometimes fail in the attempt. The response to an inability to roll upright, for whatever reason, is a wet exit, which is just what it sounds like! The paddler becomes a swimmer.

Reentering a swamped or capsized solo canoe or kayak in deep water is generally impossible without assistance or rescue equipment. The paddle float is a simple device that makes unassisted self-rescue possible for sea kayakers. The float is attached to one blade of the paddle, while the other blade is attached to a properly rigged kayak deck. The combination of float and paddle serves as a temporary outrigger, making the kayak stable enough that a paddler can, with practice, climb in over the side. I always have a paddle float secured to the deck of my sea kayak.

The most common paddle floats are inflatable bags with a pocket into which you slip one blade of a double-bladed kayak paddle and then inflate the air chambers. Some floats are made of closed-cell foam with an attachment for the paddle. Foam floats are heavier and bulkier but are faster to use since inflation is not required.

Using the float involves attaching the opposite end of the paddle to the kayak, so that the paddle sticks out at a 90-degree angle from the boat's centerline, with the float held out to the side 6 feet or so.

The paddle float should be stored very securely in a convenient place where it can be easily accessed after a wet exit. Take the float and slip it over one paddle blade; then inflate it. Force the other paddle blade under the deck rigging. Many kayaks have strong bungee cords fastened on the rear deck, just behind the cockpit coaming, precisely for this purpose. With the temporary outrigger in place, position yourself on the outrigger side of the kayak toward the bow of the outrigger and grip the paddle shaft with one hand and the coaming in the middle of the kayak with the other. Pull your chest up onto the paddle and rear deck with your face down and your head toward the rear. It helps to get one leg onto the paddle shaft while the other goes into the cockpit. When both legs are in the cockpit, carefully roll your body upright and lower yourself into the cockpit and into the seat. At all times, maintain your weight on the outrigger side of the boat to avoid capsizing in the opposite direction.

If there is water in the kayak, you'll next need to pump or bail most of the water out while the outrigger is still in place to provide stability and prevent another capsize. Only then can the paddle be retrieved so you can continue on your merry way. Notice that all of this requires that the deck be rigged with shock cord; that you hold onto the paddle or have it on a leash; that you be able to reach and inflate your paddle float; that you are dressed to survive at least temporary full immersion; that you have some way to bail; and that you be in practice and keep your wits about you. It isn't all that speedy, but it may provide a way to survive.

Additionally, the kayak must have adequate flotation in the ends to keep the boat afloat and level front to back while you reenter. Most sea kayaks with watertight compartments have adequate flotation, assuming that any hatches don't leak too fast. Other kayaks may have some foam in the ends but may benefit from installing larger flotation bags inside the bow and stern. Assume nothing. Test to be sure.

Many years ago, I experimented to verify that the same techniques work very well with canoes, and for a long time all my solo canoes have been rigged to take advantage of the paddle float. Surprisingly, I've never seen anyone else do this. But it is very easy to rig a canoe to use a paddle float. (See Figures 15.2 and 15.3.) I attach ¼-inch shock cord to each gunwale immediately behind the seat. An easy way to do this is to drill two holes in each gunwale about 7 or 8 inches apart. Pass the cord through both holes and tie it off so that the cord is tight but will stretch enough to allow the paddle blade to pass between the cord and gunwale. If you prefer, you can screw web loops or other tie-down fixtures to the insides of the gunwales to avoid holes and cords through the gunwales. (Making web loops is described later in this chapter.) Using the float does require a double-blade paddle. I like using a double-blade paddle in solo canoes anyway. When paddling with a single-blade paddle, I carry a double-blade paddle as a spare and an outrigger. For wilderness paddling, a spare paddle is on the required equipment list anyway. An ultralight, two-piece paddle stows easily. Have it securely fastened in the boat but easy to reach.

Most solo canoes have a thwart just behind the seat. This provides another option for holding the paddle outrigger firmly in place. In fact, I've successfully tested and practiced deep water reentries by securing the outrigger paddle only to the center thwart with rope or bungee cords. But it is wise to have some rigging already in place. The paddle will be more secure if you can lash it to the thwart in addition to slipping it under shock cords at the gunwales. I make bungee loops with handles for this, but the ball-bungee loops

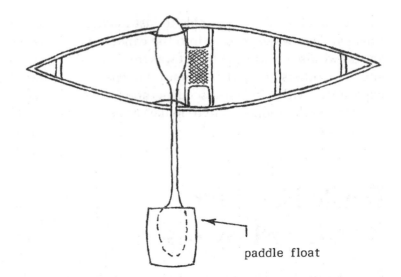

paddle float

FIGURE 15.2. *Top view of a solo canoe with a double paddle and a paddle float attached in the outrigger position.*

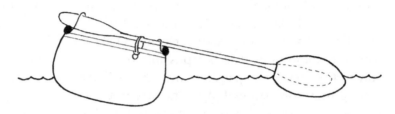

FIGURE 15.3. *End-view cross section of a canoe with a double paddle and a paddle float in the outrigger position. The paddle is attached to the gunwales and the center thwart with shock cord.*

found in camping stores work quite well. Leave one or two fastened to the thwart at all times, and you'll be good to go. Rig your gunwale shock cord to hold the paddle near the center thwart so that you have the option to use both the gunwale cords and the thwart cords at the same time.

To use a paddle float with a tandem canoe, rig the cord to hold the paddle outrigger near the center of the canoe so that you can reenter near the widest part of the canoe. That is probably where the center thwart is, and it may be enough to rig the thwart with bungee loops.

Be aware that to use the paddle float outrigger with a tandem canoe you will need to carry a kayak paddle or a pole of suitable length, perhaps 8 feet long. Don't guess. Experiment and practice first in shallow, warm water to make certain it will work for you when you really need it. If you paddle your tandem with a partner, you will have other rescue options not covered here. You can learn tandem canoe rescue methods from books, videos, and safety classes. (See Appendix B.) Even so, it may be very helpful to also have the paddle float option.

Canoe reentry starts with securing the float to a paddle blade. Pass the other blade under the shock cord on the near gunwale, and continue to pass it under the shock cord on the opposite gunwale until the tip of the blade extends several inches beyond the far gunwale. Additionally or optionally, you may lash the paddle shaft to the thwart. If the boat is not level, you may find it is easier to get the paddle in place first and then attach the float and inflate it. The outrigger won't prevent the canoe from rolling unless the paddle shaft is held firmly to the gunwale. Hold the paddle shaft and gunwale, or the paddle shaft and thwart, firmly together with one hand while you reenter the canoe similarly to the kayak procedure.

Reentering a canoe with a paddle float outrigger is slightly easier than reentering a kayak because you don't need to fit yourself into the small cockpit opening. However, to be safe and successful, you may need more flotation than came with your canoe from the manufacturer. If you have an ABS, Royalex, plastic, or aluminum canoe without end flotation, I suggest installing inflatable canoe end flotation bags in both bow and stern, as described below. If you have a Kevlar or fiberglass canoe with flotation chambers built into the ends, the flotation may or may not be sufficient to support the ends while you reenter the water-filled canoe. Be certain to test under the worst-case scenario with the canoe filled with water.

Inflatable paddle floats are light, compact, and store easily, while solid foam floats are heavier and bulkier but do not need to be inflated. Both kinds are available at kayak shops, outfitters, and through mail order and online sources, such as NRS. Pakboats, a maker of canoes and kayaks,

sells a convenient paddle float that is also a dry storage deck bag. (See Appendix A for these and other sources.) It may be safer because it doesn't need inflation and stays attached to the side of the kayak until after the paddle blade is inserted. It has worked well for me in tests, and I like the handy extra storage. I recently read about experiments with a kayak paddle with highly buoyant blades: the Buoyant Safety Paddle. (See Appendix A.) It is said to provide the reentry benefits of a paddle float with greater convenience and simplicity. It is an interesting idea.

With all these devices, techniques, and rigging, you must test them yourself and practice on your own until you are confident you can perform a deep water reentry under the most difficult conditions you expect to encounter. Don't forget that these methods may get you back in the boat but won't solve whatever condition caused you to capsize or wet-exit in the first place.

Installed Flotation

Although the paddle float outrigger is very useful, it is not ideal. It requires practice and some manipulation while in the water. The whole process of installing the outrigger while hanging on to the canoe in deep water, and then reentering, is relatively time consuming and may be much more difficult during the excitement, or panic, of a real emergency. In cold water you may not have enough time before hypothermia renders you helpless. And if the float or the paddle gets away from your grasp, you may be in deep trouble, literally. Cold water and bad weather aren't the only reasons to expedite reentry. When I'm cruising among alligators in Florida, I'd rather be able to immediately climb back into the boat and not have to fumble for several minutes attaching an outrigger.

One sees magazine advertisements for outriggers that attach more or less permanently to canoes for greatly increased stability. Other flotation aids attach to the outsides of canoe hulls below the gunwales. All of these, however, interfere in some way with the performance of the boat and the ease of paddling and use. Most add too much weight and complexity. Outriggers are subject to getting hung up on weeds, brush, rocks, and trees in the water or on the portage trails. They may provide benefits for the physically impaired and for some anglers with unruly children or dogs. However, for a majority of serious paddlers, the compromises are unacceptable.

I wanted something better, something faster, easier, simpler, and lightweight as well as safe. The most elegant solution was to provide a permanently attached "outrigger" that works inside the canoe—an "inrigger," if you will. In my canoes, flotation inside the hull, beneath the gunwales, provides some of the roll stability of an outrigger. The flotation is at the sides, away from the centerline, and located along the widest part of the hull.

In Figure 15.4, drawing A shows the end-view cross section of a canoe with antiroll flotation. With no water in the canoe, it will behave normally when tipped. In drawing B, a loss of balance, or weight applied to the gunwale, tips the canoe. However, with water in the canoe, as in drawing C, the flotation is partially submerged. This provides lift or buoyancy and a "righting moment" that resists further tipping or rolling. The resistance continues even if the gunwale is under water.

When the antiroll flotation is sufficient and properly located, it provides two great advantages: it resists capsizing when swamped, and it allows unassisted deep-water reentry in the case of a capsize and wet exit. The extra flotation also helps keep a swamped boat afloat and displaces water so that less bailing is required. It floats some hulls high enough to prevent the canoe from filling with much water if it has to be righted from an upside-down position. Since all of the flotation is inside the hull, it

will have no influence on the canoe's normal handling. Without water inside it, the boat will still tip over just as easily as ever! The "inrigger" flotation benefits occur only when there is water inside the boat. Only then is water displaced by the flotation so that the flotation "floats" and provides additional buoyancy. (See Figure 15.5.)

Note that when a canoe without antiroll flotation is swamped with water inside, it rides deeper in the water. The reduced freeboard, or distance between the waterline and the top of the gunwale, leaves little remaining resistance to roll, and capsize is imminent. Even if you could reenter, you would merely capsize and exit again.

A few kayaks and canoes have side flotation integral to their design. These include inflatable boats with side tubes as well as some of the pack-

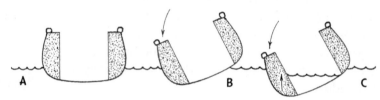

FIGURE 15.4.
A. *End-view cross section of a canoe hull with internal side flotation.*
B. *The canoe tips or rolls left.*
C. *With water inside, the flotation resists tipping.*

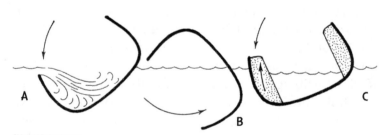

FIGURE 15.5.
A. *A loss of balance or weight at the gunwale causes the canoe to tip, or roll, and flood. Waves or leaks can also cause flooding, which greatly reduces roll stability.*
B. *When there is enough water in the canoe, stability is lost and the canoe rolls and capsizes.*
C. *When side flotation is installed, water in the canoe causes the flotation to submerge, which provides buoyancy and resists capsizing.*

able skin-on-frame boats that are tensioned by inflated air tubes in the sides. Inflatable boats and collapsible skin-on-frame boats that require assembly do not appeal to everyone, and many of the good ones are costly, but they travel and store conveniently packed into a duffle bag and some of them are reasonable in price.

I own one such reasonably priced skin-on-frame boat, a 12-foot Puffin kayak made by Pakboats (see Appendix A) that has a 28-inch beam and long side air tubes that provide excellent flotation in the sides and the ends. The flotation is configured so that one can use the reentry procedures described in the section "Testing and Self-Rescue Procedures" later in this chapter. This should work with some of the other wide-beam kayaks and canoes made by Pakboats and perhaps with other makes and models having similar air tube configurations.

Side flotation by itself is not enough to guarantee recovery. Without flotation in the ends to keep the canoe level, it will be unstable in pitch (fore and aft) when swamped. Reentry using the side flotation results in a lot of residual water in the boat. You will be unable to balance the boat fore and aft, and either the bow or stern will dive underwater. I've rigged some canoes with enough flotation in the sides to enable reentering only to find that pitch instability made them impossible to balance, bail, paddle, or control. I was safer swimming in the water! Unassisted reentry requires four-point flotation—left, right, bow, and stern. It is possible to extend the side flotation into the ends to provide this. It works in the Puffin kayak mentioned earlier. But it is simpler and will intrude less on interior space to deal with the four points of flotation separately.

Obviously, the interior of a canoe or kayak must have space in the right places to accommodate the flotation. Since the ends are rather narrow, they are not very useful for storage of gear, but they do contain sufficient volume that can be devoted to flotation. Even with flotation installed at all four points, all my gear for several weeks of camping and fishing still fits in my solo

canoes, from small, 12-foot boats to long wilderness trippers.

Outfitting and Modifying Existing Boats

Some owners object to making additions and modifications to their boats, especially if they consider the changes visually unattractive or nontraditional. But I suspect that the early native paddlers who risked their lives in walrus-hide kayaks and birchbark canoes would have loved our modern flotation. With care and creativity you can make the flotation look good, and it will go a long way toward keeping you and your beloved canoe together.

End Flotation

Some Kevlar and fiberglass canoes have small flotation chambers built into the ends. In combination with antiroll flotation, they may provide enough pitch stability for reentry. In addition, ultralight Kevlar and composite canoes often have a thin layer of foam sandwiched between the cloth and resin layers in the bottom of the hull, and some manufacturers mention this as a flotation benefit. The truth is that this foam sandwich is primarily a convenient way to manufacture hulls that are both lightweight and rigid. It offers a little flotation but not in the best location for safety. When the canoe fills with water, the bottom wants to float—and if there is no buoyant flotation in the sides, it may become more stable upside down!

Also, the rigidity makes the boat a bit brittle and delicate unless heavily built. I really love my ultralight Kevlar canoes for their intended uses, but it is wise to understand their limitations. If you have such a canoe with built-in end flotation, you will want to add the side antiroll flotation first and test to find out whether you need more end flotation. The side flotation will offset the buoyant bottom, providing much better stability when swamped.

If you have a wood, plastic, ABS, Royalex, or aluminum canoe without flotation in the ends, you will almost certainly need to add end flotation. ABS, Royalex, and cedar strip hulls are naturally buoyant, and some paddlers assume this qualifies as sufficient flotation. It might prevent a swamped boat from sinking to the bottom of a lake but, when filled with water, such hulls won't float a passenger safely and won't float the boat high enough to avoid obstructions and damage on moving water.

Inflatable flotation bags are readily available at a reasonable cost and are probably the easiest and lightest-weight option. Bags of many sizes and configurations exist to fit most kayaks and canoes. Small end bags are enough to provide sufficient end flotation in a four-point flotation system to permit reentry in nonwhitewater conditions. The small end bags made for tandem canoes also work well in solo canoes, assuming your uses will include only mild, class 2 whitewater. This should leave room for camping and fishing gear even in relatively small canoes. If you are outfitting a canoe primarily for demanding whitewater, you will want to sacrifice storage space for larger flotation bags. A good source of flotation bags and the hardware to fasten them in the boat is NRS. (See Appendix A.)

Installing bags under the decks into the ends of a kayak or decked canoe is straightforward. They can be held in place by tying them to screw-mount tie-down brackets or nylon web loops that are attached inside the kayak with the same screws that hold exterior shock cord deck rigging. If you don't already have deck rigging, you may want to add some anyway. Figure 15.6 describes how to make a web loop. Nylon webbing is available in many sporting goods stores and from kayak outfit-

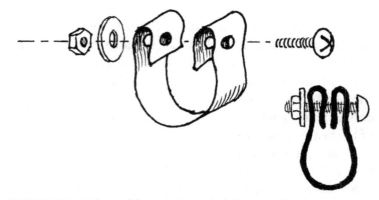

FIGURE 15.6. *Nylon web loop tie-in, exploded view and end view. Use ¾-inch-wide nylon web material and stainless steel machine screws and nuts. Start with a piece of webbing 5 to 6 inches long. After cutting, melt the ends with a candle flame to seal them from unraveling. To make the holes, melt them with a heated nail. Hold a large nail in pliers or a vise grip, and heat the tip in a candle flame. Enlarge holes until the screw fits.*

ters and suppliers, such as Chesapeake Light Craft. (See Appendix A.)

In open canoes, the flotation bags are useless if they are not fastened securely down into the boat. They must not float up away from the bottom of the canoe, or they will not float the boat as high as possible. The end bags should also be firmly pulled into the bow and the stern by the tie-down cords. To attach the cords, drill holes through the gunwales or use web loops or screw-mount tie-down brackets every 6 inches or so alongside the flotation bags. I use ⅛-inch nylon line or 3 mm lacing cord to make a cross lattice between the gunwales to hold in the bags. (See Figure 15.7.) You could also glue a D-ring patch to the floor of the hull to provide a tie-in point at the wide end of each wedge-shaped bag. (See the next section for more on installing D-ring patches.)

Inflatable bags do require some attention. They will last longer if they are not overinflated. This can happen when they are heated by exposure to sun or as temperatures warm during the day. Let out some air as needed. It is also good practice to deflate them for storage. Inflation valves, tubes, and connections have been known to fail and should be tested and inspected before and after each outing.

Side Flotation for Solo Canoes

Side flotation provides the resistance to roll and is the heart of outfitting for reentry. I offer guidelines and recommendations based on what has worked in the boats I've tested. It is easy to perform an installation, test it, and make changes or add more flotation until tests are successful.

About 0.8 cubic foot of flotation per side has worked well for me in all of the canoes and kayaks I've outfitted so far. This displaces about 50 pounds of water. More flotation is better, especially for heavier paddlers. I've successfully used as little as 0.6 cubic foot in some boats. The flotation does not need to support your weight; it only has to resist rolling over when a gunwale is submerged as you reenter. Hull designs, available space for flotation, reentry technique, and the paddler's body size and weight all have an influence. The goal is to get as much flotation as possible into the areas where it will be most effective and still leave room for comfort and cargo. The good news is that it need not add much weight to the boat.

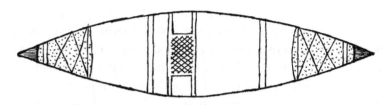

FIGURE 15.7. Top view of a solo canoe with end flotation bags tied in place.

Unfortunately, there is no ready-made inflatable flotation for the sides like there is for the ends. Those building a new boat may prefer to construct flotation chambers integral with the hull, as described below. (See Figure 15.8.) Those retrofitting existing boats have some easy-to-use options. Rigid, closed-cell polystyrene insulation foam (or Styrofoam) carved and cemented in place works okay, especially where it is not too exposed to bumps and abrasion. It comes in a variety of types and thicknesses at your local building supply store. You want the closed-cell foam, which in my local stores is blue. Saw or carve pieces of foam to fit inside the hull in the locations shown in the illustrations later in this chapter. It works fine to assemble short sections, or long narrow sections, into the long flotation areas required. Glue in at least 0.8 cubic foot of foam per side. Make shallow water tests as

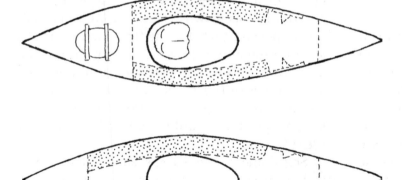

FIGURE 15.8. Kayak flotation. At the top is a kayak with a rear hatch and a large storage/flotation compartment built in. The side flotation, indicated by stippled shading, is extended as far to the rear as possible. Side flotation should also be extended as far forward as possible while leaving room for feet and foot braces. At the bottom is a kayak without a rear hatch. After end flotation is installed, extend the side flotation as far to the rear as possible. For solo reentry into a swamped kayak, you want to have a lot of flotation in the rear. You will have to get much of your body weight onto the rear deck in order to get your legs into the cockpit. And the more flotation you have, the less bailing you will have to do.

described later in this chapter in the "Testing and Self-Rescue Procedures" section. The foam can be sealed with epoxy, or covered with fiberglass, and painted to make it more durable and better looking in exposed areas.

Expanded urethane foam is another convenient flotation material. Construct partially enclosed areas from composites and/or plywood to fill and pour in the liquid foam, which expands and solidifies after mixing. Density is typically about 2 pounds per cubic foot, although some foams as light as 1.2 pounds per cubic foot are available. Two cubic feet will be enough for both sides of one canoe or kayak. It can be cut, filed, sanded, and sealed or covered with epoxy and fiberglass. It must be held firmly in place. Cost is reasonable. Some sources of boat flotation foams are listed in Appendix A.

Other interesting and more convenient options are available. While swimming in a friend's pool, I discovered something laughably simple, cheap, and effective. Foam "swim noodle" cylinders are made of flexible, closed-cell polyethylene foam and are durable and lightweight. They are sold in pool supply stores, seasonally in many chain stores including K-Mart and Wal-Mart, and online and by mail order. (See Appendix A.)

One common swim noodle form is a cylinder 4 inches in diameter and 58 inches long. (See Figure 15.9.) This is what I use most often. These forms can be simply tied into place in the boat (as shown in Figure 15.10) and are so convenient and easy to install that I recommend experimenting first with swim noodles for side flotation outfitting. Installing two of these per side provides

about 0.79 cubic foot of flotation per side, which has been sufficient in all of my solo canoes and kayaks.

You may find other diameters and lengths that can be used if they add up to similar volume. Appendix C lists data and formulae for calculating flotation volume and buoyancy of cylinders. Sometimes different sizes can be combined to fit available space better, such as using two or three noodles with a diameter of 2.5 inches instead of one with a diameter of 4 inches. And they can be cut with a band saw or a sharp knife into strips of different cross-sectional shapes. I rip long strips in different shapes to fit in the crevasses around the full-size noodles, adding as much extra flotation as I can. Their flexibility allows curving them to fit hull shapes.

If they fit, I simply tie two 4-by-58-inch foam cylinders into each side in the interior of the canoe. They are placed at the widest part of the hull, which is where they are most effective at resisting roll (as shown in Figures 15.10 and 15.11). It is important that the side flotation extends as low into the hull as possible but not toward the centerline. This will provide some roll resistance before the boat tips too far when swamped. It is also important that the side flotation extends as high as possible toward the gunwales or tops of the sides.

Solo canoes and kayaks should have their seats near the center and the widest part of the hull so that the paddler's weight is balanced in the boat fore and aft. This is also where the side flotation is most effective and important. In many recreational kayaks, the foam cylinders

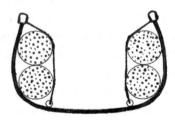

FIGURE 15.10. *Canoe end cross-section view with side flotation cylinders tied in.*

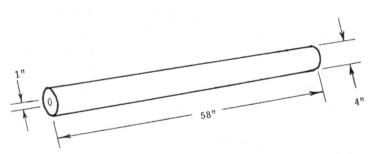

FIGURE 15.9. *Swim noodle flotation cylinder showing the center hole.*

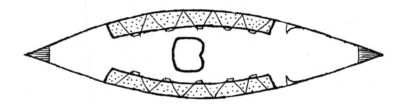

FIGURE 15.11. *Solo canoe top view with side flotation cylinders tied in.*

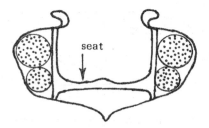

FIGURE 15.12. *Kayak end cross-section view with side flotation cylinders.*

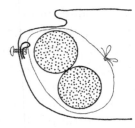

FIGURE 15.13. *Detail of cylinders being tied to a web loop tie-in. Cylinders should be held tightly to the hull side and deck. This makes a lightweight installation.*

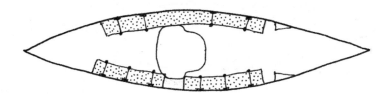

FIGURE 15.14. *The left side of the kayak (at top) shows cylinders held in place by the seat mount and four tie-in points. The right side of the kayak (at bottom) shows six tie-in points. Use six tie-in points if the seat mount will not hold the cylinders in place or if the cylinders must be cut in half in order to fit in front of and behind the seat mount.*

will fit outboard of the seat and may be held in place in the center by the seat mounting. (See Figure 5.12.) The ends of the cylinders, which are not held by the seat mounting, will need to be secured by tying them together and in place against the sides of the hull. They should be tied to web loops or tie-down brackets screwed to the inside of the hull above the waterline (as shown in Figure 15.13). Provide at least four tie-in points per side. (See Figure 15.14.) Use stainless steel machine screws and locking nuts with the heads on the outside of the hull and the nuts on the inside. An optional dab of silicone sealer can be placed under each screw head before tightening in place.

If the cylinders do not fit outboard of your kayak seat, then cut the cylinders to mount in front of the seat and behind the seat. You will need two or three tie-in points for each front section and rear section. In some kayaks there may not be space to fit two 4-inch-diameter cylinders per side. Try combinations of 4-inch

and 2.5-inch cylinders. Cut some cylinders into smaller strips of different cross sections to fill the side volume as much as possible. They cut easily with a band saw, a handsaw, or a sharp knife. Calculate or estimate the volume of the foam pieces, and try to get 0.8 cubic foot or more per side. Carve foam to fill any space outboard of the seat. You can also plug the center holes in the swim noodles to maximize their flotation volume. Carve plugs about 3 inches long from foam scraps, coat the holes with silicone sealer, and insert the plugs.

For a more secure installation in some kayaks, you may need to tie in the cylinders at the top and bottom (as shown in Figure 15.10). Use web loops or tie-down brackets at the top and D-ring patches in the bottom. The D-rings add a little more weight but control the position of the cylinders very well. If the seat mount holds the middle of the cylinders in place, or if you can tie to the bottom of the seat or mount, then one D-ring in front and one behind the seat on each

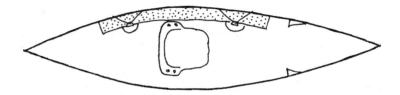

FIGURE 15.15. *Kayak D-ring locations and tie-in points for cylinders when the seat mount can hold the cylinders in place.*

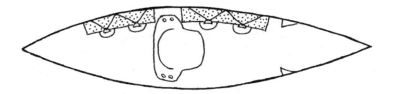

FIGURE 15.16. *Kayak D-ring locations when the cylinders must be cut in sections to fit. Four per side may be required.*

side will suffice. Use two tie-down points at the top for each one in the bottom, and angle the tie-down cord as shown in Figure 15.15. Figure 15.16 shows a kayak with four D-rings per side.

I tested a typical small, plastic, recreational kayak 10 feet long by 27 inches wide that was outfitted with flotation bags in the ends and two cylinders providing 0.79 cubic foot of flotation per side. The remaining space was quite comfortable for a paddler and some storage. Reentry over the sides was surprisingly easy, and reentry over the ends was also successful. Stability when swamped was good, although it floated low in the water. Kayaks that are a bit narrower, or that have slightly less room for side flotation, might also be successfully outfitted for reentry, but this may not work if they are significantly narrower. So far, I have not tested boats narrower than 27 inches.

If you are outfitting a solo canoe with a bench seat, fit the noodles around the seat as necessary. Cut and shape the noodles if you have to, but try to preserve as much flotation near the seat as you can. Some solo canoes have tractor-style seats that mount to the floor instead of wide bench seats that mount to the sides or gunwales. The

floor-mounted seats make it particularly easy to fit the flotation.

Because the flotation must be dependable in an emergency, the installation must be very secure. For 58-inch flotation cylinders in canoes, I use five tie-down points at the bottom and six at the top along the gunwales for each side. Skin-on-frame boats may have places to tie onto the frame, and hardware can be riveted to an aluminum hull. Holes can also be drilled through gunwales to accommodate tie-in rope; or web loops or tie-down brackets can be screwed to the insides of the gunwales.

At the bottom it will be necessary to attach fixtures to tie to. These can be D-ring patches, as mentioned earlier. Make certain that you use an adhesive that will bond well between your hull material and the patch. D-ring suppliers can help you choose the proper adhesive. For ABS or plastic hulls, a vinyl adhesive such as Vynabond works well.

Decide exactly where you want the D-rings to go, and mark the locations with a pencil. Next, hold a D-ring patch in place and trace a pencil line around the outside. Mark about an inch oversize. If you want to be especially neat, you can also use masking tape to mask around the area where the patch will go. Clean both the hull and the patch with alcohol. Apply adhesive to both surfaces to be bonded, and press them tightly into place. You may need to keep squeezing out air bubbles and pressing down the edges for a while until the adhesive starts to set. Do this operation outdoors, and wear a breathing mask that filters organic solvents. Let the bond dry a day or two before putting tension on the D-rings. Figure 15.17 shows an installed D-ring patch.

If you have a wood hull, or one made with fiberglass, Kevlar, or carbon fiber, then you have another option. You can save the cost of D-rings by making your own very strong fixtures from ½-inch-diameter plastic water pipe. If you have a

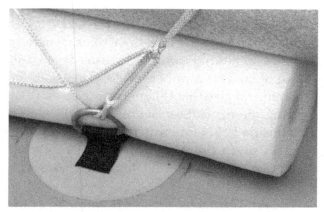

FIGURE 15.17. *D-ring and foam cylinder flotation installed in a Royalex hull.*

really beautiful wooden boat and the appearance of interior details is important, you can craft tasteful wooden fittings in place of plastic pipe and glue them to the hull. They can be shaped like the blocks for the paddle keeper cord shown in Figure 14.7 in Chapter 14. Give the blocks a large surface area for gluing.

Two feet of plastic pipe is enough to do one canoe. Cut a 2-inch length for each fixture. I cut each end at a 45-degree angle so that the cylinder wall of the pipe is 2 inches long on one side and 1 inch long on the other. Sand or rasp the long side until it is flattened and will not roll. This will be the down side, which will attach to the hull. Mark the fixture locations on the hull, and mask around them if you wish. The holes in the fittings should face fore and aft.

Epoxy and two or three layers of 6-ounce fiberglass repair cloth will hold the pipes in place. I especially like WEST System resin with 207 Hardener, which sets slowly and is ultraviolet resistant, but you can use any slow-setting fiberglass repair epoxy.

Getting a good bond will depend on preparation. Most factory-made canoes use polyester resin for fiberglass or vinylester resin for Kevlar. For an acceptable bond with your repair epoxy, you will need to sand the hull surface thoroughly. Use coarse sandpaper of 40 grit or 60 grit. It is okay to sand the resin down to the laminating cloth, but do not sand through it. It will be easy to

tell with Kevlar because it will turn fuzzy rather than sand off. Treat a fiberglass-covered wood hull as if it were fiberglass. For a wooden hull without a fiberglass cladding, sand through any paint or varnish. You may choose to finish-sand bare wood with 120-grit paper to remove coarse sanding marks. A rougher surface will provide a better bond over composites.

Cut fiberglass rectangles so that they will cover the full length of the pipe, blend into the hull along the cylindrical sides, and extend onto the hull at least 1½ inches on both sides. (See Figures 15.18, 15.19, and 15.20.) Cutting does not need to be precise. The fiberglass can be trimmed and sanded around the pipe holes after the epoxy sets.

To position the pipe sections, glue them in place with five-minute epoxy. After the epoxy has set, it is best to add the reinforcing cloth and resin to one fixture at a time. Start by mixing a batch of slow-setting epoxy, and thoroughly coat the hull area and pipe. Next, mix a small batch of epoxy with microfibers or sawdust to a thick, peanut butter consistency and use this to create

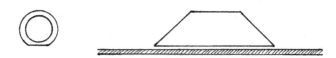

FIGURE 15.18. *Pipe tie-in fixture. On the left is an end view of the ½-inch-diameter pipe with the bottom sanded flat. On the right is a side view showing the flattened long side in place against the inside of the hull.*

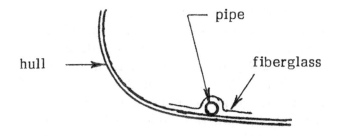

FIGURE 15.19. *Cross section of the hull, pipe, and fiberglass cloth.*

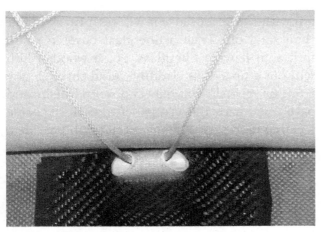

FIGURE 15.20. *Pipe tie-in fixture installed at a carbon fiber rib in a Kevlar canoe.*

a fillet between the cylindrical sides of the pipe and the hull. Lay a precut piece of fiberglass cloth in place, and smooth it into the wet epoxy. Push it down the sides of the pipe into the thickened epoxy, and fair it smoothly into the hull. Brush a layer of unthickened epoxy into the cloth. Do not trim the excess fiberglass around the angled pipe holes until after the epoxy sets dry to the touch.

You can move on to do the other fixtures and let the epoxy partially set. Before it cures entirely, come back and add a second layer of fiberglass cloth to each fixture. Finish off with another coat or two of epoxy. When it is cured, trim excess fiberglass and add two or three coats of paint or clear, ultraviolet-resistant varnish.

After the epoxy has set a few days, tie the foam cylinders in place with rope or shock cord. Use ⅛-inch nylon rope, which weighs very little and is easy to tighten, loosen, and untie to test different amounts of flotation.

A Kevlar canoe with built-in flotation in the ends can get by with a minimum of side flotation, and the weight of safety outfitting can be as little as 2 pounds. With the tie-in fixtures or D-rings well placed, you should be able to try different configurations and quantities of flotation without changing tie-in points. Check the foam flotation cylinders and ropes each season for deterioration and integrity, and replace them as needed. New ones are cheap insurance.

Side Flotation for Tandem Canoes

Tandem canoes are wider than solos, generally 33 to 40 inches in beam. The greater beam and length of tandem canoes provide more room for flotation and give that flotation more leverage or righting moment. (See Figure 15.21.) However, tandems do hold more water when they swamp, so fit as much flotation as you have room for. Water displaced by internal flotation is water you won't have to bail.

The limiting factor for side flotation in a tandem canoe will be how much space you require for cargo or for kneeling near the center when paddling solo. Enclose the volume of two or three large swim noodles, 0.8 to 1.0 cubic foot or more, in each of the sides at the widest part of the hull.

You might even extend flotation to the unused space under the seats. Swim noodles can be lengthened by doweling them together end to end through their center holes. Select a piece of plastic pipe or wooden dowel that fits the holes snugly, and glue it in place with silicone adhesive. A 6-inch dowel will extend 3 inches into each cylinder and lock them together. You might also place adhesive on the cylinder ends to be joined before pushing them together.

Whitewater Flotation

The guidelines for whitewater flotation are straightforward: fill all available volume with flotation! Whitewater can have air and air bubbles mixed, making the water less buoyant. Without maximum flotation, a swamped boat may not float high enough in the water to avoid damage from submerged rocks and objects. With a larger volume of flotation, a swamped boat will have less mass of water inside and will be easier to maneuver to safety.

A solo whitewater canoe may be outfitted with a foam pedestal and knee pads, and a kayak may have foam thigh pads and support pillars. These foam parts do not have the volume to constitute safety flotation. The ends must be filled as much as possible with flotation, and inflatable flotation bags are the handiest and most lightweight way to accomplish this.

For solo boats, choose end flotation bags that fill the areas in front of the feet and behind the seat. (See Figures 15.22 and 15.23.) In whitewater kayaks, there may be little volume left for storage, although a small dry bag can usually be stuffed somewhere. Storage float bags are available that combine the functions of both dry storage and flotation. Although they cost more, they allow efficient use of space in small kayaks. On the river you may be glad to have a dry lunch and a dry change of clothing as well as maximum flotation. Solo canoes generally have enough room for small dry bags behind the seat and between the feet or in front of the knees.

End bags for tandem canoes have to be small enough to fit behind the rear seat and in front of the bow paddler's feet (or knees when kneeling). A center float bag must fill the area between the two seats and leave enough room for the rear paddler's legs and feet. (See Figure 15.24.) For camping trips, dry bags of gear may be used to fill some of the center volume if they are tied down very well. However, some dry bags leak when submerged. On canoe camping trips, it is sometimes advisable to portage around rapids that might otherwise be run if the canoe were empty of gear and filled with flotation.

The side antiroll flotation can be just as handy for whitewater as it is for other paddling. Although one should always have companions when paddling whitewater, self-rescue flotation remains invaluable. There may be situations in which it is better to make a deep water reentry than to swim the boat to shore or wait for help. With sufficient flotation, it may even be possible to ride a swamped boat through rapids, which

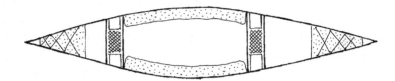

FIGURE 15.21. *Top view of a tandem canoe with end and side flotation chambers.*

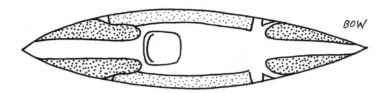

FIGURE 15.22. *Split flotation bags are available to fit on either side of center support pillars in the ends of some whitewater kayaks. If there are no pillars, a single large bag can fill each end. Side flotation cylinders are also shown. The deck is removed for clarity.*

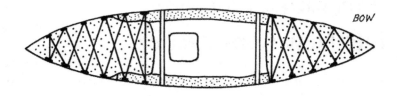

FIGURE 15.23. *A solo canoe with large flotation bags in the ends for whitewater. Side flotation cylinders are also shown.*

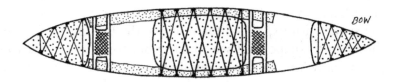

FIGURE 15.24. *A tandem canoe outfitted for whitewater. Small flotation bags fit into each end. A large center bag is tied between the seats in front of the rear paddler. Lengthened side flotation cylinders are also shown.*

is safer than swimming through them. If you do find yourself in the water, face downstream in a simulated sitting or reclining position with your feet high and pointed downstream out in front of you to fend off rocks. Keep the knees bent to absorb impacts. *Never* allow your boat to be upstream of you if you are thrown into the water. Get upstream and to the side of your boat so that it will not collide with you or pin you against rocks or obstructions.

As with the end flotation, fit as much side flotation as you have room for. In tandem canoes, tie in side flotation cylinders and extend them from under the front seat to under the rear seat. Swim noodles can be lengthened as described earlier. The center flotation bag can then be put in place and inflated to fill the remaining space between them. For flatwater use or camping, the center bag can be removed to make room for cargo. But leaving the side flotation in place will still provide resistance to capsizing if the boat should flood or if reentry becomes necessary.

Integrating Flotation into New Construction

Safety flotation can be attractively integrated into a boat during construction. This applies to most do-it-yourself methods of boat construction, including wood strip (also known as "stripper" or strip-plank), stitch-and-glue plywood, and composites like the Kevlar boats in this book.

You can use some of the methods and materials discussed earlier. You can build up flotation areas from plywood and composite materials, fill the space with expanded foam, carve the top of the foam to shape, and seal the top of the compartment with fiberglass. For lighter flotation, leave out the foam and build hollow chambers. Since built-in chambers strengthen the hull, weight can be reduced in other areas, such as gunwales, ribs, and hull thickness in sides, to keep overall weight low.

End Flotation

Most open canoes have rather small, short decks at the bow and stern. I build longer decks and place bulkheads between the deck and the hull sides to enclose end flotation chambers. The flotation volume increases dramatically as the chamber is extended farther from the ends and higher toward the gunwales. For solo canoes I typically build chambers that are about 30 inches long and as high as the gunwales. For comparison, the factory-stock chambers in my Kevlar Wenonah Advantage solo canoe are 20 inches long by 10 inches high.

I always carry cargo in packs toward the middle of the canoe, where it fits better and the weight rides better. So I don't mind sacrificing more end space to flotation. For tandem canoes you will need to leave enough room for the legs of the bow paddler, but the greater beam allows you to compensate with more flotation in the sides.

I've seen canoes with end flotation just in the bottom corners of the ends. This can make an overturned boat more difficult to turn upright while you are floating in deep water. After you have sacrificed the floor space, you might as well continue the flotation chamber up to the gunwales and get the maximum benefit.

For canoes, I make both the deck and the bulkhead from ½-inch-thick, rigid, polystyrene closed-cell foam insulation. Laminate the inside surfaces of the foam decks and bulkheads with two or three layers of 6-ounce fiberglass cloth and epoxy. After the epoxy sets, bond the decks and bulkheads into the hull with epoxy or thickened epoxy. Laminate three layers of fiberglass over the outsides of the decks and bulkheads. Let the fiberglass overlap at least 2 inches onto the hull from the bulkhead for secure attachment. Likewise, let the deck fiberglass lap 2 inches over the top and down the sides of the hull. If the gunwales are already in place, the fiberglass can lap right over them or, to save weight, the gunwales need not extend to the end—they can terminate alongside the decks. The fiberglass decks provide a lot of strength and abrasion resistance with little weight. Add at least three coats of epoxy over the fiberglass to ensure that it is watertight; then paint or varnish it to avoid deterioration from the ultraviolet radiation in sunlight.

If you are making a plywood or cedar strip canoe, you can install decks and bulkheads using the same methods. They can be painted or veneered in wood to match or contrast with the rest of the boat. Be creative. Long decks look great when they are curved side to side rather than flat. They can be readily formed with thin, flexible plywood and attractively trimmed with wood spray rails or a coaming. See Chapters 11 and 12 for more details.

End flotation in kayaks can be enclosed similarly with plywood or composite bulkheads. In kayaks or canoes, watertight hatches can be used to provide storage access to the end chambers, allowing them to be larger without sacrificing storage. This is the convention for sea kayaks. But cargo must be divided into small packs to fit through the hatches. For trips that involve portages, open canoes and decked canoes with large cockpit openings are far more convenient. Cargo can be carried in large backpacks that are ready for portaging. If you have hatches, do your best to make them watertight. Consider carrying small flotation bags inside the end chambers as insurance.

Side Flotation

Incorporating flotation molded into the sides is quite a bit more work. You may decide to save time and labor by using the foam cylinder flotation described earlier in this chapter. However, fiberglass or plywood chambers, either left hollow or filled with expanded foam, allow you to enclose volume more efficiently and to simultaneously stiffen the hull, reducing the need for ribs and heavy gunwales. And the boat interior will dry out more quickly than with foam cylinders. My preference is to build hollow side chambers from ½-inch rigid foam as described for end chamber bulkheads. This allows for extremely lightweight chambers. If possible, design each side chamber to enclose 0.8 cubic foot of volume or more.

To get the maximum flotation into the sides of solo canoes and decked boats, I make the central seating area as narrow as possible while keeping it comfortable for paddling. Vertical walls enclose the side flotation and define the seating area. For me a comfortable width is 19 inches, so my vertical walls are 19 to 20 inches apart. Paddlers of many sizes have been quite comfortable with that. The chamber walls are perfectly vertical, parallel, and equidistant apart at every point. At the fore-and-aft ends of each wall are bulkheads that attach the chambers to the sides of the interior hull.

The large interior vertical walls should be stiffened internally with layers of fiberglass or carbon fiber. If the walls are thin plywood, use wood battens. This will prevent the walls from deforming or warping, especially if you choose to mount movable seats on the walls. If you are building a decked canoe or kayak, the deck can close off and seal the tops of the chambers. For an open canoe, provide a flat top for the chambers immediately under the gunwales. Think of the possibilities for cup holders!

Structural side flotation chambers add stiffness and strength to the hull, so their added weight can be offset by weight savings in other parts of the structure. The hull can be thinner in the sides, and heavy gunwales are really not needed in the areas of structural flotation chambers. If your boat design calls for internal ribs, you can save weight by using fewer and shorter ribs. If one of your goals is manageable weight, even small savings can add up. For instance, Kayoo is 14½ feet long and in Kevlar weighs 28 pounds, including flotation, decking, adjustable seat, and portage yoke. It is quite strong and has survived numerous severe impacts with no damage.

Longer side chambers enclose more flotation volume, providing additional roll resistance and a greater safety factor. The prototype Kayoo has a beam of 29 inches with side chambers, built as above, that are 36 inches long. Each side chamber encloses a volume of 0.6 cubic foot and displaces 37.44 pounds of fresh water. Roll resistance is quite adequate but less than in later boats. Self-rescue is wonderfully successful, but more flotation makes reentry even easier and provides a greater safety factor for larger paddlers. Side chambers that are 48 inches or even 60 inches long would easily fit, providing the 0.8 to 1.0 cubic foot of volume that I prefer. Longer chambers don't interfere much with cargo space; all my canoe camping packs fit in the 20 inches between the chambers. At the front end, leave room for footrests and feet with hiking boots. I also leave room to attach rod holder tubes to the fronts of the chambers. At the rear there are no limits other than storage space. Keep in mind that with a narrower boat you would need longer side chambers to enclose sufficient volume. Also, the chambers would be closer to the boat's centerline and have a shorter lever arm to resist rolling. If you don't include enough flotation to begin with, you may need to add more later on.

If you are building a kayak, you will probably have a seat fastened to the floor. In a solo canoe, the seat can attach to the vertical walls of the side chambers if the walls are made extra stiff with braces or additional layers of fiberglass, Kevlar, or carbon fiber. My favorite way to support the seat is by attaching ledges to the walls on which the seat can rest. The ledges can be hardwood or 1-by-1-inch aluminum angle ⅛-inch thick. Screw and epoxy the ledges in place. Then add fiberglass to the tops and bottoms of the ledges overlapping 1½ inches onto the side walls. If the screws are left in place, let the fiberglass cover them and finish with several coats of epoxy to make them watertight. Figures 15.25, 15.26, and 15.27 show seats and supports; for more construction details, see Chapters 12 and 14.

For an open tandem canoe, I would complete the boat first and do some testing. It is easy to add permanent side flotation later in a tandem since side chambers need not influence the installation of seats and thwarts. Use foam cylin-

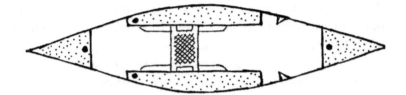

FIGURE 15.25. *The Kayoo decked canoe/kayak, top view with the deck removed to show flotation. The end and side flotation chambers show the drain hole locations as black dots. The seat slides fore and aft on rails attached to the side chambers.*

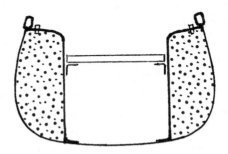

FIGURE 15.26. *End cross-section view of the side flotation chambers and sliding seat in a solo canoe.*

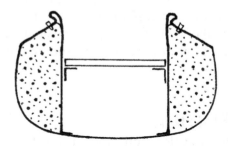

FIGURE 15.27. *End cross-section view of the side flotation chambers in a decked canoe or kayak.*

der noodles to fill to the volume you wish to test, and duct tape them in place under the thwarts. They can extend under the seats, which will hold the ends down. Test the reentry procedures in shallow water. If they don't work, let everything dry and tape in more foam. If and when you are satisfied with the compromise between recovery performance and storage space, permanently tie in flotation cylinders or build side chambers and fiberglass them in place.

Drain Holes and Plugs

Any hollow flotation chambers without hatches need to be fitted with drain holes and plugs. They allow chambers to be drained and dried for repairs if they leak. And stress and deformation that might be caused by altitude and extreme air pressure changes can be prevented. If chambers are strong, that shouldn't be much concern. But I unplug the drain holes when driving between lowland and mountains anyway. Air pressure inside can blow the plugs out, and I don't want to lose too many!

To determine where to locate the drain holes, place the boat upright and level on hull cradles or sawhorses. Locate and mark the highest points of each end flotation chamber. Drill the drain holes near those locations, so they will drain completely when the boat is upside down.

For the side flotation chambers, I like to ensure that the plugs will be out of the way so that I don't bump into them when paddling. In a solo boat, the best location is at the rear and in the corner of the chamber that is highest when the boat is upright. That corner will be inboard in a decked boat. See Figure 15.25, showing the drain plug locations in Kayoo. In a tandem canoe without a deck, interference with the side chamber plugs should be no problem. Place the plug in whichever corner is highest and least in your way.

The drain holes must be strong enough to accommodate the plugs and have a smooth internal finish. The holes should be in a material like fiberglass or hardwood and have a minimum thickness of $3/8$ inch. If the decks are thin plywood or fiberglass over foam, then harder and thicker drain hole pads are required. If the decks or tops enclosing the chambers don't meet that minimum, then epoxy a pad of hardwood or marine plywood over the spot where the drain hole will be located. The pad can be a disc 1½ inches in

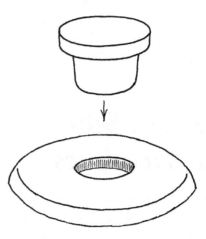

FIGURE 15.28. *A hardwood pad 1½ inches in diameter is glued on top of each flotation chamber to provide a hard point for the drain hole. The minimum thickness of the pad is ⅜ inch; the minimum hole diameter is ½ inch.*

diameter, as shown in Figure 15.28. If the pad is solid wood rather than plywood, put a layer of fiberglass over the outside of the pad to reinforce the hole area and prevent it from splitting.

Drill the drain hole in the center. Make a hole to match whatever size drain plugs you are going to use; this should be ½ inch in diameter or a little larger. Wrap sandpaper around a dowel or metal rod to sand inside the hole and round the top edge slightly. Give the pad and hole three or four coats of epoxy. Make certain that your plug will fit. You can carve a cork plug or, better yet, ream the hole out as necessary to fit a store-bought rubber plug and give the hole additional thin coats of epoxy.

The hardware sections of building supply stores may have some convenient rubber plugs. If not, check with boating and sporting goods stores. You'll find a variety of sizes and styles made for boat drains and live wells. My favorites, found at a building supply store, are rubber with brass screws that expand the plug to fit tighter. They hold tight and remove easily. Get a few extra. If you are like me, you'll lose a few. In a pinch, corks can be used to plug the holes. Check the chambers and plugs for leaks during testing. Listen for any water sloshing in the chambers whenever you carry the boat.

Testing and Self-Rescue Procedures

With your flotation outfitting completed, you will be excited to see how it works. Perform initial tests under the safest possible conditions. A swimming pool is fine for first reentry tests. Ultimately, you will want more room to test paddling maneuvers and performance limitations with water in the boat. When this time comes, pick calm, warm waters on a comfortable day with little wind. You may want to wear a wet suit if air or water temperature is cool. If you can arrange to have a safety companion during tests, by all means do so.

Before testing and rescue practice, give some attention to your most important piece of safety gear, the life jacket or personal flotation device (PFD). Wear one for all water testing. If you have an older PFD, you may be surprised by its performance—or lack of it. I once used the same life jacket for years before giving it an unexpected test. I was shocked to find that it did not allow me to swim! After a bit of experimenting, I was able to do a crude backstroke, which was not what I was hoping for. It also fit so loosely and poorly that it would not float my head above water. I had to grip it with my hands and hoist myself higher!

PFDs have come a long way since then. Look for a PFD with strong attachments and a lot of adjustment. Make certain it can be tightened well around the torso to keep it from riding up in the water. I like a PFD that can be easily and quickly tightened in the water if necessary. There are longer PFDs for canoeing and shorter ones to better suit kayaks. I especially like the fit and comfort of good kayak PFDs, and I use one for general paddling and fishing in both canoes and kayaks. PFDs with extra flotation are available for use in difficult whitewater.

Expect to pay more for a good PFD; it is worth it. Make friends with it. Give it a good inspection before each outing. You may have to trust your life to this piece of equipment, so don't wait until a real emergency to find out how well it works. Try it in the water; a swimming pool is ideal. Adjust it snugly, and learn to swim and maneuver in it. It absolutely must keep your head up and above water, even if you are unconscious. Remember, it doesn't do you any good if you aren't wearing it. Swimming ability and shallow water are no excuse for not using your PFD. People have been knocked unconscious on a gunwale or rocks and drowned in shallow water. Enough said.

A Phased Approach

I like to use a three-phase approach to solo reentry testing. First, I make some initial tests in shallow water, about waist deep. I attempt to reenter over each side and the ends. If it is more difficult over one side or the other, I'll make note of it. Second, if all goes well, I move out to shoulder-deep water, where I can make all my basic tests while floating but where my feet can still reach bottom if I have a problem. At this depth I roll overboard to simulate the experience of falling out of the boat. I also turn the boat upside down and try righting it while floating without my feet touching bottom. I test reentries over the side and end with the boat empty or partially swamped and again with the boat filled with as much water as I can get it to take on. You want to be familiar with worst-case scenarios as much as possible. Knowing the limits will help you make safer paddling decisions. I also try paddling the boat with whatever residual water remains in it after reentry, and I time how long it takes to bail.

If you encounter a failure or poor performance at any phase, stop. Try to determine the cause, correct the outfitting if possible, and test again. Continue on another day if necessary. Carefully check your flotation for leaks, especially any hollow flotation chambers.

When all is comfortable, I move on to the third phase. This is testing the most successful type of entry, usually over the side, in deeper water. It should be no different. But knowing that I cannot touch bottom puts a different edge on things. Practice keeping a cool head now, and it will be second nature in a real emergency. Absolutely do not do anything you are uncomfortable with; there is no reason to take the slightest risk during practice.

Reentry from the Side

Depending on hull configuration, your body weight and size might have some influence over the amount of flotation needed. I weigh 140 pounds, but paddlers who are much heavier have been successful with the same flotation that works for me. You can add more flotation, if needed.

Start tests by securing a paddle and something to bail with in the boat. Lash them out of the way but within easy reach, or secure them under kayak deck rigging. For bailing you can use a kayak bilge pump or the low-tech, ever-popular plastic bleach bottle with the bottom cut off. For extended trips in small open canoes, I use a collapsible water bucket, which weighs little and packs small.

Figures 15.29 through 15.33 illustrate the process for reentering an open canoe without a paddle-float outrigger. Reentering a kayak is similar except that you may need to shift a bit more toward the stern in order to fit your legs into the cockpit.

Some people might be inclined to try reentering the boat with their head toward the bow, but the method above works much better because it enables you to keep your weight lower and closer to the boat's center of buoyancy fore and aft. Reentry directly over the stern would, of course, place the head toward the bow. You can test whether or not this is possible for your boat and flotation.

For another perspective, Figures 15.34 through 15.36 (page 169) show what the reentry looks like from the side at water level.

What I've described sounds detailed. The truth is that if you just try to pull yourself into the boat in an instinctive manner, you will eventually figure out what works. The instructions above just make the learning curve easier and faster.

In a canoe, you will probably now be sitting with only your feet and ankles in the remaining water. In a kayak, a bit more of you will be in the water. Experiment with balance. The boat will not be as stable in roll as when empty of water. It may tip or heel easily until the point at which the side flotation becomes effective. But you should be able to balance and remain upright without difficulty. Test the stability by leaning side to side while trying not to tip over and out. Try to paddle with the water in the boat. It will be extremely sluggish but movable. You won't go fast with all that mass to move. But once in motion, it will continue slowly for quite a while. Test tracking straight ahead as well as turning and maneuvering. Then time how long it takes you to bail. During a real capsize, this information will help you evaluate the situation and decide whether to swim the boat to shore, reenter and paddle, or bail before paddling. You don't need to get all the water out to achieve near-normal performance and paddle to shore. But even a few inches of water might seriously affect initial roll stability.

If this combination of interior antiroll flotation and solo reentry has any downside, it is that water is required in the boat. You will definitely be left with some bailing to do. With a paddle-float outrigger, it is often possible to reenter without getting much additional water in the boat. But you will spend much more time out of the boat and may be in serious trouble if either the paddle or the float gets away from you. Fingers lose control quickly in cold water. Under most situations, I feel much safer and much happier if I can reenter quickly. With four-point flotation, the boat will be under control and you may bail at leisure.

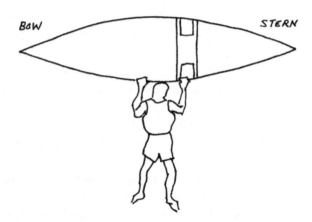

FIGURE 15.29. *Reentry, view from above. While floating in the water, position yourself facing the canoe near the wide, middle part. Grip the gunwale or coaming with both hands. Kick your feet to get your legs up near the surface of the water so that you are belly down with your head at the gunwale and your legs away from the boat at a right angle.*

FIGURE 15.31. *Get your center of balance over the center of the boat before trying to get your legs in. This requires getting your chest or abdomen over the center; your head might project beyond the far gunwale. Pull into position by holding the thwart, the seat, or the far gunwale. Grab the far gunwale with the hand that is toward the bow. Stay low to balance.*

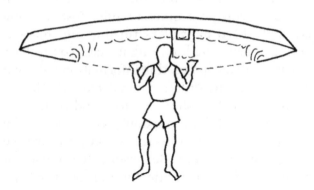

FIGURE 15.30. *Pull the gunwale down and just under the water so that water flows into the boat. Kick your legs to keep them up near the surface. If the legs are too low, reentry may be difficult or impossible. When there is enough water in the boat to make the flotation effective, you will be able to push down on the gunwale and kick and pull forward to slide over the gunwale, which will be underwater.*

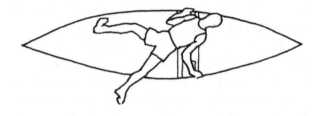

FIGURE 15.32. *Swing your legs one at a time toward the bow and into the boat while your head swings toward the stern to maintain roll balance. Try not to roll over and out the other side!*

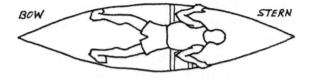

FIGURE 15.33. *You are now facing down in the boat or kneeling in front of the center seat or center thwart and facing the stern. Roll yourself upright and into the seat.*

After most of your body is out of the water, the risks of hypothermia are greatly reduced. You can deal more quickly with adverse wind and current or help others around you.

Righting the Boat

You will also want to test righting the boat in case it capsizes and remains upside down. It may float level and stable upside down on the four-point flotation. Generally, kayaks will easily roll upright. With canoes I usually duck under the gunwale and come up underneath the cockpit. You should find air to breathe there and need not be rushed. Then the boat can usually be righted by pulling down on one gunwale while pushing up on the other. Sometimes it takes bouncing up and down in the water while coordinating the push and pull.

Reentry from the End

Try a reentry over the stern or bow to learn if it is possible. Pull down on the end and pull yourself up on the deck, or push the deck into the water under you. Try to balance, straddle the boat, and work your way toward the cockpit and into the seat. A lot of water in the boat may be required to keep the opposite end from rising and the boat from rolling over. The boat may fill just from pulling the end down, or you may have to let some water in from the side first. Most of my canoes can be entered from the end. They usually take on a lot more water this way, so I normally default to the side entry. But it is good to know how different procedures may work for you in your own boats. With one of the kayaks tested, reentry from the end resulted in less water in the boat, but reentry over the side was much faster and required less effort.

Tests with Cargo

Gear may be tied into a boat loosely, securely, or not at all. The second and third choices both

FIGURE 15.34. *Solo reentry from the side with an end cross-section view of the canoe. Start by facing the gunwale in swimming position with your legs high.*

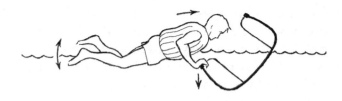

FIGURE 15.35. *Push the gunwale underwater and let water in until the flotation is effective. Then kick forward and pull yourself across the canoe.*

FIGURE 15.36. *Keeping the center of gravity as low as possible, pull your torso over the center of the canoe, balance the canoe, and get one leg at a time in.*

have their virtues, whereas the first is always a bad approach.

Much of the cargo that one carries in a canoe—such as dry bags of clothing, food, and camping gear—is lighter than water. During a capsize, packs that are not tied in may stay in the boat or float free and out of the way. (They rarely sink, even if they feel like they're loaded with bricks during portages.) If they float free, you can retrieve them after you have reentered the boat and have it under control.

Waterproof packs tied securely into the bottom can add flotation to the boat, and tie-in fixtures can be rigged to the gunwales and the bottom, or under decks, for this purpose. I have done a little testing reentering a swamped boat with packs lashed securely in place and had no problems. If you are concerned about the loads you carry, test with them or with simulated loads that are not valuable.

Packs that are merely tethered to the boat and not securely lashed down into the hull, on the other hand, can create a hazard if the boat rolls upside down. Wayward ropes and packs can get in the way of righting the boat or reentering. Gear should be tied in very securely or not at all. Before launching I try to imagine how hazardous, inconvenient, or uncomfortable it would be to capsize, get wet, and chase or lose my gear. Then I make my tie-in decision accordingly. An extra minute or two spent tying in packs is not so inconvenient.

It is possible to configure waterproof packs or dry bags to fit into the ends and be secured to perform the function of end flotation. I admit to having done this. But most dry bags are not designed for that purpose, and they do not seal well enough to guarantee staying leak free during total immersion. Unless you just cannot do without that extra cargo area, opt for the safety of dedicated flotation.

Troubleshooting

Following the outfitting guidelines just described, I have conducted successful tests with quite a variety of canoes and kayaks and found that outfitting for antiroll flotation seems to be somewhat forgiving. Requirements are few: Although more flotation is almost always better, 0.8 cubic foot of flotation per side seems adequate. Side flotation must be as far from the boat's centerline as possible, and the boat must be wide enough to provide sufficient leverage for the flotation. (As mentioned earlier, narrow kayaks may not be adaptable.)

If you have difficulty with reentry, first check your technique. If your legs are low, or dangling under the hull, reentry may be difficult or impossible. Also, the canoe might roll over if you push the gunwale down too far too fast or do not wait for enough water to enter the boat to make the side flotation effective. The gunwale needs to go down only far enough to let water in and for you to pull and kick yourself into the boat. Try to keep the boat from heeling over or rolling farther than necessary when reentering. (See Figure 15.37.) As you pull your legs back into the boat toward the bow, remember to stay low and keep your balance by moving your head and shoulders toward the stern and centerline. Otherwise, you may just roll out the other side of the boat!

Common outfitting problems are likely to include too little flotation or a poor configuration. If you do not have enough end flotation, it will be obvious. The boat will float low when swamped, and the bow or stern will try to dive underwater after reentry.

Side flotation is a little trickier. If side flotation is extended too far onto the bottom toward the centerline of the hull, the boat may try to roll upside down during reentry. Move flotation away from the centerline, or add more side flotation. Note that some flotation materials are denser than others. If your flotation is relatively heavy, it will have to displace more volume. Remember to subtract the weight of your flotation material itself from the weight of the water it displaces when calculating its flotation value or buoyancy.

Let me reiterate how important it is that flotation be secured adequately. I once fastened flexible foam noodles into the sides of a canoe just by the middles of the cylinders and left them unattached toward their ends. When they were submerged, they flexed upward enough to prevent reentry. Securing the ends of the cylinders into the canoe was all that was needed to achieve successful reentries.

Safety depends on preparation and good judgment. Inspect your flotation outfitting and safety equipment before paddling. Your carefully outfitted boat, the self-rescue skills you've acquired,

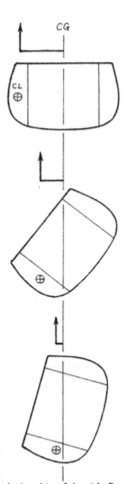

FIGURE 15.37. *Relationship of the side flotation center of lift (CL), or center of buoyancy, to the boat center of gravity (CG).*

At the top is shown the leverage of the side flotation CL relative to the vertical plane of the boat's CG when the boat is level. With the boat flooded with water but level, the lever arm is longest and the ability of the side flotation to resist tipping or rolling is good.

As the boat is tipped to reenter, the boat rotates about its fore-and-aft axis. The CL is now closer to the CG; therefore, the lever arm of the side flotation is reduced. But the side flotation is now fully submerged, providing maximum lift to aid reentry.

As rotation approaches 90 degrees, the CL approaches the CG. The lever arm of the side flotation shortens and approaches zero. At this point there is little righting moment, and the boat will very easily roll upside down. To facilitate reentry, keep rotation well short of 90 degrees and maintain some thrust into the boat by kicking with the feet and pulling with the arms.

and your confidence in using those skills will help to ensure that recoveries from upsets go smoothly and predictably. Practice is a vital element. Review your solo reentry techniques and retest your boats regularly. A good time to take a refresher is before a trip into a remote area or before that long-awaited paddling vacation. Sometimes a lovely summer day is a siren call to go paddling or swimming. Why not take advantage of that to work in a little safety practice?

Chapter 16

Three Canoe Designs (and How to Modify Them)

When Lewis and Clark explored the upper Missouri River, they met Native Americans paddling bull boats, curious round craft made with a single large buffalo hide stretched over a round framework of wood. It is difficult to imagine a less efficient and less controllable hull design than a round boat. But with these simple craft, the Indians could float on the river, and they served their purposes.

Choosing a design to build can be confusing. Sometimes all we really need is a way to get out on the water, but generally we would like to do more. A review of basic design features can help us decide what sort of canoe or kayak might mesh with our personal paddling interests.

There exists today a huge variety of craft propelled with paddles and no shortage of wonderful canoe and kayak designs to choose from. Each type has its own uses and advantages, from large but heavy oceangoing outrigger canoes and sea kayaks, to very small and delicate canoes so light that you can carry one for miles up a hilly trail to a high mountain lake, to rugged plastic and inflatable kayaks that make some of the wildest whitewater rivers safe (or at least feasible) to run.

While the canoes most of us need are somewhere between the extremes, even that useful middle ground offers a confusing array of hull shapes and sizes. A canoe suitable for fishing on a pond may be less than desirable for camping trips on large lakes or for running river rapids. Those who are new to paddling are often tempted to own a boat that feels very stable and secure on flat water, but these do not necessarily perform so well in other conditions. If in this situation, consider that you will be a beginner for a short time and that, if you are devoted to paddling, you may be an experienced veteran for a long time. If you are going to put in the time and effort to build your own boat, you may want to anticipate your own paddling goals and build one you can grow into.

I was delighted when I could afford to buy my first canoe. It was a wide and stable tandem. But I eventually wanted to paddle farther and faster with less effort. I wished that it wasn't so heavy and that it didn't get blown around so much by the wind when I paddled solo. When I acquired my first small solo canoe, it felt unstable and easy to tip because I had been used to paddling solo in large, bargelike tandems. However, before long that first solo canoe was again too wide, too slow, too stable, and too inefficient for the waters I wanted to explore. The canoes I chose as a beginner served me for a relatively short time. Boats that I built a little later are still a delight and may stay with me for a lifetime.

The designs included in this book are somewhat general in purpose. They should be suitable for paddlers of moderate and advanced experience and skills, and beginners will find them manageable, fun, and easy to paddle when the principles of design and of adjusting one's own boat are understood. For instance, stability is increased with a lower center of gravity, and you can begin by paddling your canoe from a kneeling position or from a temporary seat that positions you as low as comfortably possible. After you gain confidence and experience, the seat can be raised to a level that permits a better compromise between stability and the ability to lean or "heel" the canoe to carve turns more easily.

Design Features and Performance

Selecting a design is actually one of the most enjoyable steps of the building process. It is an opportunity to learn more about how canoes work, to reflect on your own paddling needs and styles, and to consider your paddling goals. Here are some basics of canoe and kayak design that you can consider and even use to modify the designs in this book.

Hull width or beam is a major consideration. Narrow hulls can be fast but may roll side to side more easily and capsize more easily than wider ones. Wide hulls are more stable and slower, but they make it more difficult to reach the water with a paddle. This is somewhat less a problem with tandem canoes, in which each paddler sits away from the wide center and closer to the narrow ends. But the solo paddler may be caught in the dilemma of choosing between paddling ease and stability.

One solution is for the soloist to paddle from a kneeling position, closer to one side for an easier reach with the paddle. In this position, a solo paddler can handle a large canoe and exercise a lot of control over it. On the other hand, kneeling may be uncomfortable for long paddling sessions, and many activities, such as fishing and photography, favor sitting.

Sitting has other advantages too. A double-blade paddle, which is very efficient and powerful, is always used while sitting, and a low, seated position is the most stable of all. A seat also allows the addition of a backrest for those of us with back issues.

Width is not the only feature that influences stability and speed. The cross-sectional shape of a hull plays a significant role in determining stability, handling, efficiency, and performance. The designs in this chapter all use versions of a shallow arch cross section (shown in Figure 16.1) to achieve a good blend of efficiency and stability.

The importance of cross-sectional shape extends above the waterline, as shown in Figure

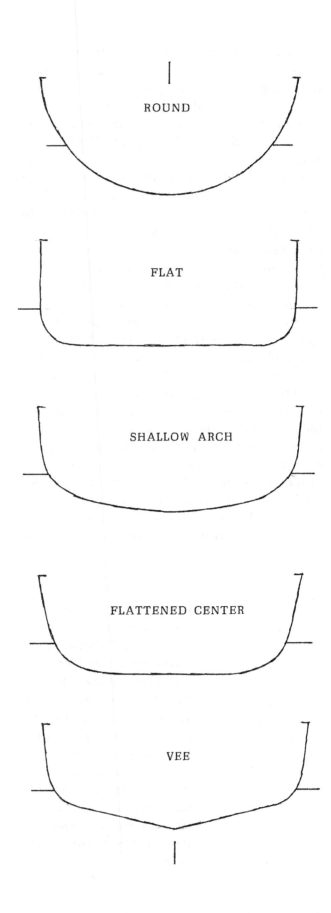

ROUND

FLAT

SHALLOW ARCH

FLATTENED CENTER

VEE

FIGURE 16.1. *Different cross-sectional hull shapes have different performance characteristics. The round shape at the top will have the least wetted area, or surface area in contact with the water below the waterline. This produces the least drag caused by friction between hull and water and tends to make it very fast. However, it has almost no resistance to rolling and capsizing and thus is not a good choice for a general-purpose canoe.*

The wide, flat bottom shape has the most stability and resistance to roll. However, waves from the side will easily lift and roll it side to side, making it uncomfortable or even hazardous on large lakes where wind and waves prevail. The flat bottom provides a lot of wetted area and drag but will float in the shallowest water. It has the least draft and is best at floating over shallow obstructions. Compared to other shapes, the flat bottom hull will weigh more, require more stiffening in the flat bottom, and be less efficient, which means it will take more paddling energy to produce speed. It won't be the best choice for paddling long distances on lakes. However, a flat bottom hull is easier to move sideways with draw and pry strokes, which is a plus for whitewater and river use.

A shallow arch hull is versatile. It provides a good compromise between stability and efficiency with minimal wetted area and moderate draft. It can be leaned or heeled in a controlled manner. This helps one maintain an upright position when struck by waves from the side and also aids in turning the boat.

A hull with a flattened bottom center and flare in the sides can provide some of the good attributes of both a flat bottom and a shallow arch. However, it doesn't match the efficiency and low wetted area of the shallow arch.

The Vee bottom hull will handle somewhat similarly to the shallow arch with some penalty in wetted area. The Vee provides good straight-line tracking and may resist turning. This makes it better for lakes than for small rivers and whitewater. Many hulls with other shapes will come to a Vee toward the ends to improve tracking and turn aside waves. The Vee has greater draft than most other shapes, making it more suitable for deep water. Abrasion and wear tend to concentrate at the apex of the Vee.

16.2. The shape of the hull below the waterline determines the boat's *initial stability*: its initial resistance to rolling away from horizontal. The shape above the waterline determines the boat's *secondary* or *final stability*: its ability to resist capsizing and return to the upright position after it has begun tipping. A hull with lots of flare above the waterline will have greater secondary stability. As the hull rolls to the side, the flared area, which encloses a lot of buoyant volume, comes into contact with the water and provides resistance to rolling farther. We might like to have a canoe that we can lean easily so as to stay level in rolling waves and to aid turning, but beyond a certain degree of roll we would like resistance to capsizing. This combination could be achieved with a hull with a round or arched bottom and flared topsides.

But as you can see, flare comes at a cost. The canoe is wider and will require a sitting paddler to reach farther to the side to paddle. This may require the paddler to sit higher and lean to the side, both of which reduce stability. It also places the paddle blade farther from the centerline of the boat, which will tend to make it turn when you want it to go straight and therefore require more energy and time for course correction, especially with a single-blade paddle.

Tumblehome is a solution for the open solo canoe. Instead of flaring, the hull gets narrower at the top between the gunwales. This enables you to place the paddle blade closer to the hull, where paddling is easier and more efficient and you are less likely to bang your elbows or the paddle on the gunwales. Notice that even with tumblehome, there can still be some flare; as shown in Figure 16.2, the tumblehome hull's widest point is still above the waterline. This allows the boat to be leaned, with resistance to rolling increasing as you lean for several degrees. But if you lean too far beyond that point, the boat will capsize abruptly as the flare disappears into tumblehome and buoyancy quickly diminishes. On the other hand, tumblehome allows the paddler to sit lower in the boat, thereby lowering the center of mass and gaining back some stability.

Instead of lowering the seat to gain stability, a canoe builder might choose to take advantage of tumblehome to raise the gunwales and gain more freeboard, the distance from the waterline to the top of the gunwales. Extra freeboard helps keep waves and spray out, and the extra depth also increases hull volume to carry more weight. Higher gunwales normally make paddling more awkward, but tumblehome reduces this difficulty. This modification especially suits large,

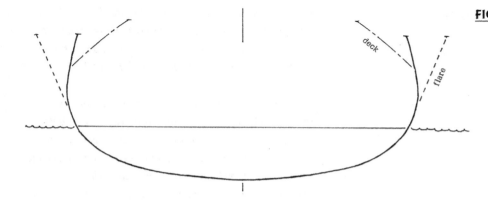

FIGURE 16.2. *When a hull gets narrower toward the top than at its maximum width or beam, it is said to have tumblehome. The solid line depicts a canoe hull with tumblehome. The dotted line shows a hull with flare; it gets wider toward the top. The interrupted line shows the hull shape when decked. From a seated position in a solo canoe, it is easier to paddle efficiently if there is tumblehome or a deck. The three solo canoe designs in this chapter all have some degree of tumblehome.*

heavy paddlers, those who want to carry a heavy load, and whitewater paddlers.

You can see from Figure 16.2 that putting a deck on the boat improves the picture even further. This is the kayak advantage. The paddler can sit even lower for greater stability while the deck keeps the water out, allowing for very low sheerline, where the hull meets the deck, and very easy paddling ergonomics, even with the low hand position typical when using a double-bladed paddle. With a low center of gravity, stability can be acceptable even if the hull is made narrow to achieve light weight and greater speed and efficiency. A deck adds complexity to a boat's construction, however, and increases its weight. If decks are low and the hull is narrow, then cargo volume will be small. Open canoes are handier for portaging and loading large backpacks. They are also generally lighter for their size and can be carried on auto roof racks without special kayak saddles.

One of the most visible features of a hull is its length. (See Figure 16.3.) Long hulls generally have a higher top speed than short ones. They may also have relatively large wetted area and drag, so it may take a lot of power to achieve or maintain that top speed. Compared to short hulls, long hulls are more difficult to turn and to maneuver in narrow streams and around obstructions. The other side of this coin is that they track better—they go straight and stay on course with fewer correction strokes. Short, wide canoes and kayaks turn more quickly, track less well, and have lower top speeds. However, if they are well designed and not too wide, they may require relatively little effort to maintain an acceptable cruising speed. On trips where endurance was more important than sprint speed, I've often seen short canoes keep up easily with longer ones.

One way to improve the turning ability of a canoe regardless of its length is to increase the amount of *rocker* in the hull. This is the curvature of the bottom when seen from the side, as shown in Figure 16.4. A small amount of rocker can reduce wetted area and drag without having much influence on tracking or turning, while a greater amount can significantly improve maneuverability at the expense of tracking. A moderate amount of rocker can be built into a hull to strike a compromise between tracking and maneuver-

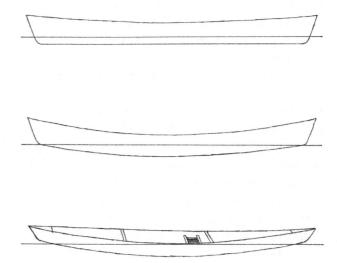

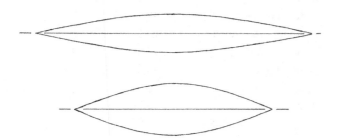

FIGURE 16.3. *Length-to-width ratio is a major determinant of top speed.*

FIGURE 16.4. *Rocker. At the top is a canoe with a straight keel line; it has no rocker. Below the waterline, the side profiles of the ends have a lot of area, which resists turning and therefore aids tracking a straight course. In the middle is a canoe with an exaggerated amount of rocker; the ends curve upward like the bottom of a rocking chair. There is much less resistance to turning. The bottom sketch shows how leaning a canoe will temporarily create the effect of increased rocker. If the canoe can be leaned far enough without swamping or capsizing, it will turn more quickly with less effort.*

ability. The ability to turn quickly is very desirable for restricted waterways, small rivers, and avoiding rocks and obstructions in shallow water and whitewater. Also, for just messing about, a boat that can turn to make small figures in the water is a lot of fun.

Many canoes and kayaks can be leaned to help turn them. As a boat leans, the wider midsection is depressed into the water, effectively creating a more highly rockered bottom and shortening the boat's waterline by lifting the bow and stern out of the water. If the boat is moving forward, leaning away from the direction you want to turn will generally start a turn in the desired direction. Note that this is the opposite of riding a bicycle, on which you lean *into* a turn. Many, but not all, canoes work this way. Of course, narrow canoes, canoes with little freeboard, and canoes with tumblehome cannot be leaned far without risk of swamping or capsizing. Waves and rough water may also argue against the leaning technique.

Volume and capacity are other important considerations. Greater hull depth provides more buoyancy and helps maintain sufficient freeboard when carrying a heavy paddler or a lot of gear. Greater width and/or fuller ends will also increase volume, but, beyond a certain point, the performance compromises are generally more suitable to tandem canoes than solos. Higher ends will help keep the boat from swamping in whitewater conditions and high waves. However, lower ends and less freeboard make the craft easier to control in strong winds. And a lower hull equates to less material and less weight. When both wind resistance and wave protection need to be maximized, a decked canoe or kayak is best. Every design decision involves compromise; there is no perfect canoe for all conditions. However, most general-use designs will be forgiving and will suit a variety of activities.

I especially like and recommend building relatively small solo canoes. The most practical canoes and kayaks are often the ones that are just large enough for your physical size and intended missions—and no more. Compared to larger tandem canoes, solos require less labor and money

to build. They weigh less, which makes them easier to portage and to transport on cartops. They are also great fun to paddle. Small size and light weight make them easy to accelerate and decelerate; they are the sports cars of paddle craft. Even for two people, it may be preferable to have two solos rather than one tandem. Instead of arguing about how to paddle, each person gets a separate boat to paddle their own way and chart their own course. Relationships have been saved by solo canoes!

There are many specialized canoe designs. The three designs in this book are solo boats for all-around use. Dragonfly is small, light, and pure fun. Kayoo is versatile and can handle a variety of wind, waves, and weather. And Wasp is radically distinctive, easy to paddle, difficult to capsize, and equally manageable for both small and large paddlers.

All three are primarily suited for flatwater lakes and rivers as well as mild river rapids, such as class 1 and class 2 whitewater. They can be easily modified and customized. Increasing and decreasing a design's length and rocker are described at the end of the chapter. Hull strength, weight, and volume can also be optimized for whitewater use or ease of transport.

Dragonfly: A Small, Light Solo Pack Canoe

DIMENSIONS	
Length	11'7.2"
Width, maximum	28"
Width at 3.75" waterline	27.3"
Width at gunwale	26.36"
Depth at bow	15.5"
Depth at center	10.5"
Depth at stern	14"
Rocker (at bow and stern)	0.8"

When weight is a major consideration and fun on protected flat waters is the mission, it is hard to beat a little solo pack-style canoe like Dragonfly. She can be built with a finished weight in the range of 12 to 22 pounds depending on choices for the hull laminate, finishing touches, and outfitting. This is the easiest project of the three and requires the least building time and materials cost. Its diminutive size and handy portability ensure that it will get a lot of use, and it is easy to store when you aren't on the water. Simplicity of design makes for less labor and easy construction. It is also ideal for making a scaled-down model for learning how to work with epoxy and the fabric form method.

For many paddlers, a small solo canoe like Dragonfly may be a better alternative to the popular plastic recreational kayaks. The open canoe is easier to get in and out of, holds more gear, is easier to fish from, and is much lighter. It is less trouble than a kayak to carry on cartops since it can just go upside down on simple load bars. Because it is upside down, no cover is needed to keep out rain and debris. On the water it moves conveniently and efficiently with a double-blade paddle, just like a kayak.

It is true that safety on whitewater and on large waters in wind, waves, and weather demand larger and stronger canoes and heavier kayaks with decks and a coaming that accommodates a sprayskirt. And Dragonfly could be built deeper, heavier, and with a deck to better handle those conditions. But for children, small adults, and many of us who have earned senior status, a manageably lightweight canoe for enjoying protected waters is much better than not getting on the water at all. Although I stay very active at age sixty-six, I recognize that I can no longer maintain as much strength and endurance as in my youth. With experience, one can develop strategies to compensate. Lightweight canoes, along with other lightweight gear, allow me to continue to enjoy extended wilderness canoeing, running some whitewater rivers, and other paddling pleasures. If I stay healthy, I will be able to lift a little pack canoe onto a cartop for a long time. Even now, for a quiet evening paddle on easy home waters, my larger, stron-

ger, and faster canoes are more boat and weight than necessary.

It is no secret that more hull area and material equals more weight. Therefore, a shorter canoe with lower sides can be lighter than a longer and higher one. To achieve the greatest portability, we want a canoe with the minimum length and freeboard required for the weight of the paddler and the intended load. Also consider the degree of rough water capability and impact protection desired. All else being equal, lighter boats are more fragile, but modern materials can produce light weight with adequate safety.

Shorter canoes have other advantages. Even when two canoes weigh the same, one that is much shorter will be easier to carry and manage. It will have less swing weight (less mass that is far from the center of gravity), making it easier to maneuver while carrying. Turning the boat is less effort, and it will go down a twisty or bumpy portage trail without hanging up in the trees and bushes.

Storage is not the least of considerations. Small boats fit into more places. If you build a boat, you will want to protect it so that it lasts a long time. To do this you need to minimize exposure to sun and weather. Small canoes fit easily into garages, carports, or basements. Some of my friends who have had to store their large canoes outdoors have watched them deteriorate, warp, weaken, and disintegrate into uselessness.

On the minus side, a shorter canoe will not track as well on the water and will have a lower top speed. These are partially offset by using the efficiency of a double-blade paddle. And the smaller hull may have less wetted area and drag, which can translate into a good cruising speed with only moderate effort.

With these considerations in mind, I suggest a more lightweight approach to building Dragonfly than for the larger designs. (See Figure 16.5.)

Stations #1 and #9 can be used as templates for end flotation bulkheads. The front thwart can be placed at a comfortable distance from the seat to provide a footrest. The rear thwart is positioned conveniently to use as a simple backrest by itself

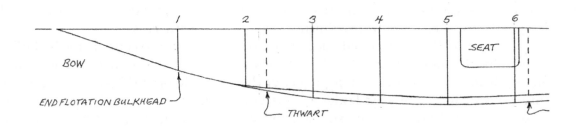

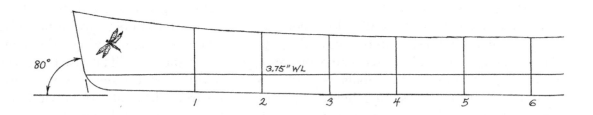

DRAGONFLY

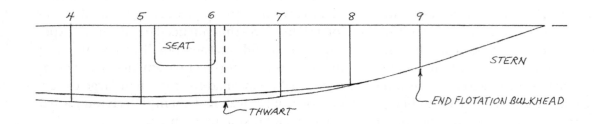

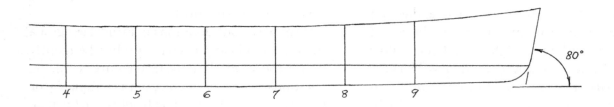

FIGURE 16.5. *Dragonfly top view and side view.*

or as part of a more elaborate and comfortable backrest: a "seat back" 4 to 6 inches high by 8 to 10 inches wide will add to comfort without interfering with paddling or safety. A taller rest can be installed, but it must be foldable so as not to interfere with the self-rescue reentry techniques described in Chapter 15. A tall backrest should also be foldable or removable so that the boat can be carried inverted on a cartop.

Figures 16.6 and 16.7 provide the drawings required to make forms for the end profiles and the stations. (See also Figure 16.8 on page 184.) Note that the end profiles and the stations are drawn to different scales. This is so that both the ends and the stations can be printed as large as possible and still fit on the page. Since Dragonfly is symmetrical fore and aft, a minimum of work is required to enlarge or plot the drawings to full size and make the forms. This ease of construction makes her ideal for first-time builders and for building as a scale model to try composite construction (Chapter 10 on building a model features Dragonfly). Although she is smaller, simpler, and quicker to build than the other designs, the shallow arch hull and balance between volume, stability, weight, and efficiency should make her useful and a lot of fun for many paddlers.

Very small and light solo canoes became popular in the Adirondacks of New York from the 1880s to around 1900, and they are again catching on with paddlers. Like those earlier pack-style canoes, Dragonfly is designed to be paddled from a very low sitting position with a double-blade paddle. I think of such canoes as being like kayaks without decks. Sitting low makes for a low center of mass that provides good stability in such a small canoe. To make it easier and more pleasant to paddle from a low seat, Dragonfly is designed with some tumblehome, a modern feature that makes the hull narrower at the gunwale than at the maximum width. A minicell foam pad placed in the bottom of the hull is all that is required for a seat.

Try test paddling with pad thicknesses of 1 to 4 inches. When you find a height that suits you, the seat can be glued in place. I like to attach a pad with Velcro, making it easy to change or to remove for drying and cleaning.

Low seating requires low and narrow gunwales so that it is not too difficult to reach the water with the paddle. While paddlers with short torsos can raise the seat, raising it too much will reduce stability. Smaller and lighter-weight paddlers will like low sides. Dragonfly is sized primarily for average-size and smaller adults. Heavier paddlers and heavy cargo will make the canoe ride deeper in the water, reducing freeboard, dryness in waves, and resistance to swamping. On small ponds and calm waters, these factors will not matter. But, for better versatility with a very small canoe like Dragonfly, it helps to size the volume and freeboard to the weight and size of the paddler.

The easiest way to do this is to change the depth of the boat (or the height of the gunwales) as described later in this chapter in the section on modifying designs. The plans show a depth at the center station #5 of 10½ inches. This should be fine for many average-size paddlers with a moderate camping load on mild waters. Small paddlers less than 120 pounds who want the lightest possible canoe might reduce the depth by 1 inch. For paddlers over 165 pounds, add 1 inch to the depth. Paddlers over 200 pounds who expect to carry some camping gear might add 2 or 3 inches, although most paddlers this large will prefer a longer and larger canoe. For whitewater use, add about 2 or 3 inches for the average paddler. (Whitewater will also demand a stronger and heavier hull laminate, as discussed below.)

Manufacturers often publish load capacities for their canoes. But this may not reveal much about how the boats will handle, how much freeboard remains, or what conditions can be managed with the advertised weight. And the capabilities and safety will differ with paddlers of varying skill and experience. So, rather than

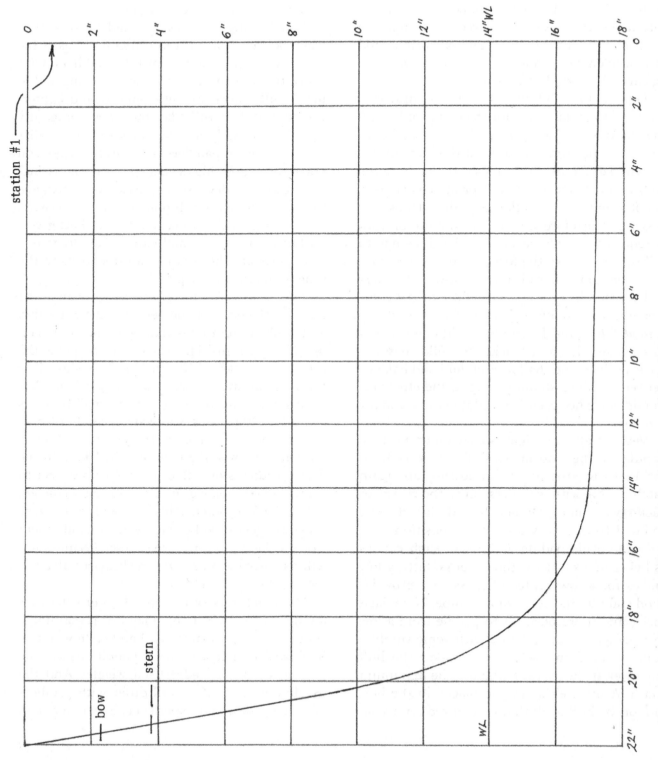

FIGURE 16.6. *Dragonfly profile for ends. Bow and stern are the same except for height.*

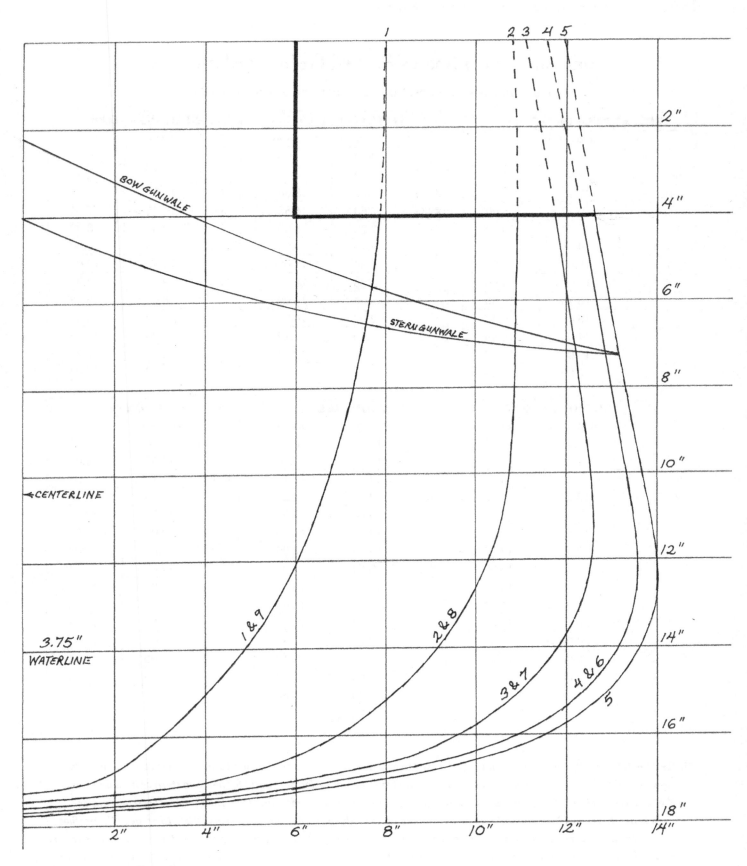

FIGURE 16.7. Dragonfly stations.

Dragonfly: Coordinates for End Profiles and Stations

Measurements in inches. Spacing between stations is 12 inches.

BOW AND STERN PROFILES	HORIZONTAL	VERTICAL
Top	22.00	0.00
Bow height	21.60	2.27
Stern height	21.36	3.79
	20.59	8.00
	20.20	10.00
	19.65	12.00
3.75" WL	18.67	14.00
	18.00	14.96
	16.75	16.00
	16.00	16.43
	14.00	16.99
	12.00	17.07
	0.00	17.24

STATIONS #1 & #9	HORIZONTAL	VERTICAL
	8.00	0.00
	7.90	4.00
#1 G	7.72	5.66
#9 G	7.60	6.52
	7.28	8.00
	6.76	10.00
	6.04	12.00
WL	4.88	14.00
	3.04	16.00
	2.00	16.76
	1.00	17.12
	0.00	17.24

STATIONS #2 & #8	HORIZONTAL	VERTICAL
	10.80	0.00
	10.94	4.00
#2 G	10.90	6.66
#8 G	10.88	7.04
	10.86	8.00
	10.76	10.00
	10.28	12.00
WL	9.16	14.00
	8.00	15.18
	6.92	16.00
	4.00	17.04
	2.00	17.28
	0.00	17.44

STATIONS #3 & #7	HORIZONTAL	VERTICAL
	11.10	0.00
	11.76	4.00
#3 G	12.18	6.98
#7 G	12.22	7.16
	12.32	8.00
	12.56	10.00
	12.56	12.00
WL	11.84	14.00
	10.00	15.78
	8.78	16.62
	6.62	17.00
	4.00	17.32
	2.00	17.46
	0.00	17.57

STATIONS #4 & #6	HORIZONTAL	VERTICAL
	11.60	0.00
	12.36	4.00
#4 G	12.85	7.17
#6 G	12.88	7.24
	13.00	8.00
	13.33	10.00
	13.58	12.00
WL	13.64	14.00
	12.00	15.37
	11.58	16.00
	10.00	16.36
	8.00	16.82
	6.00	17.18
	4.00	17.42
	2.00	17.56
	0.00	17.68

STATION #5	HORIZONTAL	VERTICAL
	11.96	0.00
	12.65	4.00
#5 G	13.18	7.27
	13.30	8.00
	13.70	10.00
	14.00	12.00
WL	13.65	14.00
	12.00	15.74
	10.00	16.55
	8.00	16.98
	6.00	17.28
	4.00	17.50
	2.00	17.64
	0.00	17.75

FIGURE 16.8. *Dragonfly coordinates. These can be used to produce full-size end profiles and stations as depicted on the grids in Figures 16.6 and 16.7. For horizontal numbers, measure from the right edge of the grid for bow and stern profiles and from the centerline at the left edge of the grid for stations; for vertical numbers, measure down from the top. Each pair of side-by-side numbers provides coordinates to plot one point. Connect the plotted points with a curved line to produce the profiles shown. The letter G indicates the gunwale position or sheerline at each station. Dragonfly is a symmetrical design: the stations forward of the center station 5 are identical to the stations to the rear. Stations 1 and 9 are the same, stations 2 and 8 are the same, and so on. The only difference is that the gunwale heights are slightly higher on stations toward the bow.*

list maximum weight capacities, I suggest the guidelines above.

The laminating guidelines given in Chapters 3 and 9 can be used for Dragonfly. If the canoe is to be used only on protected waters and rock bashing is not part of the intended mission, then light weight is often more important than strength. Weight can be saved by building a laminate with lighter or fewer layers. The laminate can be stronger in the bottom, where stiffness and impact protection are needed, and lighter in the sides to save weight. A light all-Kevlar laminate can consist of three layers of 5-ounce Kevlar or two full layers with a third partial layer covering only the bottom of the hull. Make the partial layer either the first inside layer against the form and peel ply or the second or core (middle) layer. The partial layer should cover the bottom of the hull and extend past the waterline an inch or two. If you prefer additional strength, add a third full layer. This is desirable for heavy paddlers and rough handling. Adding yet another layer would result in a very tough hull for whitewater use and a penalty of several extra pounds.

For an ultra-lightweight carbon hull laminate, start with a first inside layer of 5.8-ounce carbon over the bottom up past the waterline. Or use a full carbon layer. Next, add a full layer of 5-ounce Kevlar for toughness followed by a full outer hull layer of 5.8-ounce carbon for stiffness. Lightweight layups with only two layers in the sides will require reinforcing ribs that extend almost all the way up to the gunwales, especially in the middle sections from stations #3 to #7. The carbon hull will achieve adequate stiffness with lighter ribs than the all-Kevlar hull. But it is difficult to give precise guidelines since fabrics and layups will vary. After your hull is removed from the form, test the stiffness of the bottom and sides, adding ribs as necessary.

If the sides are more flexible than the bottom, you have the option of narrowing the sides slightly at the gunwales to increase tumblehome. This may be desirable for smaller and

lighter-weight paddlers. It can be done by making the thwarts a little short to pull the gunwales together. It should be done only in moderation, however, narrowing the gunwales by perhaps an inch. Bending the sides to increase tumblehome may reduce both rocker and secondary stability a little. However, for open solo canoes that lack the low side decks of kayaks, paddling will be more ergonomic and pleasant for smaller paddlers. If you wish to do this, install the gunwales first. Then install the thwarts. Add reinforcement ribs only after the gunwales and thwarts have established the final hull shape.

Although it is a soft wood, spruce has a very high strength-to-weight ratio, making it ideal for wood parts like gunwales in ultralight canoes. Douglas fir is heavier but stronger and is not far behind spruce in strength-to-weight ratio. Since it is heavier, it may be used in slightly smaller dimensions. Other available woods can be used for gunwales if you prefer, and the weight penalty will not be too great. A layer of lightweight fiberglass can be added over the top of softwood gunwales to protect them from bumps, scratches, and cartop load bars. Make ultra-lightweight thwarts with tubular aluminum as described in Chapter 11.

It would be possible to complete Dragonfly as a decked canoe or kayak. I have not included this in the plans in order to keep the drawings as simple and uncluttered as possible. For deck ideas and dimensions, read the design section on Kayoo later in the chapter and see Chapter 12 on decked canoes and kayaks.

Flotation is especially important for composite canoes. For small solo canoes like Dragonfly, a polyethylene foam seat glued in place can add a very small amount of flotation to help keep the hull from sinking. But it is not enough and gives no real safety for the paddler. If you wish to keep your Dragonfly project both simple and light, then use inflatable end flotation bags instead of built-in flotation. Chapter 15 has installation instructions. For paddling on mostly flat water and some class 1 and 2 rapids, small end bags intended for tandem canoes provide adequate end flotation in solo canoes. Some float bags are designed to double as dry storage bags, so you need not reduce load space to add safety. However, since storage float bags must be securely tied in to be effective, they may be a little inconvenient for portaging and cartop carrying. Inflatable bags do need extra attention; air must be let out occasionally so that they do not overinflate due to heat from exposure to sun and temperature changes. Deflate them during storage. Installing foam cylinders for side flotation (as described in Chapter 15) can add self-rescue capability for paddling on deeper and bigger waters.

I prefer to have at least minimal flotation chambers built into the ends as permanent structures. The plans indicate using the first and last stations as positions for end flotation bulkheads. This provides adequate end flotation on protected waters and, in combination with foam cylinders in the sides, sufficient buoyancy in the event of a swamping or capsize. Supplemental end flotation in the form of float bags can be added when conditions warrant (review Chapter 15 on flotation before building).

Portaging is Dragonfly's forte. If built lightly, it will be wonderfully easy to put on a cartop, portage between lakes, or even carry for miles on rough terrain to hidden lakes in high country. I carry small canoes like this for several miles to run rivers without arranging a shuttle by car. A padded portage yoke makes carrying most canoes easier and more comfortable. However, very light canoes—canoes under 22 pounds or so—are typically just carried with one gunwale over a shoulder and an arm around the rear thwart. If no portage yoke is used, they are perhaps easiest to carry on top of the head. Outdoor writer George Washington Sears, writing in 1880 under the pen name Nessmuk, advised that his 18-pound canoe made by J. H. Rushton could "easily be carried on the head in an inverted position, first placing a blanket or old coat on the head by way of cushion."

Kayoo: A Versatile Canoe/Kayak Hybrid

"That looks like a nice way to travel."

—Comment by a passing paddler in the Boundary Waters of Minnesota

DIMENSIONS

	DECKED	OPEN CANOE
Length	14'6"	14'8"
Width, maximum	29.1"	29.1"
Width at 3.75" waterline	28.4"	28.4"
Width at gunwale		27"
Width at deck	27.5"	
Width at coaming	19" to 20"	
Depth at bow	11.8"	15.8"
Depth at center	11.6"	11.6"
Depth at stern	10.3"	14.4"
Rocker (at bow and stern)	1"	1"

Kayoo was built to be a safer and more versatile alternative to conventional canoes and kayaks. Designed from the beginning to have a deck, Kayoo combines some of the best qualities of both canoes and kayaks. (See Figure 16.9.) The decked Kayoo is a very capable craft for long wilderness camping trips and moderately rough and windy conditions. Low wetted area and fine ends with flare above the waterline yield a very good cruising speed and a dry ride. The decks angle low at the sides of the paddling station for an easy paddle reach to the water without leaning or banging one's elbows on the gunwales. Kayoo can also be completed as an open canoe, which will make it a simpler and less expensive project that will take only about half the building time of the decked version. Tumblehome in the sides of the undecked version provides some of the same benefits, although to a lesser degree.

In Kayoo, one can endure long days of paddling and cover the miles in comfort and with minimal effort. With the suggested hull layup, Kayoo has an excellent balance of strength and light weight, making it my choice for long wilderness trips involving portages. The decks and low

FIGURE 16.9. *Kayoo with deck rigging and a combination seat and portage yoke with a folding backrest.*

ends provide less resistance to crosswinds than conventional canoes, so it handles windy conditions somewhat similarly to sea kayaks.

The Kayoo hull shown in Figure 16.10 was constructed with two full layers of 5-ounce Kevlar and one layer of 5.8-ounce carbon fiber. A third layer of Kevlar was added to the bottom as one of the internal core layers to add more impact protection and puncture resistance below the waterline. If you trim such a layer carefully along one of the stringers, it may not even be noticeable on the outer surface. With this layup, decks, a cockpit opening 6 feet long, and a simple 4-inch-thick polyethylene foam pad on the floor for a seat, Kayoo weighs 24 pounds. With a combination seat that converts to a portage yoke, total weight is 28 pounds.

In the side view, the gunwale line shows the gunwale height when building an open canoe. The deck sheerline is where the hull meets the deck when building the boat as a kayak or decked

canoe. For an open canoe, thwarts are required in the approximate locations shown. When the decked version is built with structural side flotation chambers, no thwarts are necessary. (See Chapter 12 on decked canoes and kayaks for details.)

The bow flotation bulkhead should be about 29 inches from the bow, and the stern flotation bulkhead should be about 27 inches from the stern. Station template #2 can be reduced in size a bit to provide the shape for the bow bulkhead. Station template #12 can be enlarged slightly for the stern bulkhead. It is also acceptable to install the bulkheads at stations #2 and #12 and use the station templates unchanged.

Forms for the end profiles and the stations may be picked up from Figures 16.11, 16.12, and 16.13. Note that the end profiles and the stations are drawn to different scales. This is so that both the ends and the stations can be printed as large as possible and still fit on the page.

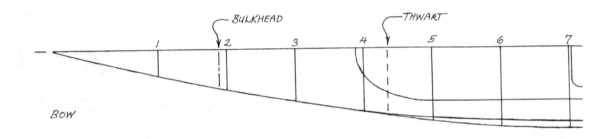

BULKHEAD

THWART

1   2   3   4   5   6   7

BOW

KAYOO

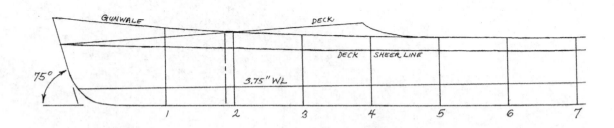

GUNWALE

DECK

DECK   SHEER LINE

75°

3.75" WL

1   2   3   4   5   6   7

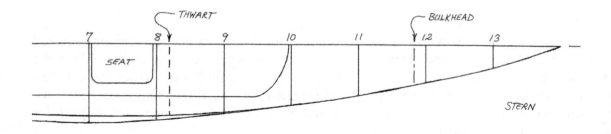

THWART

BULKHEAD

7   8   9   10   11   12   13

SEAT

STERN

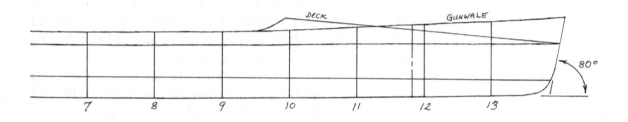

DECK

GUNWALE

80°

7   8   9   10   11   12   13

FIGURE 16.10. *Kayoo top view and side view.*

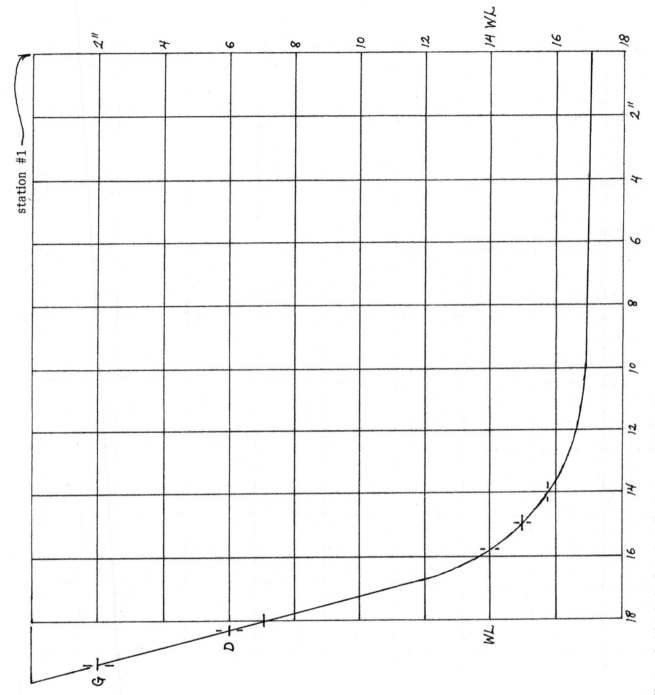

FIGURE 16.11. *Kayoo bow profile. D = deck height for decked version; G = gunwale height for open version.*

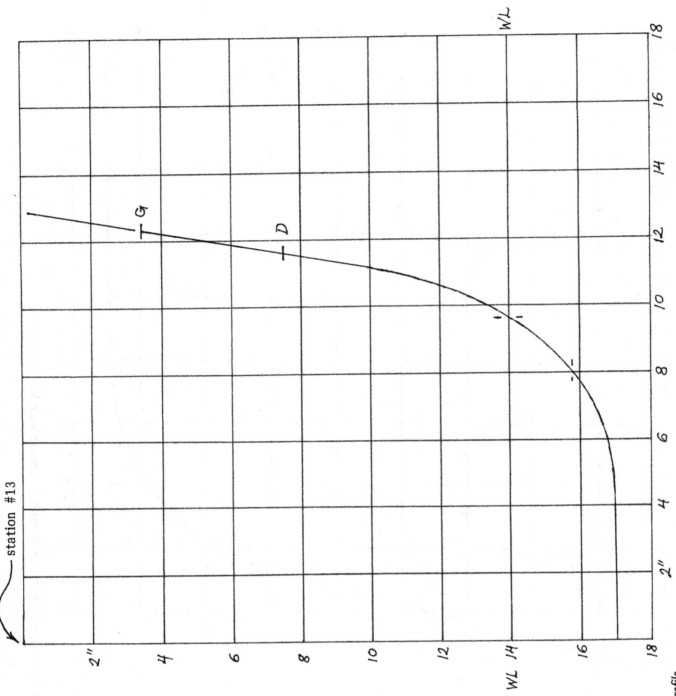

FIGURE 16.12. *Kayoo stern profile.*

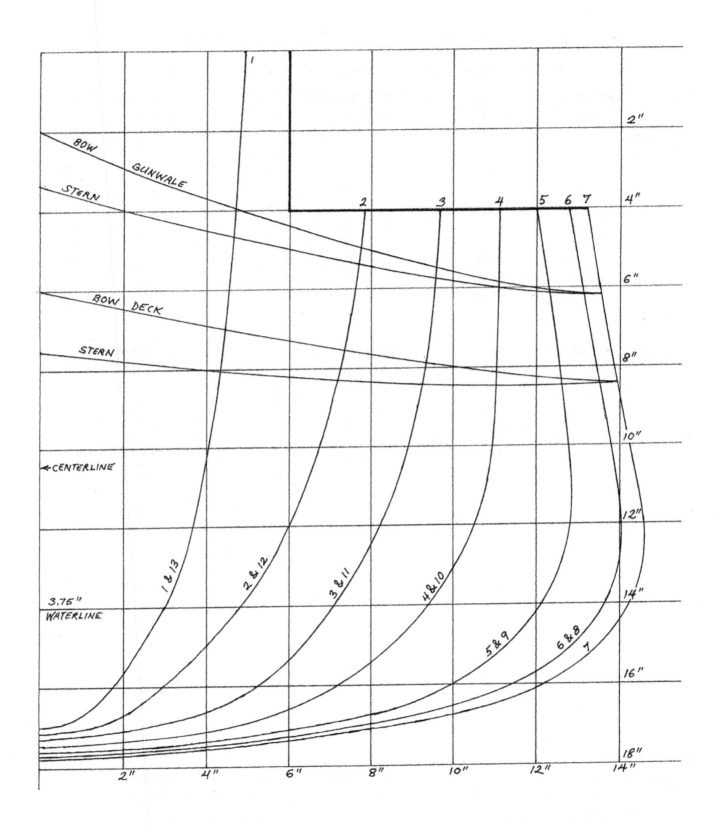

FIGURE 16.13. *Kayoo stations.*

Kayoo: Coordinates for End Profiles and Stations

Measurements in inches. Spacing between stations is 12 inches.

BOW PROFILES	HORIZONTAL	VERTICAL
gunwale-G	19.35	2.00
deck-D	18.30	6.00
	16.65	12.00
3.75″ WL	15.76	14.00
	14.96	15.00
	14.00	15.75
	12.00	16.65
	10.00	16.88
	8.00	16.90
	4.00	16.96
	0.00	17.00

STERN PROFILE	HORIZONTAL	VERTICAL
G	12.33	3.37
D	11.60	7.48
	11.15	10.00
	10.60	12.00
WL	9.65	14.00
	8.00	15.83
	6.00	16.80
	4.00	16.95
	0.00	17.00

STATIONS #1 & #13	HORIZONTAL	VERTICAL
G1	4.72	3.94
G13	4.64	4.62
D1	4.40	6.96
D13	4.28	8.00
	4.00	10.00
	3.62	12.00
WL	2.94	14.00
	1.67	16.00
	0.63	16.85
	0.00	17.00

STATIONS #2 & #12	HORIZONTAL	VERTICAL
G2	7.70	4.9
G12	7.64	5.34
D2	7.30	7.50
D12	7.14	8.24
	6.66	10.00
	5.96	12.00
WL	4.76	14.00
	2.92	16.00
	2.00	16.68
	0.00	17.14

STATIONS #3 & #11	HORIZONTAL	VERTICAL
G3	9.56	5.48
G11	9.54	5.74
D3	9.28	7.86
D11	9.20	8.40
	8.80	10.00
	8.20	12.00
WL	7.04	14.00
	6.00	15.34
	5.20	16.00
	2.25	17.04
	0.00	17.28

STATIONS #4 & #10	HORIZONTAL	VERTICAL
G4	11.06	5.84
G10	11.06	6.00
D4	11.04	8.10
D10	11.04	8.42
	10.90	10.00
	10.46	12.00
WL	9.34	14.00
	8.44	15.00
	7.12	16.00
	4.00	16.62
	2.00	17.10
	0.00	17.42

(continued on next page)

FIGURE 16.14. *Kayoo coordinates. These can be used to produce full-size end profiles and stations as depicted on the grids in Figures 16.11, 16.12, and 16.13. For horizontal numbers, measure from the left edge of the grid except for the bow profile, which is measured from the right edge of the grid; for vertical numbers, measure down from the top. Each pair of side-by-side numbers provides coordinates to plot one point. Connect the plotted points with a curved line to produce the profiles shown.*

Kayoo: Coordinates for End Profiles and Stations (continued)

STATIONS #5 & #9				STATIONS #6 & #8				STATION #7		
	HORIZONTAL	VERTICAL			HORIZONTAL	VERTICAL			HORIZONTAL	VERTICAL
G5	12.26	6.04		G6 & 8	13.12	6.16		G7	13.54	6.17
G9	12.28	6.14		D6	13.52	8.40		D7	13.92	8.40
D5	12.50	8.26		D8	13.54	8.44			14.24	10.00
D9	12.58	8.44			13.75	10.00			14.57	12.00
	12.73	10.00			14.00	12.00			14.50	13.00
	12.77	12.00		WL	13.60	14.00		WL	14.20	14.00
WL	12.08	14.00			11.34	16.00			12.00	16.10
	9.90	16.00			8.00	16.91			10.00	16.76
	6.00	17.08			6.00	17.22			8.00	17.10
	4.00	17.37			4.00	17.42			6.00	17.36
	2.00	17.54			0.00	17.68			4.00	17.55
	0.00	17.56							2.00	17.69
									0.00	17.76

As in Figure 16.10, the gunwale line indicates the height at the gunwales for building an open canoe, and the deck line indicates the height of sheerline where the hull meets the deck for building the decked version. The hull laminate should be built a few inches higher than needed and trimmed to the desired height. Note that the stations forward of station #7 are identical to the stations to the rear. Stations #1 and #13 are the same, stations #2 and #12 are the same, and so forth. This symmetry reduces your workload. However, the hull is slightly asymmetrical. The bow profile is longer than the stern profile, which gives the hull a finer entry as it moves through the water. Also, the gunwale and deck sheerlines are higher toward the bow than toward the stern to give a bit more protection from waves.

With the dimensions given in the accompanying plans and coordinates (Figures 16.10 to 16.14), Kayoo is most suitable for paddlers up to 170 pounds with a moderate camping load or for somewhat heavier paddlers without gear. Although the boat will float much more weight, the hull will sink lower, reducing freeboard and protection from waves. Heavier paddlers may

want to increase the volume by making the hull higher at the gunwales or deck. Increasing depth by 1 inch will add roughly 80 pounds to the capacity. Add as many inches as you like, but remember that lower sides make solo paddling more comfortable for paddlers with shorter torsos. Higher sides are definitely better for waves and whitewater, but more area is presented to the wind, and the hull will be heavier.

Figure 16.15 shows how to use station templates #5 and #9 to make bulkheads for the Kayoo side flotation chambers described in Chapter 12.

Figure 16.16 shows the cross-sectional curve of Kayoo's deck at the front and rear of the coaming and at the bow and stern flotation bulkheads, which support the deck. Reinforced plywood arches are made that support the deck at the front and rear of the coaming. The curves shown can be used to produce jigs for making the arches. Although Figure 16.17 (page 196) gives the coordinates to generate full-size templates, the shapes are not critical. The decks were sized and shaped relatively high to enclose the backpacks I like to use for camping and portaging. Higher decks will enclose greater volume to accommodate larger

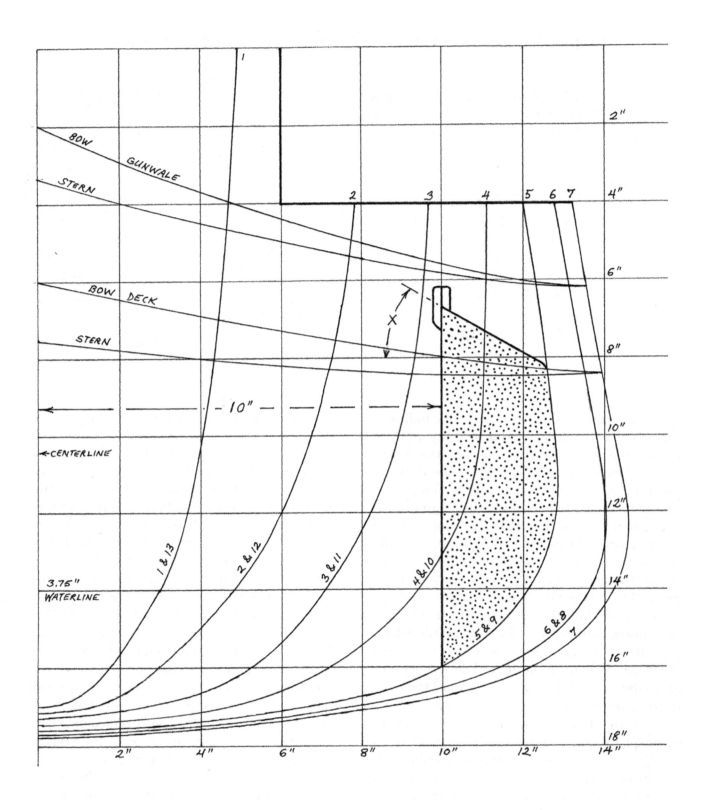

FIGURE 16.15. *The template for stations 5 and 9 can be marked to trace or draw the bulkheads for side flotation chambers. Deck angle X will be about 30 degrees to produce the design coaming height of 11.6 inches.*

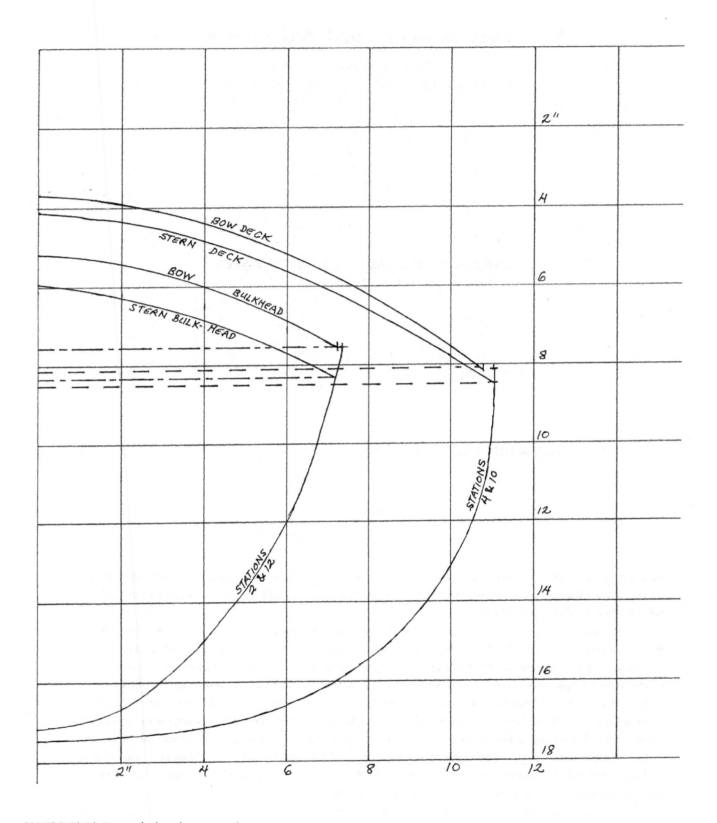

FIGURE 16.16. *Kayoo deck arch cross sections.*

Kayoo: Coordinates for Deck Arch Cross Sections

Measurements in inches.

BOW DECK BULKHEAD	
HORIZONTAL	VERTICAL
0.00	5.20
2.00	5.42
4.00	6.00
6.00	6.86
7.22	7.50

BOW DECK ARCH	
HORIZONTAL	VERTICAL
0.00	3.68
2.00	3.90
4.00	4.40
6.00	5.18
8.00	6.24
10.00	7.52
10.80	8.12

STERN DECK BULKHEAD	
HORIZONTAL	VERTICAL
0.00	5.92
2.00	6.28
4.00	6.84
6.00	7.70
7.20	8.30

STERN DECK ARCH	
HORIZONTAL	VERTICAL
0.00	4.12
2.00	4.34
4.00	4.84
6.00	5.62
8.00	6.60
10.00	7.78
11.04	8.42

FIGURE 16.17. *Kayoo deck arch coordinates.*

From the Kayoo Paddling Log

For the initial trials, I paddled a few hours, covered over 7 miles, and did some tests. I used a temporary seat, and other minor finishwork was still incomplete. Weight was around 24 pounds. Although I chose a secluded area, one fisherman did ask, "What kind of kayak is that?"

The boat does exactly what it was designed to do. It is wonderfully easy and comfortable to paddle. Although the decked design is intended to facilitate using a double-blade paddle, the easy reach to the water also makes it very nice for using a single-blade paddle, nicer and drier than in a conventional solo canoe. It is stable and easy to fish from; I caught some bluegills on a fly rod. I was lucky to have some occasional 20-knot winds for testing. It handles wind similarly to my sea kayaks, noticeably better and safer than my open canoes. Wind has less influence on the low ends and covered deck. Plus, the moderate length and rocker ease turning and better enable maintaining control and desired angle on the wind. It is easily leaned to aid turning. Light weight and low wetted area result in easy cruising speed and fast acceleration. It does not maintain glide and direction quite like my 16½-foot Wenonah Advantage solo canoe, but with no rocker and a long waterline, the Advantage is very slow to turn, which is especially annoying in unfavorable winds or current, or when chasing down snagged lures while fishing.

Kayoo's sloped deck allows a relatively low seating position that is extremely stable. In rough or windy conditions, it can actually be paddled okay sitting right on the floor. It was still easy to reach the water with the paddle. For fishing in calmer conditions, I sat high on a stack of cushions under a fabric canoe chair. A good all-around seat position seems to be 5 or 6 inches off the floor, an inch or two lower and more stable than in my other solo canoes.

On day two of paddling, I completed the primary water tests. Everything worked fine. I tested a movable seat with side rails and bungee hold-downs. The seat moves forward and aft, both to trim the boat and to aid loading and unloading packs. This will be a useful feature. Loading and seat trim are further simplified because, unlike other solo canoes, there is no thwart behind the seat. Carbon fiber arches molded under the decks combined with the rigid side flotation chambers seem sufficient.

The boat was loaded with my usual camping/tripping load. A large backpack/portage pack fits behind the seat and under the rear deck, and my food pack fits forward under the bow deck. There was lots of extra room forward where I was able to fit a portable toilet and a 5-gallon water jug (necessary for some of the remote western river trips where safe water is not available and portable water filters are not adequate for some of the contaminants). My loaded backpack weighs 40 pounds, and my food pack is 15 pounds. With me and a bit more gear, there was a little over 200 pounds in the boat. With this load, stability was still excellent and there was plenty of freeboard. Tracking was noticeably better with a load, and it still felt very safe for leaning to aid turning. For me this is an ideal tripping canoe. Paddlers who are a lot heavier who also want to carry a heavy camping load might prefer a hull with more volume. (Read about making modifications later in this chapter.)

Finally, I performed the flotation and rescue tests. When capsized, the boat floats high and stable either right side up or upside down. It is easy to roll it right side up while floating in the water wearing a PFD. The boat is so light that in rolling upright it floats high on a side flotation chamber and takes on very little water. However, it has to have water inside for the flotation to provide buoyancy and stability for reentry. The solo self-rescue reentry procedures were surprisingly easy, and I was able to make reentries from deep water over the sides and the ends.

The sun was setting on the lake, and my "work" at self-rescue testing was done. A relaxing 6-mile paddle down the calm lake and back would make an enjoyable evening. I cast behind the canoe and trolled as I paddled in the twilight between ospreys and herons. Suddenly, I was startled by a strike and a heavy fish. After a twenty-five-minute struggle, a 30-inch northern pike appeared alongside the canoe! She was actually a little bigger than the pike I've caught this year on "real" fishing trips. Go figure. Keeping my fingers well-separated from pike teeth, I released the fish. A slender crescent moon just above the mountainous west horizon illuminated bats picking insects right off the deck of my bow. I wondered what other magical journeys this new boat and I would share.

Kayoo is finally completed, more or less. It is still in rough finish; I will sand it eventually and add more accessories and rigging details. With the combination seat and portage yoke and mounting rails installed, and with neoprene-padded gunwales, the weight is 28 pounds. Most ultralight canoes this size will weigh more without including self-rescue flotation, portage yoke, or decking. I'm pleased.

Seat rails mounted to the side flotation chambers allow the seat to move fore and aft through a wide range. Thus, the trim range is very great for coping with a variety of wind conditions, and no extra weight or ballast is required to do this. The seat can be mounted in high position for general use, fishing, and comfort, or in low position for maximum stability in whitewater or dangerous wind and wave conditions. Remounting the seat in the portage yoke position takes only a few seconds. Unlike other solo canoe or kayak portage yokes, this one can be left in place in the yoke position for cartopping, which is incredibly convenient. The canoe slides off the car rack and right onto the shoulders, and away you go to the water.

With the sloped deck, it is easier and much more comfortable to reach the water with the paddle, single or double blade, making paddling a joy. This also encourages using a shorter, lighter paddle. For fishing and travel on lakes and large rivers, I like using a double-blade paddle. Although I need a longer paddle with other solo canoes and some kayaks, a paddle length of 220 cm seems just right for Kayoo.

It is really a joy to use this boat; each outing teaches me more. Although I've paddled and owned solo canoes that excel at one specialty or another, Kayoo is the most versatile. She does lots of different things rather well.

Since those initial tests, Kayoo has endured many years of hard use, including extended wilderness trips, class 2 and 3 rapids, and almost daily workouts and fishing duty on the Upper Potomac River. It has come through everything with flying colors and still remains one of my all-time favorite canoes or kayaks because of its versatility, safety, comfort, light weight, and all around ease of use.

packs and camping gear. Lower decks will look slimmer and more streamlined and will reduce windage. You can bend a piece of thin plywood to make an arch of any height you desire.

Kayoo's decks have a straight taper from the arches at the coaming to the ends. This encloses a large volume for flotation and makes it easier to form the decks with thin plywood. If you redesign the deck heights to your own liking, you will need to shape the flotation bulkheads to fit.

Wasp: A Uniquely Safe and Ergonomic Solo Tripping and Fishing Canoe

DIMENSIONS

	WITH LOW ENDS	WITH HIGH ENDS
Length	14′8.4″	14′10″
Width, maximum	30″	30″
Width at 3.63″ waterline	27.5″	27.5″
Width, gunwale at paddler's station	20.5″	20.5″
Width at 3.63″ waterline at paddler's station	26″	26″
Depth at bow	11.6″	16.6″
Depth at center	12.5″	12.5″
Depth at stern	10″	14.6″
Rocker (at bow and stern)	0.9″	0.9″

Many people have mistaken Wasp for a kayak on first sight, even though it is really an open canoe with decks only at the ends to enclose large flotation chambers (see Figures 6.1 and 11.28 in earlier chapters). It does combine many attributes of both a solo canoe and a kayak but in a different manner than Kayoo does. A lot of flare and volume toward the ends enables Wasp to ride over waves and carry a large load for canoe camping. (See Figure 16.18.) Yet it is light, highly maneuverable, fast when not heavily loaded, and a joy to paddle. It offers an extremely ergonomic,

easy reach to the water with the paddle, whether using a single- or double-blade paddle. This short reach to the water encourages using a shorter, and therefore lighter and less fatiguing, paddle. The paddle stroke can be made closer to the hull centerline so that the canoe tracks straight with less energy wasted on correcting strokes.

Where Kayoo has structural flotation chambers and a moderately low seat to enhance safety and stability, Wasp takes a different approach. The narrow waist allows one to remain closer to the center of gravity while getting closer to the water. Polyethylene flotation, in the sides at the wide portions of the hull, provides the self-rescue capability as outlined in Chapter 15. Just getting into and out of the boat is easier with the narrow waist because it is a shorter step into the center of balance, and the boat is more difficult to tip.

The flared areas of the hull help resist capsizing. The flare and volume toward the bow and stern encourage Wasp to ride over waves rather

FIGURE 16.18. *Wasp with plenty of room for camping equipment.*

than plow into them. Moderate width at the waterline makes for a good turn of speed, while the combination of flared ends and low seat provides good secondary stability. The narrow gunwales and waterline at the paddler's station also make it easy to reach a hand into the water without tipping, an attribute that makes Wasp my absolute favorite for aquatic research and fishing. It is hands down the safest-feeling and most ergonomic open solo canoe I've paddled.

As built, Wasp has low ends with large decks, enabling it to handle windy conditions with ease. I built this example with more rocker than the plans call for, which allows Wasp to turn on a dime with little effort. The enhanced maneuverability helps in negotiating tricky rock gardens and whitewater. Ability to turn also helps when trying to steer a straight course and hold a navigation line in a strong quartering wind. My long, fast canoes with straight keel lines and no rocker become difficult to manage in such conditions. Quartering tailwinds are a special problem, and the situation can be hazardous if the boat is pushed sideways to wind and waves. For sea kayaks, a rudder or a skeg can be helpful, but they add weight, complexity, and mechanical apparatus that can fail. For canoes and recreational kayaks, I prefer the simplest and lightest approach: a hull that will turn with moderate ease.

Both Wasp and Kayoo turn acceptably well if built to the plans. With extra rocker, most boats will turn more easily but require more work to track a straight line. Wasp makes that task easier by allowing you to make the paddle stroke closer to the boat's centerline. A double-blade kayak paddle also works wonderfully well with Wasp's narrow gunwales. Alternating power strokes on each side keeps you tracking in the desired direction with little effort. If tracking straight across flat waters is your goal, then build Wasp exactly to the plans. (See Figures 16.19 through 16.26.) If you would like to try the extra rocker, that is easily done when cutting out and setting up the stations on the strongback and will be described below.

Wasp was built with three layers of 5-ounce Kevlar and an outer layer of 4-ounce fiber-glass. The outer fiberglass layer will allow me to do some sanding if I decide to eventually smooth and paint the hull. The hull has about the same puncture and impact resistance as the Kayoo example shown earlier in this chapter, but it is more flexible and requires more ribs for reinforcement. This greater number of ribs, combined with the larger hull surface area requiring more cloth and epoxy, makes Wasp a little heavier than Kayoo. With the low ends and large decked flotation chambers shown in the plans and pictured in Figures 6.1 and 11.28, and with a 4-inch-thick polyethylene foam seat fitted on the floor, Wasp originally weighed 28 pounds. With a more elaborate combination folding seat, backrest, and portage yoke, and the associated hanger panels and hardware, the weight went up to 36 pounds.

Because I had not made side flotation an integral part of the boat, I added tie-in points and installed about 0.9 cubic foot of polyethylene foam into each side. Since the hull is narrow at the center paddling station, the flotation was added in the more widely flared areas to the front and rear. These additions boosted the final weight to 38 pounds. This is still quite light for a strong solo canoe outfitted this well. A bit more weight could be saved by using inner and outer layers of carbon fiber, omitting the fiberglass outer layer, and perhaps building in ultra-lightweight flotation chambers.

I recommend building Wasp to the plans with long, low end decks as shown in Figure 16.19. However, I've included drawings and coordinates for those who prefer to build it with higher ends and smaller, simpler decks.

Most canoe and kayaks plans, including those for Dragonfly and Kayoo, show all the stations on a single sheet. This generally works well, given the simple lines of most boats. But Wasp has a far more complex shape than most canoes. Not only is it asymmetric (that is, its bow and stern stations are not identical), but it is "wasp-waisted": its waterlines curve somewhat like a soda bottle or a mountain dulcimer. If drawn on a single sheet, there would be a confusing overlapping of lines, so I have drawn the stations on four sheets for clarity.

Wasp is quite versatile as is, and there are few reasons to make changes. It might be lengthened for greater straight-line top speed on big waters with large loads. If you do this, keep in mind that it is still not a tandem canoe. The narrow center paddling station and wide ends suit solo use only. I recommend strongly against shortening this design. Shortening the narrow center section will reduce the room to swing a paddle, while shortening the ends will make them blunter and will reduce performance.

Wasp Tests

The tests of Wasp were conducted with my prototype, which has low ends with relatively large flotation chambers covered with peaked decks and spray rails. Also, the prototype was built with more rocker in the ends than is shown in the plans. Total rocker is about 2¼ inches in each end, while the plans call for about ⁹/₁₀ inch.

Note that performance characteristics will depend on the shape of the hull you build, your size and weight, your paddling skill, and the center of gravity. The seat should be positioned so that your weight is balanced fore and aft. Make the seat height as low as is comfortable while allowing you to paddle without banging the paddle shaft or any body parts on the gunwales. The top of my seat is about 5½ inches from the inside bottom of the hull. While Wasp can readily be paddled while kneeling, it is most convenient and more stable to paddle from the low seated position. In this regard Wasp is much like a kayak with a high seat, making it easy on both the knees and the back.

Initial tests demonstrated Wasp has very pleasant stability for paddlers with some experience. Wasp can be leaned easily to carve turns or to remain vertical when broadside to rolling waves. Yet the more it is leaned the more it resists rolling farther. I feel as though I would have to fall out before capsizing. The large amount of rocker in the prototype makes it very easy to

turn and maneuver, even without leaning. It also tracks quite well when paddled close to the side or when using a double-blade paddle. For me, double-blade paddle lengths of 205 to 220 cm work nicely. The shorter length with a high-angle stroke works surprisingly well, allowing power strokes close to the side for better tracking. The longer paddle is better for keeping water drips out of the boat.

Wasp is both lightweight and moderate in length, and it accelerates and decelerates easily and quickly. Combined with its maneuverability, these characteristics make it a delight on twisty streams. The large rocker of the prototype does not produce the straight-line glide of long hulls that have no rocker. However, a relatively narrow beam at the waterline produces a very good cruise speed, and tracking is more than adequate, especially with a double paddle. If your main mission involves flatwater lakes, you might prefer to build it with the ⁹/₁₀-inch rocker of the plans, which will result in better straight-line tracking. Friends who paddled the prototype on rivers liked the sprightly acceleration and maneuverability.

Wasp's speed performance can be deceptive and difficult to gauge at first. It does accelerate quickly, which gives it a very sporty feel. The view from the sitting position shows the bulbous-looking bow at the flared sheerline compared to the more pointed ends of traditional solo canoes. However, the hull entry lines at the waterline are quite streamlined, and the beam at the waterline is relatively narrow. These combine to give a good cruising speed without much effort. I paddled the same 4-mile course, using the same paddle, with both Wasp and my Wenonah Advantage, a slender and very fast solo canoe that is 16½ feet long. Wasp was faster by a few minutes. I wouldn't consider this conclusive evidence for a precise speed comparison, and these are definitely not racing canoes. But it certainly indicates that Wasp, with my weight loading, is about as speedy for cruising as a rather fast solo canoe.

Wasp has a large-volume hull, making it possible to carry large loads and readily negotiate some whitewater. The light weight and added

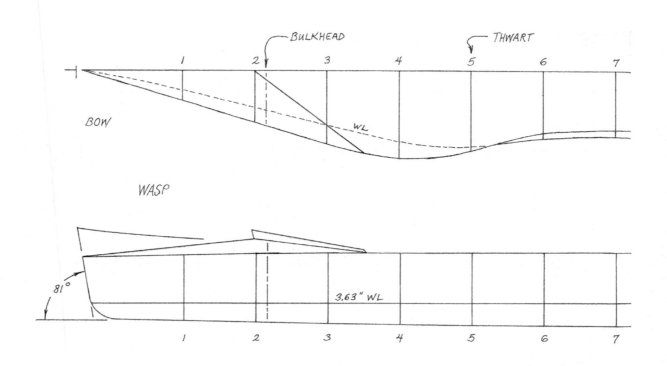

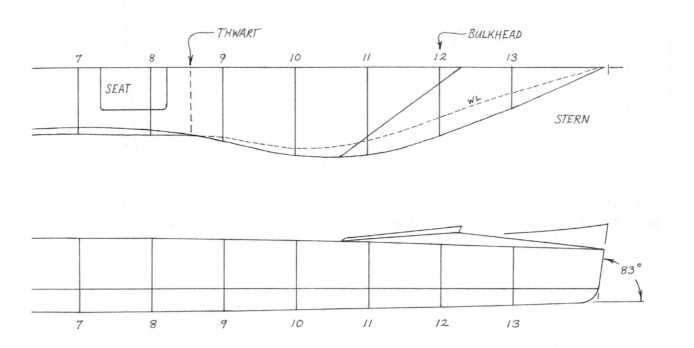

FIGURE 16.19. *Wasp top view and side view. The flotation chamber bulkheads are raised in the center about 2 inches above the sheerline to create peaked end decks.*

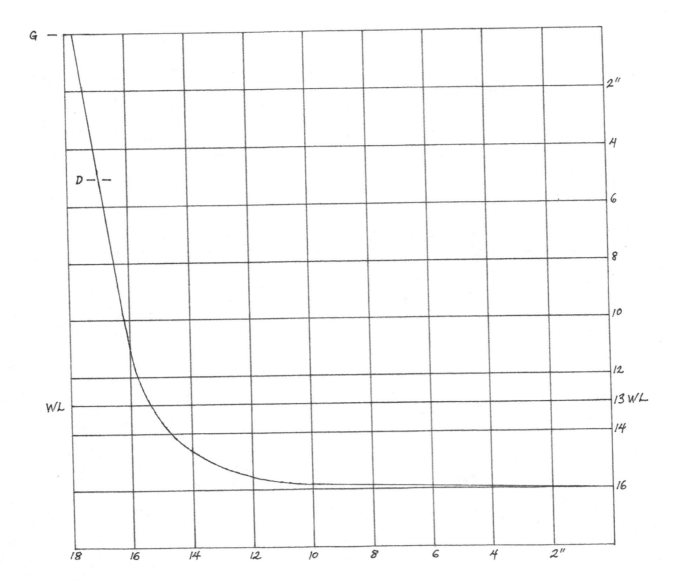

FIGURE 16.20. *Wasp bow profile. G indicates the bow and stern heights for building with high ends and gunwales extended to the ends; D indicates the heights for low ends with large end decks.*

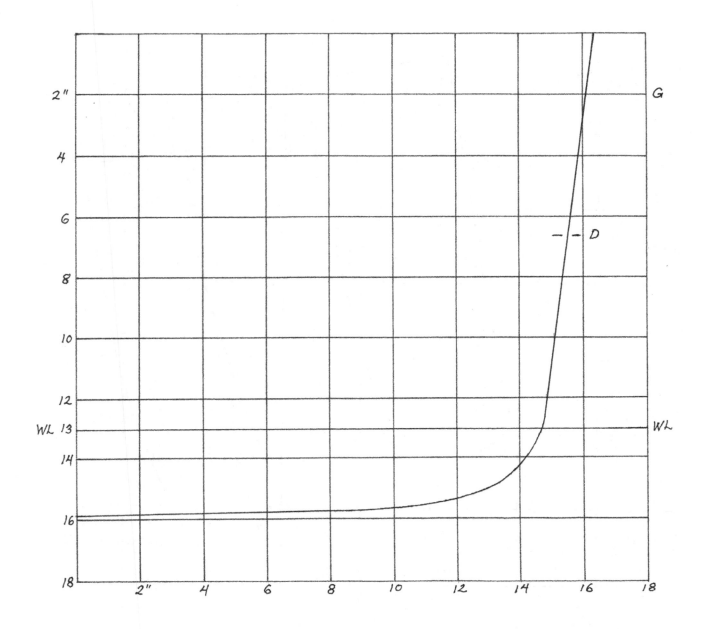

FIGURE 16.21. *Wasp stern profile.*

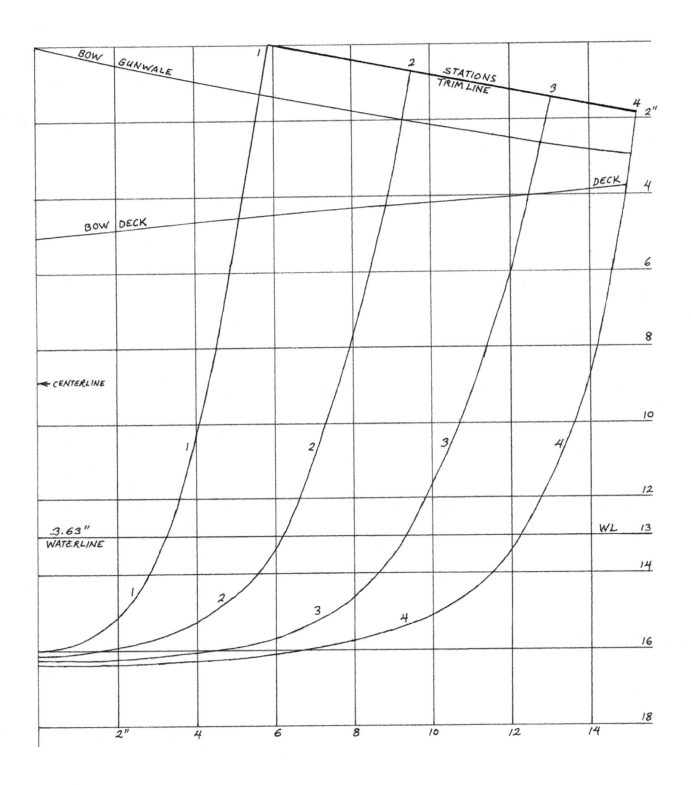

FIGURE 16.22. *Wasp stations 1 through 4.*

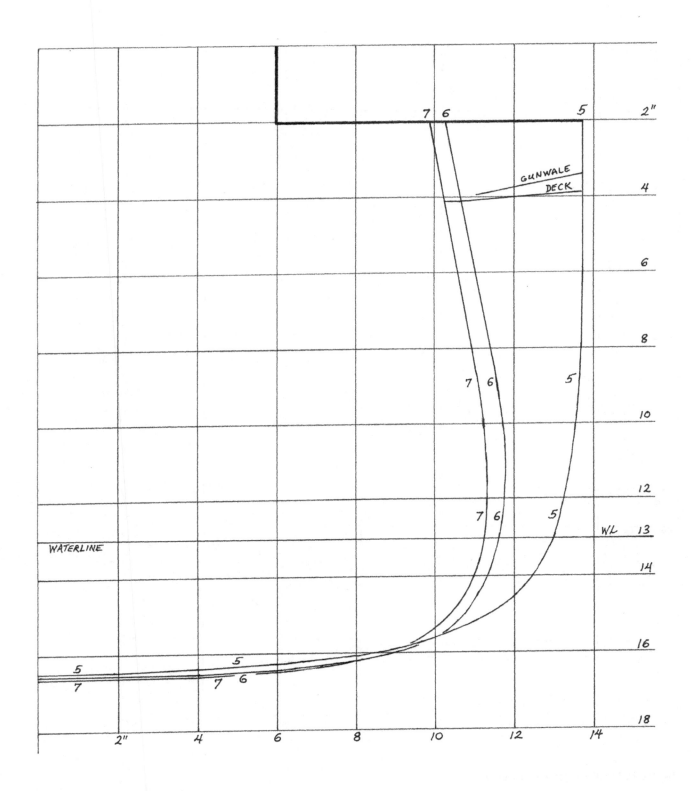

FIGURE 16.23. *Wasp stations 5 through 7.*

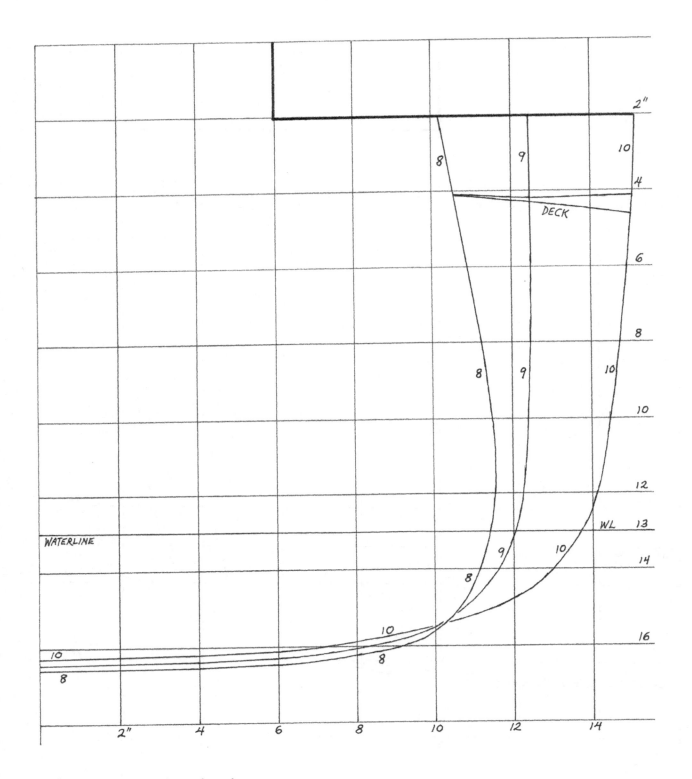

FIGURE 16.24. Wasp stations 8 through 10.

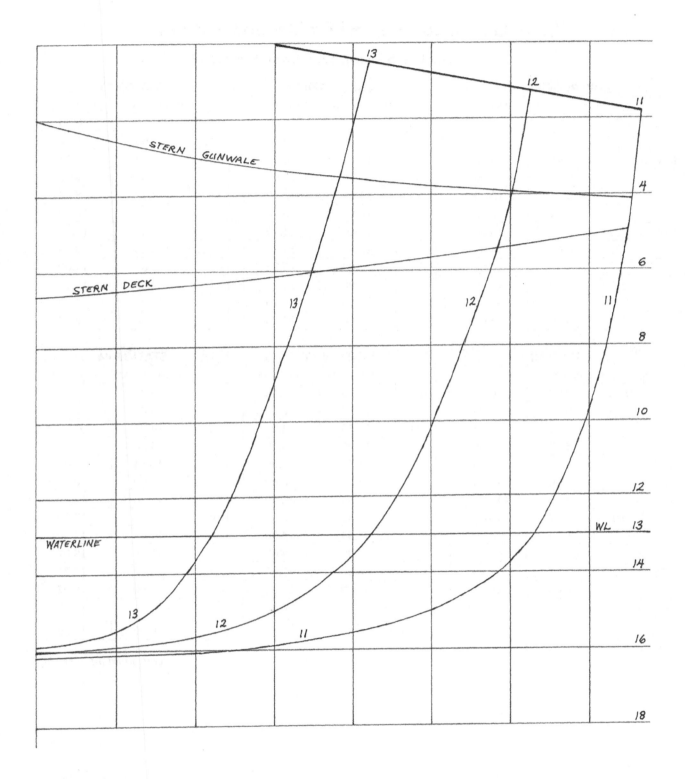

FIGURE 16.25. *Wasp stations 11 through 13.*

Wasp: Coordinates for End Profiles and Stations

Measurements in inches. Spacing between stations is 12 inches.

BOW PROFILE			STERN PROFILE			STATION #1		
	HORIZONTAL	VERTICAL		HORIZONTAL	VERTICAL		HORIZONTAL	VERTICAL
gunwale-G	17.70	0.00	trim	16.33	0.00		5.85	0.00
	17.39	2.00	G	16.09	2.00	G	5.66	1.27
deck-D	16.91	5.05	D	15.51	6.62	D	5.12	4.45
	16.44	8.00		15.10	10.00		4.85	6.00
	16.13	10.00		14.86	12.00		4.50	8.00
	15.72	12.00	WL	14.69	13.00		4.07	10.00
3.63″ WL	15.33	13.00		14.20	14.00		3.57	12.00
	14.67	14.00		13.30	14.85	WL	3.25	13.00
	14.00	14.62		12.00	15.36		2.80	14.00
	12.00	15.58		10.00	15.65		2.00	15.12
	10.00	15.81		8.00	15.70		1.00	15.78
	0.00	16.00		0.00	15.90		0.00	16.00

STATION #2			STATION #3			STATION #4		
	HORIZONTAL	VERTICAL		HORIZONTAL	VERTICAL		HORIZONTAL	VERTICAL
trim	9.50	0.70	trim	13.05	1.40	trim	15.22	1.85
G	9.28	1.95	G	12.80	2.60	G	15.06	2.95
D	8.83	4.23	D	12.46	4.00	D	14.95	3.72
	8.42	6.00		12.00	6.00		14.56	6.00
	7.90	8.00		11.41	8.00		14.14	8.00
	7.26	10.00		10.70	10.00		13.60	10.00
	6.56	12.00		9.84	12.00		12.76	12.00
WL	6.14	13.00	WL	9.31	13.00	WL	12.22	13.00
	5.54	14.00		8.64	14.00		11.48	14.00
	4.00	15.22		8.00	14.63		10.00	15.07
	2.00	15.93		6.00	15.65		8.00	15.71
	0.00	16.12		4.00	16.04		6.00	16.07
				0.00	16.24		4.00	16.26
							0.00	16.36

(continued on next page)

FIGURE 16.26. *Wasp coordinates. These can be used to produce full-size end profiles and stations as depicted on the grids in Figures 16.20 through 16.25. For horizontal numbers, measure from the left edge of the grid except for the bow profile, which is measured from the right edge of the grid; for vertical numbers, measure down from the top. Each pair of side-by-side numbers provides coordinates to plot one point. Connect the plotted points with a curved line to produce the profiles shown.*

Wasp: Coordinates for End Profiles and Stations (continued)

STATION #5	HORIZONTAL	VERTICAL
trim	13.72	2.00
G	13.72	3.42
D	13.72	3.88
	13.71	6.00
	13.68	8.00
	13.56	10.00
	13.24	12.00
WL	13.02	13.00
	12.50	14.00
	12.00	14.55
	11.17	15.15
	10.00	15.60
	8.00	16.04
	6.00	16.26
	4.00	16.36
	2.00	16.43
	0.00	16.47

STATION #6	HORIZONTAL	VERTICAL
trim	10.25	2.00
G	10.65	4.05
D	10.66	4.10
	11.40	8.00
	11.71	10.00
	11.75	12.00
WL	11.61	13.00
	11.31	14.00
	10.80	14.90
	10.00	15.60
	8.00	16.18
	6.00	16.44
	4.00	16.53
	0.00	16.56

STATION #7	HORIZONTAL	VERTICAL
trim	9.85	2.00
G&D	10.23	4.11
	10.92	8.00
	11.23	10.00
	11.28	12.00
WL	11.20	13.00
	10.95	14.00
	10.00	15.32
	8.00	16.22
	6.00	16.48
	4.00	16.58
	0.00	16.63

STATION #8	HORIZONTAL	VERTICAL
trim	10.17	2.00
G	10.53	4.07
D	10.53	4.10
	11.22	8.00
	11.48	10.00
	11.54	12.00
WL	11.42	13.00
	11.13	14.00
	10.00	15.60
	8.00	16.20
	6.00	16.45
	4.00	16.54
	0.00	16.56

STATION #9	HORIZONTAL	VERTICAL
trim	12.45	2.00
G	12.46	4.19
D	12.47	4.26
	12.46	8.00
	12.39	10.00
	12.23	12.00
WL	12.03	13.00
	11.63	14.00
	11.00	14.80
	10.00	15.51
	8.00	16.03
	6.00	16.27
	4.00	16.38
	0.00	16.45

STATION #10	HORIZONTAL	VERTICAL
trim	15.14	2.00
G	15.05	4.11
D	15.02	4.62
	14.92	6.00
	14.72	8.00
	14.45	10.00
	14.13	12.00
WL	13.75	13.00
	13.01	14.00
	12.00	14.78
	10.00	15.50
	8.00	15.87
	6.00	16.12
	4.00	16.23
	0.00	16.30

(continued on next page)

Wasp: Coordinates for End Profiles and Stations (continued)

STATION #11				STATION #12				STATION #13		
	HORIZONTAL	VERTICAL			HORIZONTAL	VERTICAL			HORIZONTAL	VERTICAL
trim	15.30	1.80		trim	12.50	1.28		trim	8.40	0.46
G	15.06	4.07		G	12.06	3.92		G	7.66	3.50
D	14.95	4.89		D	11.72	5.37		D	6.96	6.00
	14.79	6.00			10.84	8.00			6.35	8.00
	14.44	8.00			10.08	10.00			5.64	10.00
	13.90	10.00			9.13	12.00			4.87	12.00
	13.14	12.00		WL	8.51	13.00		WL	4.41	13.00
WL	12.61	13.00			7.50	14.00			3.78	14.00
	11.73	14.00			6.00	14.95			3.00	14.85
	10.00	14.99			4.00	15.62			2.00	15.48
	8.00	15.53			0.00	16.02			0.00	15.90
	6.00	15.87								
	4.00	16.05								
	0.00	16.15								

rocker of the prototype provide good maneuverability for whitewater. It also draws less water than my other canoes and kayaks, allowing it to float easily over obstructions and travel shallows that would make my other boats run aground. In the lightweight hull layup described, I've used Wasp for class 2 rapids. But I would build heavier for more serious whitewater. And, to tell the truth, when the mission is whitewater only, I often bring a sacrificial plastic boat and leave the handmade composite boats for the situations in which light weight and efficient paddling are more appreciated.

Wasp is unusual in that it is suitable for paddlers of almost any size and weight. Due to the narrow waist, it is especially easy for a small person to paddle but will also carry a large paddler and a heavy load. Kayoo is similar in length and somewhat similar in paddling performance to Wasp, but Kayoo is designed more specifically for lightweight portaging and efficient wilderness camping with a slightly smaller load.

Although Wasp is a little larger and heavier, it will carry more weight and is extremely forgiving for a wide range of paddler sizes. And it's just great for fishing!

Modifying Canoe and Kayak Designs

Any boat design can be modified, but will the change be for the better? Certain modifications have predictable results but may have unintended consequences elsewhere. For example, making a design narrower overall will predictably make it faster. It will also probably make it less stable, but by how much? If you plan to load the narrower hull with the same amount of heavy camping gear, it will sit lower in the water than the wider version, adding back some of the wetted surface that you took away when you made the hull narrower, and possibly making the boat slower, not faster. Freeboard will also be reduced, making it more subject to swamping but simultaneously reducing the influence of wind on the boat's progress and direction. On the other hand, the narrower boat will be lighter, which will counteract its reduced buoyancy to an extent.

It is indeed tricky to change a design and predict all of the consequences—especially if you haven't paddled the original design. Nonetheless, paddlers with some experience who recognize the basic performance characteristics of a boat design often say to themselves, "That would be perfect, if only…" So let's look at some of the more common and straightforward changes that you might wish to make, and discuss how to accomplish them.

Depth

Depth or gunwale height is often easy to modify, and is often desirable, as discussed in the section on Dragonfly earlier in this chapter. Higher gunwales increase freeboard, carrying capacity, windage, and weight, while reducing ease of paddling. Lower gunwales have the opposite effects.

Add any extra depth equally over the entire length of the canoe, from bow to stern. When drawing out full-size forms, make the gunwale marks the same distance higher at each station and at both ends. I extend the station lines on my plans and provide coordinates beyond the designed sheerline for my designs to make increasing the gunwale height

easy. You can draw out and cut the stations to their full-drawn height, build the hull accordingly, and then simply trim the hull to whatever height is desired.

Many designers terminate the station lines at the sheerline and provide no coordinates beyond that point. If you wish to raise the gunwales on a design where this is the case, use a flexible curve or a French curve to extend the stations upward in a pleasing and logical curve.

Length

Increasing a boat's length is another way to increase its volume and load capacity. It will also improve straight-line tracking and top speed, at the expense of added weight, slower turning, and increased wetted surface area and drag. Heavier, larger, and stronger paddlers may like this trade-off for traveling on large lakes and carrying large camping loads.

To increase length, add an equal distance between each station and to each end profile. Make the end profile additions where they meet the first and last stations. Adding just 1 inch between each station and at the ends has a significant effect. For Kayoo, with thirteen stations, the boat will grow by 14 inches—from 14 feet 6 inches to 15 feet 8 inches for the decked version and from 14 feet 8 inches to 15 feet 10 inches for the open canoe. Adding 1½ inches between stations increases the length by 21 inches.

A design can be shortened in a similar fashion to make the canoe more maneuverable in narrow twisty streams or rock gardens, to reduce the weight a bit for easier portaging and transporting, or to accommodate storage space constraints. Since shortening the hull will reduce its volume, it will also reduce freeboard, load capacity, and stability. This may be fine for lighter-weight paddlers and day trips on ponds and protected flat waters, and you can mount the seat lower to improve stability. You could also gain back some of the freeboard and load capacity by raising the gunwales. While excess capacity can sometimes be useful, it is also a burden to carry around a bigger and heavier boat than you actually need or to paddle with gunwales higher than necessary.

When lengthening a design, the stringers will span a greater distance between the station molds.

And when the polyester fabric is heat-shrunk during construction, it may deform the stringers a little and make for an unsightly, slightly wavy hull shape. To counteract this, use thicker stock for the stringers and adjust the dimensions of the station forms accordingly.

Rocker

Rocker can also be changed to fine-tune a design's balance between tracking and turning. For general flatwater use, most paddlers prefer better tracking over quicker turning. The designs in this book all have about 1 inch of rocker at both bow and stern. This provides good tracking and fairly good maneuverability, and turning can be quickened by heeling or leaning the boat. However, rocker can be increased to provide greater maneuverability in whitewater and narrow creeks. On Kayoo and Wasp, rocker of 2 to 2¼ inches at both bow and stern will provide a good balance between turning ease for small rivers and acceptable tracking for crossing lakes. Three inches of rocker will produce a very quick-turning boat, with a noticeable sacrifice in tracking. Given the very modest amount of rocker on these designs, I do not recommend reducing it below the designed specification.

Rocker is increased by changing the heights at which stations are mounted on the strongback. Since the hull is built upside down on the strongback, the keel line must curve down at the ends or up in the middle when setting up stations. To do this, mount each station progressively higher from the bow toward the middle station and then lower again toward the stern. This can be done with shims or by leaving extra material at the top reference line (where station meets strongback) when you cut out the plywood stations.

Let's assume that there are thirteen stations and that station #7 is the middle station (which is the case for both Kayoo and Wasp). Let's also assume that there is a designed 0.8 inch of rocker at each end and you want to increase it by 1.2 inches, for a total of 2 inches at each end. Mount the bow profile form and station #1 normally at the designed height. Add 0.2 inch to the plans height of station #2, and continue adding an additional 0.2 inch to each station up to the middle station, so that station #3 is 0.4 inch higher, station #4 is 0.6 inch higher, station #5 is 0.8 inch higher, station #6 is 1 inch higher, and station #7 is 1.2 inches higher. With 1.2 inches added to the original 0.8 inch of rocker, there is now a total of 2 inches of rocker from bow to middle. Toward the stern the stations will be progressively lower than station #7. Add 1 inch to the plan's height of station #8, 0.8 inch to station #9, 0.6 inch to station #10, 0.4 inch to station #11, and 0.2 inch to station #12. Station #13 is mounted at the plan's height like station #1.

You may read some references to differential rocker, and some manufacturers claim a benefit for more rocker at the bow or less at the stern. Actually, this effect is easily produced by adjusting fore-and-aft trim or weight balance. For instance, placing the seat and the paddler's weight more to the rear will make the bow ride higher in the water, resulting in the effect of more rocker in the bow and less in the stern. Since weight loading and seat position can be changed easily, moving them is a convenient way to experiment with the effects of trim and differential rocker on handling. Trimming the bow low makes it easier to track into a strong headwind, and trimming the stern low facilitates tracking downwind. Although a movable seat is convenient for trim

changes, repositioning the weight of cargo works as well. I almost always have a dry bag, fishing kit, or water bottle that can be moved from one end to the other. In a pinch, a rock can provide ballast.

Before you change the rocker, keep in mind that the boat's length also influences its turning ability. A shorter canoe will turn readily with less rocker. With a length of less than 12 feet, Dragonfly will turn well enough for most uses and you may not wish to compromise her tracking any further. Even a modest increase in rocker would be desirable only for making a version specifically for whitewater. Dragonfly's sides should also be raised a few inches (or a deck added) to reduce the chances of swamping in rapids.

Flare and Tumblehome

Most open canoe hulls are flexible enough to change the amount of flare or tumblehome by altering the length of the thwarts. Shortening the thwarts reduces the width at the gunwales and increases tumblehome or reduces flare. Deforming of the hull in this manner is also likely to round the bottom more in cross section, increase the depth, reduce rocker, and reduce stability. Lengthening the thwarts and increasing the hull's width will reduce tumblehome or increase flare; depth will also be reduced, and rocker and stability may increase.

Chapter 17

Making a Lightweight Paddle

Composite materials are ideal for creating ultra-lightweight paddles. It is a relatively quick and simple project to make a paddle with foam, wood, epoxy, and carbon fiber or fiberglass.

(See Figure 17.1.) Creating your own custom paddle is also an excellent way to introduce yourself to working with epoxy and a variety of composite techniques. It can help you gain confidence with the materials before undertaking the much bigger task of building a canoe.

The Process

The materials needed are urethane foam (available from Aircraft Spruce; see Appendix A), wood for the shaft, carbon fiber or fiberglass cloth, and epoxy to bond it all together. (See Figure 17.2.) Spruce has great strength for its weight and is an ideal choice for the shaft. Lighter-weight western red cedar can be used to save weight. A cedar shaft needs to be sheathed in fiberglass to increase strength and keep it from splintering. Many other woods can and have been used for paddle shafts, including ash and soft maple, but most of them will be heavier. The wood must have straight grain and no knots or flaws. (See Figures 17.3 to 17.9.)

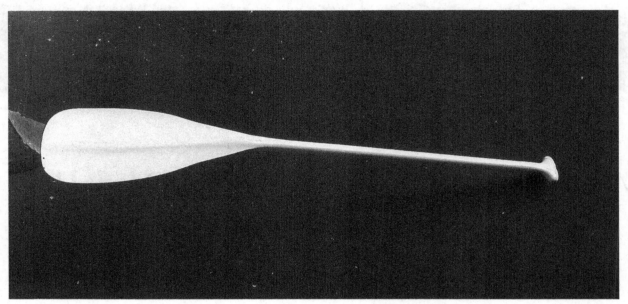

FIGURE 17.1. *This bent-shaft paddle is made with carbon fiber over a core of foam and cedar. Weight is less than 10 ounces, making it almost effortless to paddle all day. A spare like this can be carried on wilderness trips without increasing the burden on long portages.*

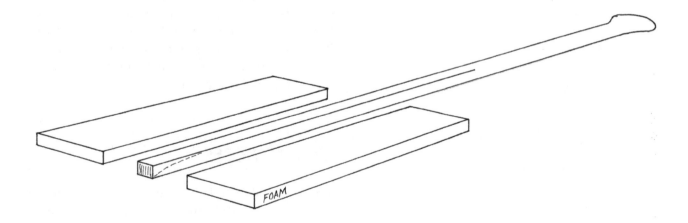

FIGURE 17.2. *An exploded view shows the parts of a single-blade paddle; a double-blade paddle is made the same way. The shaft is wood, to which two pieces of lightweight, rigid urethane foam are glued for the blade. Note the orientation of the wood grain, which runs through the shaft from front to back, not side to side. Trim the blade end of the shaft to a taper more or less like the dotted line (see also Figure 17.6). The taper can also be a straight line (as shown in Figure 17.5). Greater curve provides more volume and buoyancy in the blade, which I've come to like. The foam can be thicker than the wood at this stage; it will be easy to cut and shape later. Use a few small dabs of quick-setting epoxy to glue the foam to the wood so that they form a flat surface across one side of the blade (as shown in Figures 17.6 and 17.7).*

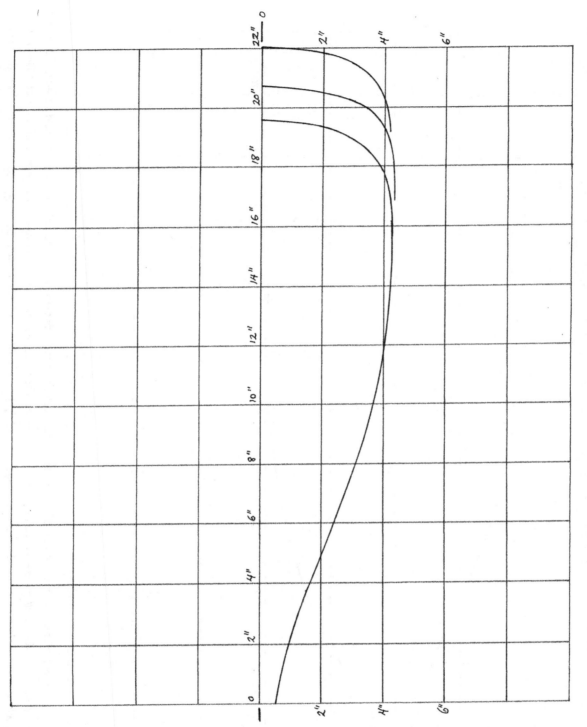

FIGURE 17.3. This is a good, all-around blade shape for a single-blade paddle. Expanding the grid to 2-inch squares will provide a full-size pattern. The blade is symmetrical. Cut out the half blade shown, and trace both sides to make a template. There are three alternative blade ends. The short 19.6-inch blade makes a paddle that can be used as a compact and very light spare on wilderness trips. It also works well with a bent shaft. The 20.75-inch blade has more area and power suited to all-around paddling with either a straight or a bent shaft. The long 22-inch blade on a straight shaft is appropriate for deep water and large paddlers in tandem canoes.

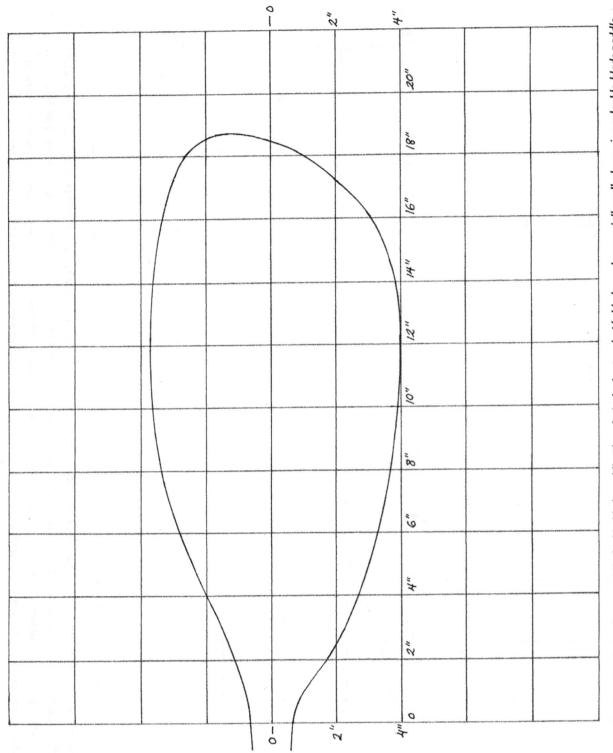

FIGURE 17.4. *Here is one of my favorite shapes for a versatile double-blade paddle. The relatively short and wide blade works especially well when using a double-blade paddle with a solo canoe; it is very good for kayaks as well. An asymmetric shape provides moderate blade area and power without having to dig too deep into the water. The long side is up when paddling. When you carve the blades, make them mirror images left and right, making certain that both blades have their tips on the same side of the shaft.*

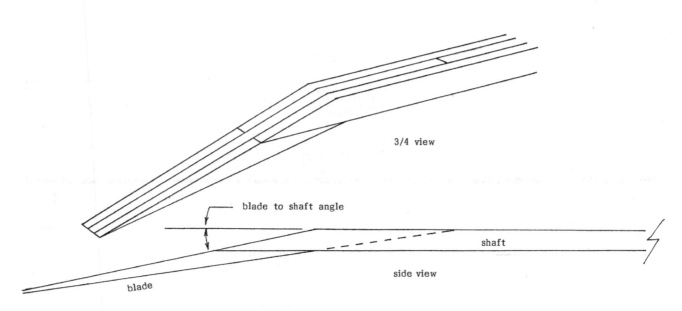

3/4 view

blade to shaft angle

shaft

side view

blade

FIGURE 17.5. *To create the bend in a single-blade, bent-shaft paddle, laminate wood with epoxy in at least three overlapping layers as shown. For three layers, each layer should be approximately 0.4 inch thick. An angle of 12 degrees between the shaft and the power face of the blade is my preference for general paddling.*

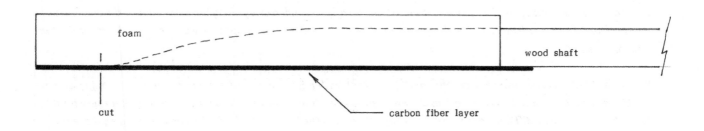

foam

wood shaft

cut

carbon fiber layer

FIGURE 17.6. *Final shaping of the paddle will be easier if you taper the end of the shaft approximately to the dotted line before gluing the foam pieces to the sides. Then, with the foam glued in place, cover the flat, level side of the blade with a layer of carbon fiber or fiberglass cloth; do not use Kevlar (also see Figure 17.7). First, saturate the foam and wood blade surface with epoxy. Then lay the cloth in place and saturate it with epoxy. Use 10- to 12-ounce carbon fiber for a very strong blade. Or, use 5.8-ounce carbon fiber for an ultralight paddle; note that it will not be as strong and must be used with care. Several layers of 6-ounce fiberglass are an inexpensive but heavier alternative.*

After the epoxy sets, carefully saw the blade to its finished profile shape using a fine-tooth blade in a band saw or a tabletop jigsaw, or a hacksaw blade. The saw blade should cut from the fabric side toward the foam or else the fabric will pull away from the foam. Next, the foam is carved and sanded to the dotted line profile. Urethane foam cuts and sands with very little effort, so proceed with care. The flat side will be the power face — the side of the paddle that pushes the water when you take a stroke. Shapes other than a flat power face are possible, but flat is easy to fabricate and paddles well.

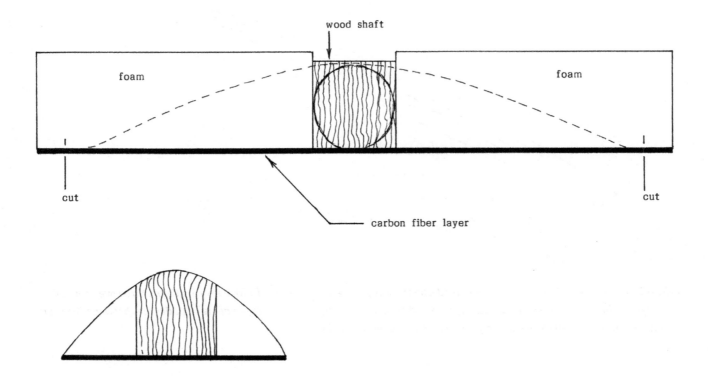

FIGURE 17.7. *This is an end-view cross section of the blade. Note the orientation of the wood grain at right angles to the blade. After the cloth-and-epoxy-covered blade is sawn to its profile shape, carve and sand the foam to the dotted-line cross section. Taper and feather the edge of the foam as shown so that the foam is sanded away along the outer edge of the blade, exposing the cloth for 0.4 to 0.5 inch along the blade's perimeter. This will permit a stronger bond between the cloth layers on the two sides of the paddle.*

Where the blade gets narrower toward the shaft and throat, within 5 or 6 inches of the throat, the foam should just meet the blade edge in a pointed intersection (as shown in the lower left inset). If you try to form a curved taper there for a cloth to cloth bond, it will be difficult to make carbon cloth conform to the bend. Techniques like vacuum bagging make sharper bends and more complex shapes possible, but such techniques and the equipment they require are not needed for the projects in this book.

Notice that the foam is left rather thick. This creates a blade with a lot of volume and buoyancy. A buoyant paddle feels great in the water. It will provide some extra lift for bracing and save you energy while lifting the paddle at the end of a stroke. The paddle almost jumps out of the water.

If you are making a double paddle, try to make both blades match as well as you can. When the foam shape meets your approval, cover it with fabric and epoxy just as you did the flat side. Start by placing a layer of plastic wrap on your work surface. Then place the blade flat side down on the plastic wrap and start applying epoxy and cloth to the curved foam. The carbon or fiberglass fabric should extend beyond the blade edges. Trim it with a saw, and sandpaper the edges after the epoxy sets.

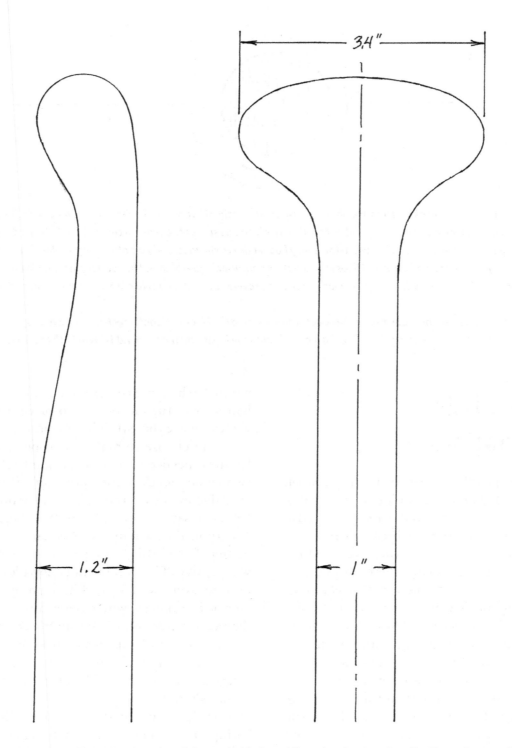

FIGURE 17.8. *Glue blocks of wood to the sides of the single-blade paddle end and carve a handle. Shape the rest of the shaft and handle after the blade is covered with cloth and epoxy or before gluing the blade foam to the shaft blank. Carve the shaft to a pleasing oval cross-section shape. A sharp spokeshave is the most convenient tool for this, and wood rasps are handy for final shaping before sanding. Size the shaft to suit your grip. The dimensions given are minimums; larger will be stronger. A spruce or cedar shaft must be relatively large in diameter to maintain adequate strength.*

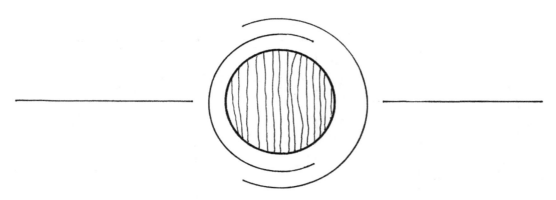

FIGURE 17.9. *If you've used a weak and lightweight wood like cedar for the shaft, you will need to reinforce it with fiberglass or lightweight carbon fiber cloth. Add epoxy and a strip of cloth along one side of the shaft to cover about two-thirds of the shaft diameter (as shown in the cross section). When the epoxy has set dry to the touch, add a cloth and epoxy layer from the other side, overlapping as shown. The horizontal lines indicate the orientation of the blades. The overlapping double layers of cloth are at right angles to the blades, just like the wood grain. This provides extra strength to absorb the energy of paddle strokes.*

On a bent-shaft paddle, reinforce the area of the paddle throat, where the blade and shaft meet, with an extra layer of carbon fiber or fiberglass cloth about 6 inches long, lapping it equally onto the blade and the shaft. Add this to both the front and back.

Double-Blade Considerations

Double blade paddlers have to decide between straight (parallel) and feathered (angled) blades, and between a one-piece and a two-piece (also known as a take-apart or a breakdown) shaft. One-piece paddles are less expensive to build, but their length can make them difficult to transport and store. One-piece paddles are limited to a single-blade orientation, either straight or feathered. Two-piece paddles allow you to switch at will between straight- and feathered-blade orientation. Feathered blades can reduce wind resistance, especially when battling into a headwind. Straight blades are an advantage going downwind. A two-piece shaft allows you to switch. Straight blades may be easier on your wrist, reducing the prospect of tendonitis. Some people find straight blades easier to use; others have no difficulty adopting the proper technique for a feathered paddle.

If you are building a one-piece paddle with a wood shaft, I recommend making the blades parallel, which is easiest. You can always cut it in half later to turn it into a two-piece paddle that you can use either straight or feathered.

If you choose to make a two-piece paddle, a ferrule is needed to serve as the joint between the two equal-length sections of shaft. Ferrules are available in both carbon fiber and stainless steel from Chesapeake Light Craft. (See Appendix A.) A carbon fiber ferrule is more costly but much lighter. The ferrule is bonded to the paddle shaft with epoxy. The carbon fiber ferrules that I've used fit over the shaft and have an inside diameter of 1.17 inches, which determines the shaft's diameter at the joint. The shaft's diameter and shape at the hand grip areas can be slightly different to suit your hands but—to maintain adequate strength—should not be less than 1.1 inch for a spruce shaft.

Ferrules come with holes predrilled for a spring-loaded locking pin that enables the two halves to come apart. There are alternate holes for locking the shaft with the blades straight or feathered. With a ferrule installed, you can experiment with the angled positions and drill new holes for the locking pin if the default angles don't suit you. Feather angles of about 55 to 75 degrees are common. My personal preference is about 60 degrees so that the wrist doesn't have to bend too much.

Feathered blades can be angled for right-hand control or left-hand control. To determine this, hold the paddle in paddling position. Make certain that the long sides of the asymmetric blades are up. If the top of the left blade is rotated forward of the right blade, then the paddle is right-hand control. The blades can be rotated the other way for left-hand control, and holes can be drilled in the ferrule to suit either.

Take-apart ferrules can sometimes stick if they become dirty, and the locking mechanism can fail. I've had locking pin springs break, but they are easily replaced. The simplicity of one-piece paddles generally makes them trouble free, but two-piece paddles are versatile and convenient.

How Long?

Choosing the right length is an important aspect of paddle making. The best way to do this is to sit or kneel in your canoe in the position that you plan to use when paddling. With a single-blade paddle, the correct stroke is with the paddle held vertical. If you hold a paddle vertically with the hand grip at about chin height, the paddle throat should be at the waterline and the paddle blade should just be submerged. In other words, chin height to waterline should equal the distance from the top of the grip to the throat, where the shaft meets the blade.

If you don't have a canoe or a paddle at this stage, sit down in a chair and measure your torso length from your chin to the seat. Add to this the estimated height of the canoe seat above the waterline, not above the bottom of the boat (about 3 to 6 inches is average for a solo canoe). Adding these two measurements will yield the distance from the top of the grip to the throat. There is some leeway and room for personal preference, and an inch or two longer or shorter is not critical.

Most manufactured paddles are sized by their overall length, but it is the shaft length, from the grip to the throat, that is most important. I like a somewhat short bent-shaft paddle for speedy cruising but may switch to a longer length if using a straight-shaft paddle in a tandem canoe.

Choosing the length of a double-blade paddle is more subjective. Wider boats and higher gunwales require longer paddles. If the boat is narrow, you can paddle with a short paddle and a high angle to the water or a long paddle and a low angle. A longer paddle is slightly heavier. I prefer a light paddle and accept a medium-high angle. For canoes like Dragonfly and Kayoo without a deck, try a double paddle with overall length of about 90½ inches or 230 cm. Very tall paddlers may want a paddle about 2 inches longer. My height is 5 feet 7 inches, and for the decked version of Kayoo, I use a paddle length of 86½ inches or 220 cm. This is also an average paddle length suitable for many sea kayaks, touring kayaks, and recreational kayaks. A length of 90½ inches may be preferable for tall paddlers or relatively wide kayaks. For very narrow kayaks or shorter paddlers, experiment with shorter paddles. Whitewater kayak paddles are as short as 191 to 200 cm.

Because of her narrow waist, Wasp can be happily motivated with a relatively short double paddle. Ergonomically, I enjoy her with paddles as short as 80½ inches or 205 cm, but a high paddling angle results, which drips water on my legs and in the boat unless a spray cover is used. So I usually use an 86½-inch or 220 cm paddle. A paddle 2 inches shorter might be very nice for Wasp. I should quit writing and go build another paddle!

After your paddle is shaped and sanded, it should be epoxy sealed and finished with paint or a UV-blocking varnish. For a double-blade paddle, add a pair of drip rings (available from outfitters) to the shaft near the blades.

The best part of building a paddle is the need to test it. So . . . go paddling!

Farewell To the Walleye

Sam Rizzetta © 2006

Thanks to Mark Jones who suggested the song and title on the last morning of a north country wilderness canoe trip.

Afterword

Wasp on a tributary of the Shenandoah River. Aerial photograph by Lee Jones.

"In our tradition the water is respected. The River is considered a living creature like the animals and the plants. We call it The Long Human Being. The Old Elders would gather us together and lead us down to the water for a plunging ceremony. The Old Elders would ask the River permission to enter its body."

—From a conversation with Hawk Littlejohn

To respect the river, and all waters, as native traditions teach, we must be thankful for what we take from the water and be moderate in its use. We must also be mindful of what we leave for others and careful of what we put into the water. The lives and health of many creatures and many other people will depend on our behaviors, as our lives and health are, in turn, influenced by the actions of others. Somehow, it is easier to be mindful of these things in a canoe. For what is paddling but caressing the water?

Canoes and kayaks connect us intimately with the water and keep us humbly aware of our place in nature. They allow a quiet, contemplative outdoor experience that silences the mind and sharpens the senses. They encourage solitude and provide the freedom and joy of moving over the water by our own power. That sense of freedom is enhanced by knowing that these simple craft, with modern materials, designs, and flotation, might take us farther with less risk.

Paddle more. Smile more. Be mindful. And stay safe. See you on the water.

Appendix A

Sources of Supplies

Aircraft Spruce & Specialty Co.
P.O. Box 4000
Corona, CA 92878-4000
aircraftspruce.com

Thin and flexible aircraft plywood, composite materials, fiberglass, Kevlar, carbon graphite, epoxies, rigid foams, vacuum bagging supplies, interesting catalog. Good prices for epoxies.

Applied Vehicle Technology
5641 Massachusetts Avenue
Indianapolis, IN 46218
http://avtcomposites.com

Good prices and availability for carbon fiber fabrics.

Buoyant Safety Paddle
buoyantsafetypaddle.com
Chesapeake Light Craft
1805 George Avenue
Annapolis, MD 21401
clcboats.com

Oakume marine plywood, stitch-and-glue kayak and canoe kits, supplies, epoxy, fiberglass, paddle floats, marine paints and varnishes, and ferrules for making take-apart kayak paddles.

Clark Craft
16-99 Aqua Lane
Tonawanda, NY 14150
clarkcraft.com

Expanded urethane foam flotation, supplies.

Fiberglass Warehouse
fiberglasswarehouse.com

Fiberglass, carbon fiber, and Kevlar.

Fibre Glast
95 Mosier Parkway
Brookville, OH 45309
fibreglast.com

Fiberglass, carbon fiber, and Kevlar.

Foam Factory Inc.
22800 Hall Road
Clinton Township, MI 48036
thefoamfactory.com
closedcellfoams.com/polyethylene.html

Polyethylene foam sheets and cylinders.

Infinity Composites Inc.
P.O. Box 1277
Ashtabula, OH 44005-1277
infinitycomposites.com

Good prices and availability for Kevlar 49 in both 38-inch and handy 50-inch widths. Also, Kevlar scissors.

Jamestown Distributors
17 Peckham Drive
Bristol, RI 02809
JamestownDistributors.com

Almost everything for boatbuilding.

John Greer & Associates
4128 Napier Street
San Diego, CA 92110
jgreer.com

Polyurethane pour foam flotation.

NRS
2009 South Main Street
Moscow, ID 83843
nrsweb.com

Flotation bags, paddle floats, bilge pumps, D-rings, adhesives, dry bags, wet suits, and dry suits.

Pakboats
P.O. Box 700
Enfield, NH 03748
pakboats.com

Folding boats and a nifty combination paddle float/ dry bag/deck bag.

**Piragis Northwoods Company and the Boundary
     Waters Catalog**
105 North Central Avenue
Ely, MN 55731
piragis.com

Accessories, including canoe seats, portage yokes, paddles, and canoe camping gear.

PoolToy
617 Innovation Drive, Suite 102
Chesapeake, VA 23320
http://pooltoy.com

Swim noodle flotation cylinders.

Stewart-MacDonald
21 North Shafer Street
Box 900
Athens, OH 45701
http://stewmac.com

Cam clamps, tools, and materials for building and repairing stringed instruments, several of which are useful for composite boat building.

Sweet Composites
6211 Ridge Drive
Bethesda, MD 20816
http://sweetcomposites.com

Fiberglass, Kevlar, graphite, and epoxy.

Wenonah Canoe Inc.
P.O. Box 247
Winona, MN 55987
wenonah.com

Manufacturer of a wide variety of canoes and kayaks. Their annual catalog is a good primer on canoe design and materials.

West System Inc.
100 Patterson Avenue
Bay City, MI 48707
westsystem.com

WEST System epoxies, fiberglass, and instruction manuals. The WEST System user's manual is required reading.

Appendix B

Sources of Information

American Canoe Association
1340 Central Park Boulevard, Suite 210
Fredericksburg, VA 22401
americancanoe.org

> Canoe and kayak safety information and instruction.

Basic Essentials Solo Canoeing, by Cliff Jacobson
Globe Pequot Press, P.O. Box 480, Guilford, CT 06437
globepequot.com

> Includes good tips on outfitting.

Building a Strip Canoe, by Gil Gilpatrick
DeLorme Publishers, P.O. Box 298, Yarmouth, ME 04096
delorme.com

> Includes plans.

Building Your Kevlar Canoe, by James Moran
International Marine/Ragged Mountain Press,
130 E. Randolph Street, Suite 900, Chicago, IL, 60601
mhprofessional.com

> Includes plans.

Canoecraft, by Ted Moores
Firefly Books (U.S.) Inc., P.O. Box 1338, Ellicott Station,
Buffalo, NY 14205
fireflybooks.com

> Includes plans.

Fiberglass & Composite Materials, by Forbes Aird
HP Books, The Berkley Publishing Group, 375 Hudson Street,
New York, NY 10014
hp.com/hpbooks

> Provides a good general background on composites.

Paddling.net
paddling.net

> A good source of paddling information, safety information, books, product reviews, and classified adds.

The Strip-Built Sea Kayak, by Nick Schade
International Marine/Ragged Mountain Press, P.O. Box 220,
Camden, ME 04843
mhprofessional.com

> Includes plans and a good description of how designs influence performance.

Appendix C

Data and Formulae for Calculating Flotation Volume

The specific gravity of fresh water = 1.0

Weight of fresh water = 62.4 pounds per cubic foot

The specific gravity of seawater = 1.03

Weight of seawater = 64.3 pounds per cubic foot

One cubic foot = 1,728 cubic inches

Volume of a cylinder = area of cross section (a circle) times the length

Area of a circle = πr^2

π = 3.14159

r = radius

Index

Page numbers followed by an "f" or "t" refer to figures or tables respectively.

CPSIA information can be obtained at www.ICGtesting.com
Printed in the USA
LVOW04s2120231014

410305LV00008B/117/P